FISK'S HOMER, WILLIE'S CATCH AND
THE SHOT HEARD ROUND THE WORLD

Colin
There are some nice
stories about Brooklyn
here . especially 1955 .
Good to see you. Stay in
Dick Touch

FISK'S HOMER, WILLIE'S CATCH AND THE SHOT HEARD ROUND THE WORLD

Classic Moments from Postseason Baseball, 1940–1996

by G. RICHARD MCKELVEY

McFarland & Company, Inc., Publishers
Jefferson, North Carolina, and London

Front cover photograph: Bill Bevens at the 1947 World Series
(COURTESY NATIONAL BASEBALL LIBRARY AND ARCHIVE, COOPERSTOWN, N.Y.)

British Library Cataloguing-in-Publication data are available

Library of Congress Cataloguing-in-Publication Data

McKelvey, G. Richard, 1935–
    Fisks homer, Willie's catch and the shot heard round the world :
classic moments from postseason baseball, 1940–1996 / by G. Richard
McKelvey.
      p.   cm.
    Includes bibliographical references and index.
    ISBN 0-7864-0515-5 (sewn softcover : 50# alk. paper)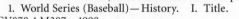
    1. World Series (Baseball)—History.   I. Title.
GV878.4.M387   1998
796.357'646 — dc21
                                   98-17880
                                       CIP

Manufactured in the United States of America

McFarland & Company, Inc., Publishers
  Box 611, Jefferson, North Carolina 28640

Dedicated to my wife, Joan,
and our children,
Stephen, Rick, Mark, Kevin and Kathy

Acknowledgments

My wife, Joan, gave me enthusiastic and steady support throughout the lengthy process of researching and writing this book. I give my very special thanks to her.

Our children contributed their talents to the completion of this project. I am indebted to Mark for transcribing the early manuscript from handwritten pages to the computer, to Steve and Kevin for their insightful editorial comments, and to Rick and Kathy for their typical optimism and sincere interest in my writing. Our extended family — Diane, Liza, Lynn and Patrick, who have joined us through marriage — were supportive partners throughout the process.

I appreciate the assistance of my colleagues at Deerfield Academy, especially the library and computer technology staffs, who shared their resources and expertise with me.

I am especially grateful to the many ballplayers and other baseball personnel who, through letters and over the telephone, contributed their remembrances about these great moments. They include Dick Bartell, Bobby Brown, Albert B. Chandler, Dom DiMaggio, Bobby Doerr, Carl Erskine, Dave Ferriss, Bob Friend, Charlie Gehringer, Lou Gorman, Harvey Haddix, Mel Harder, Tommy Holmes, Monte Irvin, Larry Jansen, Eddie Joost, Tony Kubek, Vernon Law, Don Liddle, Whitey Lockman, Gil McDougald, Mickey Owen, Johnny Pesky, Dave Philley, Johnny Podres, Phil Rizzuto, Brooks Robinson, Al Rosen, Bobby Shantz, Sibbi Sisti, Clyde Sukeforth, Ron Swoboda, Bobby Thomson, Earl Torgeson, Mickey Vernon, Bill Virdon, Wally Westlake, Wes Westrum and Davey Williams.

Contents

Introduction

It has been called "The Shot Heard Round the World" and "The Miracle of Coogan's Bluff": When a stunned radio audience heard Russ Hodges cry, "It's gonna be … I believe … The Giants win the pennant! The Giants win the pennant! The Giants win the pennant!"[1] the climax of a local rivalry turned into an electrifying national event.

It has been called "The Catch": Number 24 of the New York Giants caught the fly ball with his back to home plate in the Polo Grounds. He made the catch as he raced to the right of the "old Club House" in dead center field. In seemingly one motion, he planted his foot, whirled and made a gargantuan throw back to the infield to prevent the runner on second base from tagging up and scoring the go-ahead run.

It has been called "The All-Time Thriller": The Boston Red Sox were batting in the bottom of the twelfth inning. The score had been tied since the eighth. With the crack of the bat, the ball soared toward the left-field foul pole. The tall, powerful, right-handed hitter took a stride toward first base. He stopped and looked toward the Green Monster. And then taking five bounding sidesteps down the baseline, he rooted the ball into fair territory for a homer before finishing his jubilant jaunt around the bases.

These are just three of the many unforgettable images from baseball's great contests — events that occurred either in a playoff for a league pennant or in the annual ritual called the World Series, which determines the champion of the universe of baseball. These and other events have served to memorialize men like Owen, Thomson, Branca, Lavagetto, Larsen, Mazeroski, Fisk, and Buckner. Their names remain arguably more recognizable than those of many greats of the game — players, managers, umpires, and executives — enshrined in the Baseball Hall of Fame in Cooperstown.

Since 1940 a number of playoffs and World Series have produced magical moments. There were the great catches that saved games, and painful errors that delivered defeat. There were home runs that ended close contests, and hits that shattered no-hitters. There was the elation of the perfect-game pitcher, and there was the frustration of the hurler who, in an instant, lost both a no-hitter and a ball game. (In this book the inning in which the "magic

1

moment" begins is highlighted for the reader in the box score at the beginning of each chapter.)

George Will, syndicated columnist of the *Washington Post*, wrote in Major League Baseball's 1988 Official World Series Program, "Yes, bad bounces and journeymen players, as well as dazzling plays and Hall of Famers, make up the mosaic of memories that surround the World Series."[2] There is something within the Great American Pastime that seems to make it unusually fertile ground for such singular memories. Perhaps it is baseball's uniqueness in nature and design. The sudden event fills the void of anticipation and stands out more vividly and poignantly in this sport than in faster-paced games such as basketball, where amazing athletic feats are sometimes lost to our eyes in the rush of the game.

Baseball is a pastoral game. It was created to be played outdoors in the summertime under a comfortable and warming sun and at a leisurely pace. The legend of its birth in rural Cooperstown, New York, bespeaks the "countrified" flavor of the game.

The stories of baseball make up a rich American tableau. Fans leave their cares outside the ballpark, relax in shirtsleeves, eat hot dogs, drink something cool and refreshing, and cheer for their favorite teams and their special heroes. Some who have never developed a "feel" for the game complain about its slow pace. Missing is the "rock 'em, sock 'em" element of other contests. But the visible action and the hidden strategy of baseball is the true aficionado's delight. Red Smith said it best: "Baseball is a dull game only for those with dull minds."[3]

Baseball can be played in vast open spaces or wherever a player's mind can fantasize a field. For some, it is nine against nine on a mixture of brown earth and green grass carefully manicured for beauty and ease of play. Others make do with sandlots, side streets, or overgrown fields — the sites of some of the greatest baseball games ever played! There are the meticulously laid-out foul lines and limed bases, and there are the imagined dimensions with bags made from the shirts off the players' backs.

When Jim Lefebvre was a kid, he dreamed of playing for Los Angeles. In the many games he played with his brothers, his yard was magically transformed into Dodger Stadium. Years later, after a lengthy career in the majors, he said, "Once the stars are gone and the media has left the field and all the hype and hoopla is done, you go out and play baseball just like we played in the back yard. The game stays the same, the stage just changes."[4]

The nature of the game was so deeply ingrained in those who played and watched it that its integrity was unshaken when President Franklin Delano Roosevelt, from his office in Washington, D.C., switched on the lights in Cincinnati's Crosley Field for the first night game on May 24, 1935. Baseball retained the brown-and-green geometry of the playing field even after it moved indoors at the Houston Astrodome in 1965. Today it is played in a number of stadiums that never see the direct light of day or know a live blade of grass. Still the game remains essentially as it has always been.

In W. R. Kinsella's novel *Shoeless Joe* a struggling farmer fashions a fantasy "field of dreams" from the fertile soil of an Iowa cornfield and welcomes back deceased stars from bygone days to relive the thrill of the game they once played. When it appears that foreclosure on his house and farm will be the only realistic result of this fantasy trip into baseball's hallowed history, J. D. Salinger — who himself has been captured in the farmer's strange Eden — offers a vision of hope. He prophesies that people from all over the country will be drawn to that special spot in Iowa to take part in its magic. And each one will be willing to pay $20 to do so! Salinger adds, "They'll walk out to the bleachers and sit in shirtsleeves in the perfect evening or they'll find they have reserved seats somewhere in the grandstand or along one of the baselines — wherever they sat when they were children and cheered their heroes, in whatever park it was, whatever leaf-shaded town in Maine, or Ohio, or California."[5]

Baseball is a game predicated on order. There is uncanny symmetry in its design. Three outs, three strikes, and three times three innings provide the basic structure. Three sets of three players divide the playing field into segments for their defensive responsibilities in left, center, and right.

Baseball is a game rarely influenced by the ticking of a clock. An inning measured by two sets of three outs determines the contest's progress. Time doesn't matter; the game matters. In this sense, the Great American Pastime is beyond time. Only rarely does an external force limit the contest. It may be the setting of the sun or the coming of rain. Sometimes a city ordinance brings a game to an end in the wee hours of the morning. Most of the time, however, the game proceeds in an orderly manner to its own completion, out by out and inning by inning. There are even those occasions when the players play extra innings, but never is it an "overtime."

Through its rituals, baseball brings lives together across the generations. Children play endless games of "catch" with their dads. Tossing a ball back and forth is often as much a vehicle of unspoken communication as a means of improving the child's skills in the sport itself. David Halberstam, recalling such special moments, has written:

> Men of my age are still bonded by baseball. I cannot vouch for young men who grew up in subsequent generations in greater affluence with greater stimuli at their disposal, but for the generation I know best — men in their late 40s and in their 50s — baseball still turns us into boys again. I think I know some of the reasons now. I am bonded to my father through baseball, because he took me to Yankee Stadium when I was 5 and pointed out the great DiMaggio, and from then on we often went to Yankee Stadium together. It might have been the first thing from this world that he shared with me. I saw this game through his eyes.[6]

Baseball plays a key role in family histories. Families develop intense loyalties to their favorite teams and share in the emotions of their club's successes and failures. Families cherish the memorable moments shared celebrating their team.

Baseball is a part of individual histories as well. John Updike describes the continuity of a pastime that has been repeated summer after summer: "There is an unbroken continuum of great games that you've seen merged with games that you've played in as a child, so that all exercises in oral memory are a way of recapturing your life, and living it and saying that it mattered....To enter back into those games is a way of entering back into your youth and reversing the flow of time for awhile."[7]

Baseball is built upon essentials taught to the young as part of their initiation into the ways of the game. One is how to choose up teams. It involves going hand over hand up the bat's handle to the knob, followed by the "last-chance" kick. There is an "official" way to keep a box score, noting the difference between a swinging strikeout and a called third strike. And "whatever the field, whoever is playing the game, there's a way to talk, a way to stand, a way to move, and when the ball comes at you a way to make it look easy."[8]

But above all, there is something magical about baseball when it is played in late September and October. It is a different game, and the great catch, the big hit, or the ghastly error stands out in bold relief, to become deeply etched in the memories of those who share the moment. Later, fans recall the setting, the pitch, the swing of the bat, where they were when the happiness or the horror happened, and the emotions that were set loose.

Each fall, during the postseason, a new spirit of anticipation electrifies this orderly, timeless, and pastoral game. In *How Life Imitates the World Series*, Thomas Boswell reminds us that "baseball is played at two wildly different paces — regular-season and post season, the six months of April through September, and then October. They present different strains and require almost antithetical responses. The regular season rewards a phlegmatic stability, a capacity to endure long aggravation and ignore many losses and embarrassments. The post season asks the opposite — a knack for instant resiliency and an intolerance of even one defeat."[9]

The following stories are intended to create a mosaic of memorable moments for the fans of the Great American Pastime to remember and enjoy once again. The journey begins with a fellow named "Bobo" Newsom in the 1940 World Series and culminates with a part-time player named Jim Leyritz in the fourth game of the 1996 World Series. Each story is examined within the context of the playoff or the series in which it occurred. But ultimately, each event stands alone for what it is and for the place it holds in the memory of baseball fans. Each is a part of baseball's legacy to future generations. For the sake of those generations, let us pass the stories on.

1940

World Series

Cincinnati Reds and Detroit Tigers

Fifth Game — October 6 at Detroit

Cincinnati	0	0	0		0	0	0		0	0	0	0	3	0
Detroit	0	0	3		4	0	0		0	1	x	8	13	0

Thompson, Moore[4], Vander Meer[5], Hutchings[8]
Newsom

Seventh Game — October 8 at Cincinnati

Detroit	0	0	1		0	0	0		0	0	0	1	7	0
Cincinnati	0	0	0		0	0	0		2	0	x	2	7	1

Newsom
Derringer

In the fall of 1940, Americans looked east and west to see dark war clouds hanging over each horizon. Hitler's horrific power had swept through France and was pounding Great Britain from the air. The British Royal Air Force was making retaliatory bombing raids on Berlin. Across the Pacific, Japan had turned its military might toward the Chinese mainland.

At home, the World Series began on October 2 at Cincinnati's Crosley Field and "came along as a most welcome diversion from bombs, communiqués, crisis talk and politics. In Washington, members of The House recessed and hurried home to listen in on radios."[1]

The Detroit Tigers clinched the American League pennant on September 27, the final Friday of the campaign, when they beat the Cleveland Indians, who had been nipping at their heels. The Tigers finished the season a single game ahead of the Indians and two up on the New York Yankees.

Detroit's opponents were the Cincinnati Reds, who were in the Fall Classic for the second straight year. The previous October, the Reds had dropped four straight games to the Bronx Bombers. When the Reds defeated the Pittsburgh Pirates on the last day of the 1940 season, they became only the third team since 1913 to collect 100 victories in a season. On their way to the series,

Cincinnati outdistanced the runner-up Brooklyn Dodgers by 12 games. Under manager Bill McKechnie, the Reds hoped to capture their first World Championship in 21 seasons. Their last had come against the infamous 1919 Chicago White Sox, the year they became the "Black Sox."

Many experts gave Cincinnati a good shot at achieving its goal. During the American League's many years of World Series dominance, its pennant winner had usually outdistanced the closest AL rivals by a comfortable margin. The Yankees of the 20s and 30s were the prime example of domination. On the other hand, the National League specialized in down-to-the-wire pennant fights, and rarely had its annual entry proved a match for the Junior Circuit's champion. John Drebinger of the *New York Times,* anticipating a "new world order" in baseball, wrote about the Reds' chances:

> For the first time in a number of years the National League is coming up to a world series with what is generally conceded to be an even, or perhaps a better than even, chance to win.
> In fact, not since 1934, when Frankie Frisch and his swashbuckling Cardinals battered down another Detroit club in seven bruising games, has the senior loop entered the Fall classic holding such excellent prospects as do the Reds in their forthcoming clash with the Tigers.[2]

The Tigers traveled to Crosley Field for the series opener, with the offensive power of Rudy York and Hank Greenberg in tow. Cincinnati countered with a deep and talented pitching staff, headed by 21-game winners Paul Derringer and Bucky Walters. The Red Stockings also boasted a staunch and reliable defense aimed at short-circuiting Detroit's bid for the World Championship.

True to the pundits, the 1940 World Series provided an exciting "back and forth" set of seven games. A compelling "story within the story" focused on the heart-tugging heroics of a grief-stricken competitor. The lasting memory of Bobo Newsom creating a living memorial to his dad was a very special "moment." With the World Championship hanging in the balance, one brief instant in the final contest opened the door to victory, altered the rhythmical pattern of the series, and produced another of baseball's moments to remember.

For the hometown Cincinnati fans, game one was a painful reminder of the trauma of the previous season's four-game sweep at the hands of the Yankees. The Tigers scored five times in the second inning on five singles, coupled with several defensive lapses by the fumbling Reds. Detroit added two more runs in the fifth on a York triple and a Bruce Campbell home run. Derringer, the pride of the National Leaguer's staff, was chased from the mound during the rally in the second. The Tigers were in command all the way.

Louis Norman "Bobo" Newsom, a strapping right-hander, cruised to the victory in the 7–2 Detroit win. In the final innings, Newsom couldn't resist the temptation to do a little "showboating." He unveiled his celebrated "balloon ball" and challenged the batters to hit it. The Reds had no more success with that pitch than they had with any of his other offerings.

Bobo was on top of the world that fall afternoon. After 12 years of toiling for major league also-rans, the 1940 season was Bobo's first with a pennant winner. He had come to Detroit, his sixth major league home, from the St. Louis Browns during the 1939 campaign. He had gone 21-5 with the Tigers, registering his third consecutive 20-win season. Newsom's final two regular-season victories had come on the same day in an old-fashioned "iron man" feat. On Wednesday, September 25, during the final week of the campaign, the Tigers stood 1½ games ahead of Cleveland. They faced Chicago in a crucial doubleheader. Bobo pitched the last two innings of the first game to pick up a win when Detroit beat the White Sox, 10–9, in the tenth. He came back and hurled a complete game in the nightcap. The Tigers won, 3–2, sweeping the twin bill.

Bobo was delighted to have his family at Crosley Field for game one of the World Series. His father had never seen a series game and had been in a major league park only once before. For some time, the elder Newsom had suffered from a heart ailment. Before leaving home for the trip to Cincinnati, he told some of his close friends that he would not be back again, sensing perhaps the fate that was in store for him.

On October 2, he sat in the stands as his son picked up his first postseason victory. After the game Bobo exclaimed, "I feel great over this one because my father was out there watching me…. His name is Henry Quillan Bufkin Newsom, and he came from home in Hartsville, S.C., to see the game."[3] After the Tigers' triumph, Bobo and his dad, stepmother, and three sisters celebrated. It was a joyous family gathering with toasts for "son" Newsom's long-awaited World Series and "father" Newsom's presence at the game. Mr. Newsom went to bed early, exhausted from the day's events.

About 2:30 A.M., Bobo was awakened by a phone call; his father had suffered a heart attack. When he arrived at his dad's hotel room, Mr. Newsom seemed to be feeling better. After a short chat, Bobo went back to his room to get some sleep. Near daybreak, Bobo's 68-year-old father died. The family held a simple service for Mr. Newsom in the chapel of a Cincinnati mortuary. Bobo grieved over his loss. While the rest of the family returned to Hartsville for the burial, Newsom anguished over his responsibility to his dad, his family, his team, and himself. He decided to stay and pitch again in the World Series.

Game two established the pattern for the next five contests. Victory would go first to one team and then to the other. The second game began much like the opener. Bucky Walters walked Detroit's Dick Bartell and Barney McCosky. Charlie Gehringer, the third batter, singled home Bartell, giving the Tigers a quick 1–0 lead. Greenberg grounded into a double play, and McCosky scored.

However, Cincinnati rebounded and captured the game, 5–3, on the strength of Jimmy Ripple's two-run homer into the right-field bleachers.

The teams moved to Detroit's Briggs Stadium for game three. The Tigers, playing before a wild crowd of 52,877 fans, downed the Reds, 7–4. Going into the bottom of the seventh inning, Jim Turner and Tommy Bridges were hooked up in a 1-1 pitchers' duel. But York and Frank "Pinky" Higgins each connected for two-run homers off Turner, and Detroit went on to their second series win.

Derringer, who had been routed in the second inning of his first start for Cincinnati, went the distance in the fourth game, leading the Reds to a 5–2 win and tying the series at two games apiece.

Game five featured the emotional return of Bobo Newsom. On the afternoon of October 6, he celebrated the life of his dad, climbing the mound in Briggs Stadium — high above his personal grief — and pitching the Tigers to their third win. Supported by a three-run homer off the bat of Greenberg, Newsom fashioned a three-hitter and shutout the Reds, 8–0.

John Gardner recounted the game in "The One and Only Bobo," writing, "He had a thought in mind, a kind and richly sentimental thought that appealed to the depths of his sentimental soul. On the day of the fifth game, in Detroit, with tears streaming down the big, round, dark bearded face, Bobo announced that he was 'dedicating' this one to his dead father."[4]

When Newsom reached the Tigers' solemn dressing room, a flood of emotion washed over him. The hulking man sat sobbing on the stool in front of his locker. In a moving scene, teammates wandered by to offer Bobo both their congratulations and condolences. Finally, he spoke to the waiting reporters about the importance of the game for him: "It was the hardest game I ever wanted to win," he said as tears filled his eyes.... "I felt great. No kidding. Naturally I didn't feel as good as I should have. I pitched this game for my dad and I hope he knows what I accomplished. I knew in my heart he wanted me to win. This was the one I wanted to win most."[5]

The Fall Classic returned to Cincinnati for the crucial sixth game. Walters, who had won game two for the Reds, posted a complete-game shutout, 4–0, to even the series up.

Cincinnati's pitching was set for game seven. Their normal rotation had their ace, Derringer, rested for his third start. Detroit was not as fortunate. Manager Del Baker didn't have as easy a choice since each of his potential starters was injured or tired or both. However, with only one day's rest, Newsom requested the starting assignment and convinced Baker "he could win the pay-off collision."[6] As Tiger fans knew, "Ol Bobo pitches in and out of turn all the time."[7] In taking the ball, he was attempting to become the first pitcher to win three series games since 1922, when the Fall Classic was changed from a best-of-nine- to a best-of-seven-game format.

The Tigers helped Newsom's cause by scoring a run in the top of the third inning. Billy Sullivan, after beating out an infield single and being sacrificed to second, scored on Reds' third baseman Bill Werber's throwing error on a Gehringer ground ball.

John Kieran, covering the series for the *New York Times*, set the tone for the game at that stage:

> Just consider the situation. The Tigers had a run and they were always dangerous, no matter who was pitching. The Reds had nothing. They were facing a pitcher who breezed to victory over them in the opener and shut them out with three hits the next time he faced them. With [Ernie] Lombardi out, the Reds had only one real power hitter in their line-up, Frank McCormick, and Frank hadn't been any ball of fire at bat in the series.
>
> On the other hand, the Tigers had McCosky, Gehringer, Greenberg, York, Campbell and Higgins coming up in that order regularly. For Derringer or Walters or anybody else that was a tough array of hitters to keep in subjection.[8]

Entering the bottom of the seventh, Detroit held a narrow 1–0 lead, with Newsom having posted a string of 16 consecutive shutout innings against the Reds. It was at that point in the game, that a second memorable event was about to happen. It proved fatal for the Tigers, and pivotal in Cincinnati's victory.

Bobo's first pitch in the seventh was a fastball, and McCormick, who was hitting .185, slammed it off the left-field fence for a double. Ripple, also swinging on the first pitch, crossed up the Tigers, who were expecting a sacrifice bunt, and lined the ball off the top of the right-field screen, narrowly missing a home run. Campbell retrieved the ball quickly and threw it back into the infield to Bartell. With the fans on their feet screaming and with his teammates yelling, Bartell — with his back to home plate — held the ball for an instant as McCormick scored the Reds' first run to tie the game. That moment of hesitation would be replayed over and over again in telling the tale of the 1940 Fall Classic.

Bartell's play was immediately cloaked in controversy. Why was the play at home close at all? Even though he was slow of foot, McCormick should have scored easily.

After the game Bartell said, "I figured that by the time I got the ball, McCormick had scored standing up. So I was interested only in keeping Ripple from advancing. I didn't think there possibly could be a play at the plate."[9] The Tiger shortstop added:

> What I don't see is that McCormick apparently hesitated after rounding third. Billy Sullivan was catching. He said McCormick seemed completely disorganized at that point, like he didn't know what to do, like maybe the ball had been caught, and he held up. I don't know. And I can't ask

him any more. But it seemed to Sullivan like McCormick hesitated at third for all of five minutes. Sully was flapping his arms, jumping up and down, yelling for the ball. The third base coach was yelling at McCormick. Everybody was yelling, "Home! Home!" at me. It was bedlam. If I'd heard anybody yelling at me, I would have turned and thrown home in one motion. By the time I did turn around McCormick still hadn't scored. He must have gone by way of left field or stopped in the dugout for a drink on the way or something. But it was clearly too late to get him by then.[10]

Bartell also raised a question about the cut-off coverage involving himself and Gehringer. In his recollection of the event, he commented, "On a hit to right Gehringer is supposed to go out and take the relay. He says I went out and caught it and he was behind me. I say he went out and the ball came in over his head and I had to go over and get it before it rolled away from all of us."[11]

Referring to McCormick's slow trip home and Bartell's hesitation, sportswriter Grantland Rice wrote, "So here was a great series almost lost and finally won on two stars lost in a fog."[12]

Reporters pulled no punches in describing what they witnessed. One writer described the moment involving Bartell, saying the Tiger shortstop was standing at second base "slapping the ball back and forth between his bare hand and his glove."[13] Another account, appearing in the *Boston Evening Globe*, reported what Bartell did after receiving Campbell's relay throw: "He was sound asleep, the best bit of snoozing since Ernie Lombardi retired here in the final game of last year's Series in this same ball park."[14] The reference was to an event in the top of the tenth inning of the fourth game of the 1939 World Series. Lombardi never had control of a relay throw to home as Charlie Keller slid across the plate, making the score 6–4 in favor of the Yankees. While the Reds' catcher lay rolling on the ground with the ball lying a few feet from him, Joe DiMaggio, who had hit the single to drive in Keller, continued to circle the bases and scored while "Lombardi snoozed."

Cincinnati second baseman Eddie Joost, who had witnessed the plays involving both Lombardi and Bartell, wrote about his teammate's fateful moment: "As to Lombardi, ... Keller in his stride to the plate hit Lombardi in the jaw and throat with his knee, knocking him out. No one attempted to get to the ball so Lombardi was unfairly blamed for sleeping at the plate."[15] He was less generous about the Tiger player, writing, "Bartell took the relay from the outfield just behind shortstop, turned and watched McCormick score standing up. If he had thrown the ball McCormick would not have scored. As it turned out it was the winning run and The World Championship."[16]

Many years later, Gehringer said, "Bartell had a good chance to throw out McCormick at home plate, but never made the throw. It was the winning run."[17]

Confusion about the play was the result of both the excitement of the moment and the quickness with which it happened. That was illustrated by both Joost's and Gehringer's erroneous references to McCormick's score that tied the game as the winning run. They bear witness to how the run's importance has changed with the passage of time.

Time had to be called in order to give the grounds crew a chance to clean up the paper and cushions that had been strewn on the field by the exuberant Cincinnati fans. When the game resumed, Ripple was sacrificed to third by Jimmy Wilson and scored the go-ahead run on Billy Myers's deep fly to center field. It was enough to bring them a 2–1 win and their first championship in more than two decades.

Cincinnati became only the second team in World Series history to win the title while being outscored by the opposition. In 1912 the Boston Red Sox had scored 25 runs and defeated the New York Giants, who put 31 on the board. In 1940 the Reds had scored 22 runs, and the Tigers crossed the plate 28 times.

Bobo Newsom, pitching his third complete game — and doing it with only one day's rest — did not capture his third victory for the Tigers and for his dad. He did not finish his memorial in the manner he hoped he would. Dick Bartell went down in the annals of baseball history for a throw he didn't make. Recalling his momentous hesitation, the Tiger shortstop said, "And I knew exactly how Fred Merkle felt when he was dogged by his so-called boner in 1908, and Tony Lazzeri in 1926, and especially Ernie Lombardi in the fourth game of the 1939 Series."[18]

Later he added, "Frankly, I heard so many versions of what happened that day that I am eager to bury it. There were good and bad remarks about me, but somehow it is always the bad remarks that are remembered. For that reason, as far as I am concerned, it is a closed issue."[19]

Bartell's overall contributions to the Tigers during the entire 1940 season should be remembered far more than that one instant in time on October 8. He had come to a team that had finished in fifth place and 26½ games behind the Yankees the previous year. Graham Hovey of International News Service gave an assessment of what Bartell meant to Detroit's drive to the pennant:

> Here's a plea for a little guy a lot of you are about to tag the goat of the 1940 World Series. The scales of sporting justice must have been off center when Dick Bartell took that relay throw and stood there with the ball in his hand while Frank McCormick loped home with the tying run.... But let's take a look at the record. Why were those old men nicknamed the Tigers in the World Series at all?... What transformed them from the fifth placers to a fighting crew, good enough to win the hottest American League pennant fight since 1908? The credit goes to Bartell.[20]

Dick Bartell, the 32-year-old 5'9" firebrand, had come to the Tigers from the Chicago Cubs for the 1940 season. His leadership, drive, and spirit had been major ingredients in the club's successful climb to the American League pennant. Then, in one brief instant, all had seemingly been lost. Something had prevented one of the best arms in baseball from getting the ball to an eagerly waiting catcher.

1941
World Series
Brooklyn Dodgers and New York Yankees

Fourth Game — October 5 at Brooklyn

New York	1	0	0	2	0	0	0	0	*4*	7	12	0
Brooklyn	0	0	0	2	2	0	0	0	0	4	9	1

Donald, Breuer[5], Murphy[8]
Higbe, French[4], Allen[5], Casey[5]

By the end of the summer of 1941, the German army had moved into Russia as the nightmare of Hitler's march to conquer Europe continued. Across the Pacific, Japan had added to its conquests in China. Winds of war were blowing with increasing intensity across the waters flanking America on both east and west.

In October, against the backdrop of distressing world affairs, the eyes of baseball fans across the country were riveted on the battle of New York City. The club from the Bronx was pitted against the team from Flatbush.

The New York Yankees were poised in one corner for the baseball world's annual October prizefight. Their presence in the Fall Classic was no surprise. Joe McCarthy's Bronx Bombers had won the American League crown by an incredible 17 games. Having finished in third place a year earlier, 1941 was their fifth trip to the series in six seasons. They had been successful in each of the four years from 1936 through 1939.

The Yankees had ridden the crest of Joe DiMaggio's spectacular 56-game hitting streak, extending from May 15 until July 17. In Cleveland, more than two months after the streak began, third baseman Ken Keltner's defensive magic brought an end to one of the game's greatest achievements.

The Brooklyn Dodgers stood in the opposite corner for the upcoming World Series. For the team from Flatbush, it was only their third postseason appearance and their first since 1920. Unlike the Yankees, with their enviable assortment of trophies collected throughout the 20s and 30s, the Dodgers were seeking their first-ever world championship.

The fortunes of the franchise, both on and off the field, had been resurrected since the arrival of Leland S. "Larry" MacPhail in 1938 as the new president of the organization. When he took over, the Dodgers were over $1 million in debt. Bills had not been paid, and the phones in the club's offices had been disconnected. MacPhail, one of baseball's great innovators, had been a successful promoter in Cincinnati. In Brooklyn he spruced up Ebbets Field, giving it a coat of bright orange paint. He introduced night games and coaxed the fans back into the stands.

On the field, Brooklyn had been noncompetitive. Leo Durocher, the St. Louis Cardinal "Gas House Gang" shortstop, also arrived in Brooklyn in 1938. After Durocher's first season of play, MacPhail gave him an additional responsibility, making him the manager of the team. Larry had assembled a team of veterans, including Dolph Camilli, Joe Medwick, Billy Herman, Whitlow Wyatt, and "Fat Freddie" Fitzsimmons. He also added youngsters to the mix. He spent $75,000 — an exorbitant amount in the minds of many — for an unproven shortstop named "Pee Wee" Reese. On the other hand, he paid a mere $100 for the contract of "Pistol Pete" Reiser.

Under the fiery leadership of Durocher, the Dodgers entered the series as Flatbush's Beloved, Beautiful Bums. They had beaten back the St. Louis Cardinals' late-season rush and had captured the flag by 2½ games.

The World Series of 1941 marked the first-ever postseason meeting between the crosstown rivals. It was the first of many to take place before the team from Ebbets Field headed west to the Los Angeles Coliseum in 1958.

John Kieran, writing in the "Sports of the Times" column that appeared on the series' opening day, October 1, captured the enthusiasm in New York City and its environs:

> It's all too wonderful. Who could be sedate, restrained, logical or statistical with the dauntless Dodgers whooping into the Bronx to take after the haughty Yankees? It's the common people against the aristocrats; the unwashed against the precious; revolt of the masses against the luxurious overlords of established authority.
>
> It's the crowd from the wrong side of the railroad tracks invading the restricted residential area, bent on mischief. It's the uprising of the downtrodden, the poor against the plutocrats. At least, it's all of that to some Dodger rooters and some of that to all Dodger rooters.[1]

Yankee Stadium, the site of the opener, was bursting at the seams with a record crowd of 68,540. The American League champs beat the Dodgers, 3–2, behind the six-hit pitching of 37-year-old right-hander Charles "Red" Ruffing. A home run by Joe Gordon put McCarthy's Bronx Bombers ahead, 1–0. Bill Dickey and Gordon added key hits later in the contest to drive in the deciding runs.

A sensational catch by outfielder Joe Medwick in the opener might have remained in the forefront of baseball's memorable moments had the series ended differently. With one out in the bottom of the fourth, DiMaggio hit a ball toward the densely packed left-field grandstand. "Timing the ball accurately, Medwick was waiting in front of the stand for it to descend, leaped high, speared the horsehide with his gloved hand, then toppled over, holding firmly to the ball despite his fall."[2] But history would drape a pall over that remarkable homer-robbing catch and hoist the remembrance of a spectacular miss in its place.

Brooklyn turned the tables on New York the following day, when Wyatt went the distance in the Dodgers' 3–2 victory. After the Yankees jumped out to a lead with single runs in the second and third frames, the Beloved Bums tied the game, 2–2, in the fifth. The first run was scored by Medwick. His double was followed by a walk. A low throw to first by Gordon in an attempt to complete a double play allowed Joe to come home with the first tally. Then Mickey Owen lined a single to left to tie the score. In Brooklyn's next at bat, the winning run crossed the plate, when Camilli singled home Dixie Walker, who had reached base on an error.

An event in game three, played in Ebbets Field, provided an omen of the ultimate disappointment in store for Brooklyn fans. Fitzsimmons, the 40-year-old Dodger veteran, and the Yanks' Marius Russo, a young Brooklyn-born-and-raised southpaw, were hooked up in a classic scoreless pitchers' duel. With two outs in the top of the seventh inning, Russo lined a shot off the knee of Fitzsimmons. The ricochet was caught on the fly by Reese for the third out of the inning. However, Fitzsimmons was unable to continue in the eighth, and Durocher turned the scoreless game over to his ace reliever Hugh Casey.

In the top of the eighth inning, the Yankees stroked four straight hits off Casey and scored two quick runs. They went on to nail down a 2–1 victory and a 2–1 lead in the series.

The next day, 33,813 fans turned out to resurrect hope for the Dodgers. Late in the afternoon — a warm, bright, and sunny Sunday — Brooklyn's Beloved, Beautiful Bums were one strike away from being even with the Bronx Bombers at two games apiece. After that, the Dodgers dreamed of picking up one more win — in friendly Ebbets Field — before taking a 3–2 lead across town to Yankee Stadium, where they hoped to wrap up their first championship.

Brooklyn held a 4–3 lead in the top of the ninth. There were two outs, the bases were empty, and Casey had a 3-2 count on the Yankees' Tommy Henrich. The Dodger right-hander wound up and delivered. Henrich swung and missed. In an instant, fans exploded over the railings of the stands to join the victory celebration. Police raced onto the field to protect it and the players from exuberant Dodger rooters. Yankee shortstop Phil Rizzuto later recounted, "I was sitting on the bench. I was holding the gloves of the guys who were batting that inning — DiMaggio, Keller, Dickey, and Gordon. In Brooklyn those kids would run down after the third out and take anything

October 5, 1941: Catcher Mickey Owen of the Dodgers misses the ball after strike three, and Yankee Tom Henrich heads for first. Note the umpire's hand already raised for the "out" sign — a futile gesture, since Henrich made it safely to base, changing the course of the game (AP/ Wide World).

they could. When Henrich swung and missed that pitch, we all started for the runway in the dugout."[3]

But the pitch, whatever pitch it was, caromed off the catcher Owen's glove, allowing an alert Henrich to reach first base safely. At some point, during Owen's desperate dash to the front of the Dodgers' dugout to retrieve the ball, his name was chiseled deep into baseball's lore. The Yanks were on their way to an amazing comeback victory.

The next three Bronx Bombers — DiMaggio, Keller, and Dickey — also reached base. Before the Dodgers could get the third out, the four Yankee baserunners scored. Brooklyn went down in the bottom of the ninth on a pop foul and two ground balls. The Yankees won, 7–4, took a 3–1 series lead, and the Dodger dream had all but come to an end.

The impact on the 24-year-old backstop, who had come to the Dodgers from St. Louis the previous winter, was evident in the words he spoke shortly after the game's disappointing conclusion. "It isn't being the 'goat' that bothers me, though. That doesn't worry me in the least. What I'm really broken up about is the other boys on our club who did so well and certainly deserved to win."[4]

The Dodger catcher's nightmare was reported the following day under the chilling front-page headline: "OWEN WEEPS AT FATAL MUFF"— "Arnold Malcolm 'Mickey' Owen, whose catching for the Dodgers had been one of the features of the Battle of the Boroughs up until now, was suddenly transformed into one of the most bedeviled 'goat' prospects in all World Series annals this afternoon."[5]

Brooklyn fans could not believe what had passed so quickly before their eyes — some glistening with tears, others filled with rage. After the game, a group of Dodgers followers lined the ramp above the walkway to the club's locker room. As their defeated and dejected team came by, "they gave them a rousing Brooklyn hoot, with 'Yeah, Owen, ya bum!' the chief cheer."[6] Their seething anger also was vented in other directions. "A tear-faced kid walked out of the ball park, turned to the man with him and cried, 'Pop, it shoulda happened to Hitler.'"[7]

John Lardner, writing in the *Boston Daily Globe*, gave another glimpse of the reactions to the Dodgers' shocking loss in game four: "The faithful of Brooklyn, 30,000 strong, shuffled out of Ebbets Field in the Autumn twilight today and moved dumbly, unresistingly, where the traffic cops herded them, too stunned to speak of what happened or to think about the future."[8]

A new day brought renewed hope for many of the Flatbush Faithful. When Mickey Owen came to bat in the second inning of the fifth game, the Dodgers' fans gave him a rousing cheer.

Hope and cheers were not enough to stem the tide. New York won the game, 3–1, to wrap up the title. Ernie Bonham became the third Yankee pitcher to hurl a complete-game victory in the series. In winning the 1941 World Championship, the Bronx Bombers had beaten Brooklyn in all three of the games played in Ebbets Field.

John Drebinger, of the *New York Times*, wrote of the finale: "Oddly, the crowd, which totaled 34,072, was larger than either of the gatherings that had turned out for the two weekend games in Flatbush. The appearance of the additional few hundred in the sweltering arena doubtless was inspired by a desire to see whether the Dodgers could conceive of still one more way of losing a ballgame."[9]

For the Dodgers, too much had been lost the previous afternoon in the agonizing ninth inning. Billy Herman summed it up after the demoralized Bums went tamely to the champion Yankees, saying, "I don't think we could have beaten a girls' team the next day."[10]

What happened in Ebbets Field in the last inning of the fourth game is crystal clear. How it happened has raised questions almost from the moment it occurred.

Owen claimed full responsibility for the missed third strike. As Roscoe McGowen reported in the *New York Times* of October 6, the catcher said, "'It was all my fault.... It wasn't a strike. It was a great, breaking curve that I should have had. But I guess the ball hit the side of my glove. It got away from me and by the time I got hold of it near the corner of the Brooklyn dugout, I couldn't have thrown anyone out at first.'"[11]

Nearly 50 years later, in 1988, in an interview with Dave Anderson of the same newspaper, Owen commented, "The big mistake I made was not going out to the mound to tell Casey that I blew it. I just stood there behind the plate. I should have gone out to tell Casey that I blew it and to settle him down. But all of us were in shock from what happened."[12]

With the perspective of time and a sense of humor, the catcher commented on the fateful moment, writing, "I look at the photo of the play. I say yep, that's you ole Mick."[13]

Henrich, the batter, had his version of the pitch: "Hugh Casey threw me one of the widest breaking curves I ever saw in my nearly 20 years as a professional player. The pitch, which fooled me completely, dropped down suddenly and it must have hit at least a foot in front of the plate. Mickey Owen, who was obviously fooled by the pitch, didn't have much of a chance of stopping the ball, but he became the scapegoat of the Series. Owen was an excellent catcher…. Unfortunately, he got a bad rap."[14]

The unanswered question has been, "How did it happen?" It has been asked, "What pitch did Hugh Casey throw?" Was it a breaking curve ball as Owen and Henrich reported, or was it a spitter as Casey claimed? The pitcher, now deceased, said the pitch was a spitball. In his conversation with Anderson in 1988, Owen countered, "But if Casey threw a spitball, he threw it on his own…. It never looked like a spitball to me. It was a curveball. That's what I called for."[15]

Durocher, in *Nice Guys Finish Last*, was even more certain it hadn't been "the wet one":

> How the story got started that Casey had crossed Owen up by throwing a spitball is something I will never know. Nothing was said about any spitter at the time, you know. It was months before I first heard it. Maybe as long as a year. I do know that nothing I can say here is going to change it. It makes a better story that way. The cheater outsmarts himself and virtue triumphs. Considering how often virtue gets to triumph these days, maybe I'd better leave it alone. It just isn't true, though. Hugh Casey didn't even know how to throw a spitball. Why should he? Casey had a natural sinker — that's why he was a relief pitcher.[16]

Owen philosophically summed up his remembrance of one of baseball's most memorable moments and his most painful one, saying, "Three players all failed at the same time in the part of the game of baseball we were the best at."[17] His reference was to the fact that Casey had the highest winning percentage of any relief pitcher in the history of the game, and Henrich was "one of the finest batters ever to play in the major leagues."[18] And, as Owen would remind the reader: "One catcher holds the national league record for the most chances in succession without an error (509). This record was set during the seasons of 1941 and 1942, believe it or not. The catcher holding the record is Mickey Owen catching for the Brooklyn Dodgers. The missed third strike doesn't count because the world series games don't count in the regular seasons records."[19]

Whatever the pitch, whatever the reason, the ball got away from Owen, the championship dream died, and the Beloved, Beautiful Bums fell from grace in the hearts of many of their fans.

1946

World Series

Boston Red Sox and St. Louis Cardinals

Seventh Game — October 15 at St. Louis

Boston	1	0	0	0	0	0	0	2	0		3	8	0
St. Louis	0	1	0	0	2	0	0	*1*	x		4	9	1

Ferriss, Dobson[5], Klinger[8], Johnson[8]
Dickson, Brecheen[8]

The 1988 National Old-Timers Baseball Classic was held in Buffalo, New York. In that game, Enos "Country" Slaughter hit a ground ball off the glove of Johnny Pesky, driving in two runs. Crossing home plate with the second run was Lou Brock, who broke into laughter as he passed catcher Bill Freehan. Twenty years earlier, Brock had not been as fortunate or frolicky. In a 1968 World Series game between St. Louis and Detroit, the Cardinal outfielder had been tagged out at home by Freehan, the Tiger catcher when he failed to slide. A newspaper account of the Old-Timers game commented on the historic irony, reporting, "On a warm Monday night near the corner of Washington and Swan Street in the center of downtown, two pairs of World Series veterans — one linked by a decisive moment in 1946 and the other by a controversial play 20 Octobers ago — were suddenly connected in one disjointed memory."[1]

The decisive moment in 1946 featured the Cardinals' Slaughter and the Red Sox's Pesky. It was mentioned in the *New York Times* report on the final game of that season's World Series: "Eddie Dyer's Cardinals, an amazing club that simply refused to accept defeat, hurtled to the top of the baseball universe today. Underdogs from the beginning of the world series they defeated the heavily favored Red Sox in the seventh and deciding game, 4–3. The decisive moment, which threw a wildly cheering crowd of 36,143 into a frenzy of excitement, came in the eighth inning.[2]

Boston was the prohibitive favorite to win the 1946 World Series. The only question seemed to be whether St. Louis could prolong the series beyond four games. Joe Cronin's Fenway bunch had an outstanding hitting attack, featuring Ted Williams, Rudy York, Bobby Doerr, Dom DiMaggio, and Pesky. The Sox mound corps was led by two 20-game winners, Tex Hughson and Dave "Boo" Ferriss. The Beantowners had rolled to the American League crown, finishing with a 12-game cushion.

Williams was the soon-to-be-acclaimed American League's Most Valuable Player. In 1941 "the Splendid Splinter" had become one of baseball's few .400 hitters. Following the 1942 campaign, he put a promising career on hold and enlisted in the armed services, serving as a pilot instructor in the Marines through 1945. Williams returned to the Red Sox for the '46 campaign, and his accomplishments were staggering. Leading the majors in runs scored (142) and walks (156), he also finished number one in total bases (343). His batting average was .342, and he added 38 home runs and 132 RBIs to his impressive list of statistics. Williams's four hits in the All-Star Game, including a towering home run off Rip Sewell's "Eephus Ball," a pitch with a towering 20-foot-high arc, had powered the American League to a 12–0 shellacking of the National Leaguers and provided further ammunition to support the supremacy of the Junior Circuit in 1946.

The Cardinals featured first baseman Stan Musial, who had hit a league-leading .365. Musial, a military veteran like Williams, also returned from the service in 1946. It was expected that the National Leaguers, who relied on speed and experience, would finish second best to the power and pitching of their rivals from Boston. Under rookie manager Eddie Dyer, the Red Birds had ended the season in a first-place tie with Brooklyn. They went on to beat the Dodgers two straight games in baseball's first postseason playoff.

There seemed to be a mystique about the Boston Red Sox and the World Series. Although they had not been in a Fall Classic since 1918, their record was enviable—five attempts and five World Championships. For those making predictions about the outcome of the upcoming series, the record of former Red Sox successes was an important consideration. Together with past history, Boston had also dominated the American League in 1946, and although the Cardinals had captured the pennant in four of the past five seasons — and had been the World Champions twice — Dyer's Red Birds were thought to be overmatched by Cronin's Red Sox.

The opener took place in St. Louis's Sportsman's Park on October 6. York, the Boston first baseman, was the hero for the victorious Red Sox in games one and three. His tenth inning home run on opening day provided the winning margin in the 3–2 triumph. In the third contest, his first-inning blast with two teammates on base staked Ferriss to a lead. The season's leading-percentage pitcher, with a 25–6 record, held the Cards in check, 4–0.

St. Louis tied the series with victories in games two and four. Harry "The Cat" Brecheen tossed a 3–0 shutout at the Bosox in St. Louis, picking up the Cards' first win. The fourth game had an altogether different script from the three preceding it. As Donald Honig recounted in *The World Series*, "The next day the Cardinals tied a record set by the Giants in the 1921 Series by crashing out 20 hits in a 12–3 strafing of six Boston pitchers."[3] His military imagery gave an accurate assessment of the damage done to the Red Sox pitching staff that afternoon. Every Cardinal in the lineup hit safely, with the middle of the order — Slaughter, Whitey Kurowski, and Joe Garagiola — leading the way with four hits apiece.

Boston recovered and captured game five in Fenway Park with a 6–3 victory behind the four-hit pitching of Joe Dobson.

The Red Sox held a 3–2 lead, and the series appeared to be moving toward its anticipated outcome. However, Williams, who had been expected to power Boston to the World Championship, was having a mighty struggle at the plate. His bunt single in the third game sparked a front-page headline in a Boston newspaper. Williams carried his anger about the report for some time and commented in *My Turn at Bat: The Story of My Life:* "'Williams Bunts,' not the score, not the result of the damn game, just 'Williams Bunts.'"[4]

Williams was possibly distracted by the trade rumors swirling around the events taking place on the field. Reports in Boston had "the Splendid Splinter" going elsewhere for 1947 — perhaps to the New York Yankees. The picture of an intense organizational struggle among Red Sox decision makers was painted in the press for Beantown readers. Manager Cronin appeared to be pushing for a trade, but club owner Tom Yawkey was adamant about retaining the left-handed superstar. All the while, the Boston slugger's hitting was highlighted in a special box in the *Boston Evening Globe* entitled, "What Williams Did."[5] The daily reports were very discouraging.

The magic bat of "the Splendid Splinter" was nearly silent as Ted battled through a "five-singles series." Suffering with a sore elbow, he was also hitting into the teeth of the newly devised "Dyer shift," a modification of the defense Lou Boudreau had sprung on him in the second game of a doubleheader on July 14. Williams described the special defense: "Eddie Dyer was the Cardinal manager and he had been quoted before the game as saying he planned no changes for me, but when I got up to lead off the second inning the Cardinals started moving around. They were going into a shift, all right, but they were waiting until the last second to show it, I suppose to give me a little psychological jolt. I can't say I was surprised. By this time shifts were nothing new to me."[6]

Dyer had Marty Marion cover his regular shortstop area and moved third baseman Kurowski behind second. He positioned the other infielders and outfielders a little toward the right-field line. In the third game, Williams went against the shift and bunted down the third-base line for one of the five hits he would get. It was that single that prompted the newspaper headline and forced Dyer to modify his defense. However, Williams, as great a hitter as he was, never found a groove during the series.

As the teams took the field at Sportsman's Park for the sixth game, the favored Red Sox were one game from the 1946 World Championship.

Brecheen went to the mound for the Cardinals. When the power-packed Bosox finally scored in the top of the seventh, it was the first run they had chalked up against the "Cat" in 16 innings. That run would not be enough, as St. Louis went on to win, 4–1, evening the series. Slaughter, who had been hit on the elbow by a pitch in the final game in Boston, was barely able to hold the bat. He did, however, manage to get a key hit in the third inning, when the Cards broke on top, 3–0.

On October 15, the stage was set for the finale. For only the third time in World Series history, the teams had alternated wins in the process of arriving at the final contest. Going into the bottom of the eighth inning, with the games tied at 3–3 and the score tied at 3–3, the hometown Redbirds came to bat.

The decisive moment was near. Slaughter led off with a single to center field. The next two batters were retired, and Enos was unable to advance. With Harry Walker at the plate, Slaughter broke for second base on a 3-2 pitch. Walker lined the ball over shortstop into left–center field. Leon Culberson, who had just replaced the injured DiMaggio, chased the ball down, fumbled it momentarily, and then threw it to Pesky, who was out beyond shortstop. Pesky appeared to hesitate briefly before throwing the ball to the plate. Slaughter, having rounded third, headed for home. As "Country" steamed toward

October 15, 1946: Enos "Country" Slaughter beats Johnny Pesky's throw to score the winning run against the Red Sox (AP/Wide World).

the plate, catcher Roy Partee took Pesky's throw on a short hop. Slaughter slid across the plate and scored what proved to be the winning run.

There was irony in the events that forced DiMaggio to leave the game. In the top of the eighth, with Boston trailing 3–1, the Red Sox bounced back to tie the game. Dom hit a solid double that drove in the two runs. On the play, Slaughter hustled to retrieve the ball at the base of the fence and made a relay throw to Terry Moore. DiMaggio pulled up lame as he reached second base. Unable to return to his position when the Cards came to bat in the bottom half of the eighth inning, the flawless-fielding "Little Professor" was replaced by Culberson in center field.

Boston — dazed by the dash — battled back and had runners on first and third with one out in the top of the ninth. Brecheen, who had relieved Murray Dickson in the eighth, retired the next two Red Sox hitters to pick up his third victory and end the series.

St. Louis's World Championship was forged out of Enos's wild dash. A *Boston Daily Globe* headline bore special meaning for the disappointed Beantowners: "Slaughter Run Like Paul Revere's Ride."[7]

Pesky wore the "horns" at the series' conclusion. Immediately after the game he remarked:

> I had the ball in my hand. I hesitated and gave Slaughter six steps. When I saw him I couldn't have thrown him out with a .22. Nobody paid any attention to him.
> I couldn't hear anybody. There was too much yelling. It looked like an ordinary single. I thought he'd hold up at third so late in the game.[8]

Pesky, looking back over forty years later, described the moment a little differently: "Slaughter was stealing 2nd base when Harry Walker hit the ball. I was covering and had to go back to left-center. Enos kept on running and my throw was late. My only thought was to get the ball to the plate."[9] And after a half century, he said, "1996 will be 50 years of that play. I'll just go along and say to myself I wasn't at fault. If people want to blame me — so be it."[10]

Some years later, DiMaggio said, "I vividly recall Slaughter putting his foot on third base like he was going to stop and then he dashed toward home. He told me later that he went when he realized that I wasn't in center field." And then Dom added, "They weren't going to take any chances since I had already thrown out four [three] runners in the Series."[11]

Williams described his team's response to Enos's electrifying sprint around the bases: "Johnny Pesky took the relay and held the ball. Nobody yelled to him, not Doerr or Higgins or anybody, so you can't blame Pesky. And Slaughter just kept on running. By the time the ball got to the plate Slaughter was there, and the Cardinals had won, 4–3."[12]

Ferriss, the Red Sox starting pitcher that afternoon, said that the players "did holler [at Pesky] but crowd noise drowned them out."[13] Doerr elaborated on the conditions that caused the momentary confusion and identified with the shortstop's difficulty: "I keep hearing where Doerr nor [Pinky] Higgins called out the play. With 36,000 [36,143] fans yelling, Pesky wouldn't of heard us. I think if the ball would of been hit in right center and I would of taken the throw, the same thing probably would of happen[ed] to me."[14]

As with many of the events in baseball's mosaic of memorable moments, one has to wonder how many fans and sportswriters were focused on the key elements of the play as it was unfolding. Before television's instant replay, the observer either saw it or missed it. Those who thought they had seen it told others about the details through the written or spoken word. If the observer was Red Smith, many would believe his observations and descriptions. About the '46 event, the famed sportswriter reported, "Pesky stood morosely studying Ford Frick's signature on the ball.... At length, he turned dreamily, gave a small start of astonishment ... and then threw in a sudden panic."[15]

On the other hand, John B. Holway, after reviewing the official major league movie of the game, said, "I have played the tape again and again, in slow motion, and in stop action. I have timed it with a stop watch. The verdict: If Pesky held the ball, the camera didn't see him do it.... The camera shows Pesky taking the throw, whirling to the left, and throwing home in one continuous motion. Catch, wheel, throw."[16]

Whatever Pesky did or didn't do—whether or not his teammates were yelling to him — a large measure of credit belongs to Enos "Country" Slaughter for "finishing a three-base dash that is in many minds the most spectacular play in World Series history."[17] Remembering the circumstances, the hero wrote:

> Earlier in the Series [third base coach] Mike Gonzalez had stopped me at third and the throw went through the catcher and I could have scored. Eddie Dyer told me after that to go if I thought I had a chance and he would take the blame. So I never looked at Gonzalez and I was told later he tried to hold me up. If they hadn't taken Dom DiMaggio out of the game I wouldn't have tried to come home but Culberson didn't have the arm that DiMaggio had. They blame Pesky for holding the ball but if someone had hollered to him and he'd heard, he could have had a chance to get me. I started to slide when I was 10 feet in front of the plate. Partee took the ball on the first hop but I was safe easy. I had never done that, go all the way from first to home on a hit like that, ever before in my career. And I never did it after, either.[18]

John Drebinger, writing in the *New York Times*, summed up the series: "Threading their way to the final victory, the Cardinals followed a pattern seen only once before in world series history. That was in 1940 when the Reds, losing the first, third and fifth games to the Tigers, drew even three times and went on to win the seventh and deciding engagement for the only time they were to show in front."[19]

Drebinger overlooked the fact that Washington had beaten the New York Giants in the same pattern in 1924! More interesting, he had neglected to remind his readers how the Reds had won the series in 1940 — on a "hesitation" play involving Dick Bartell and Frank McCormick!

1947

World Series

Brooklyn Dodgers and New York Yankees

Fourth Game — October 3 at Brooklyn

New York	1	0	0	1	0	0	0	0	0	2	8	1
Brooklyn	0	0	0	0	1	0	0	0	2	3	1	3

Bevens

Taylor, Gregg[1], Behrman[8], Casey[9]

Sixth Game — October 5 at New York

Brooklyn	2	0	2	0	0	4	0	0	0	8	12	1
New York	0	0	4	1	0	0	0	0	1	6	15	2

Lombardi, Branca[3], Hatten[6], Casey[9]

Reynolds, Drews[3], Page[5], Newsom[6], Raschi[7], Wensloff[8]

One day prior to the start of the 1947 World Series between the New York Yankees and the Brooklyn Dodgers, the following advertisement appeared in the *New York Times:*

> It's great news for hundreds of thousands of baseball fans that, for the first time in history, all World Series games will be telecast this year! For the tens of thousands who already own RCA Victor Eye Witness receivers it means a real "Eye Witness" view, play by play, in their own homes![1]

Thus, a new era was ushered in for millions of sports fans who would be eye witnesses to baseball's postseason pageantry. They would watch in "living" black and white. Cameras were limited in what they could capture for the viewing audience, and television screens were minuscule compared to what the future would offer. Sportswriters' comments about the unspectacular play during the first three games of the series suggested that viewers had been mercifully spared by the limitations of the new electronic marvel. However, games four and six brought the screens to life, and produced two of the greatest memories in World Series history.

The series would be "black and white" in another respect as well. The

Dodgers' rookie first baseman, Jackie Robinson, added a special historic significance to the events that took place in Yankee Stadium and Ebbets Field that October. On his arrival from Montreal of the International League in the spring of 1947, Robinson removed the rusted lock on the main gate to the Great American Pastime. Others of his race, as well as members of other minority groups, soon followed Robinson and secured a place in the sport. Pitcher Don Bankhead had already joined him on the Dodgers' World Series roster.

The 1947 season was the first full year for another player who, during his lengthy career, would add lasting color to the game. Lawrence "Yogi" Berra, a Yankee outfielder and catcher, had made a token major-league appearance at the end of the 1946 season, but 1947 marked his official rookie season. He was playing in the first of his record-setting 14 World Series. Throughout a career of philosophical utterances, he would add wit and wisdom to both the game of baseball and the game of life.

There was a special reminder of the 1941 Series in the '47 renewal of the crosstown rivalry. Tommy Henrich still roamed the outfield for the Yankees, and Hugh Casey anchored the bullpen for the Dodgers. However, Leo Durocher, Brooklyn's manager in the '41 Fall Classic, was not there. Burt Shotton was the Dodgers' skipper, filling in for Leo during his year in exile from the game. On April 9, Commissioner Albert B. "Happy" Chandler had suspended Durocher for incidents perceived to be detrimental to baseball. The most commonly heard assumption was that Leo had associated with gamblers, but Chandler refused to state the specific charges.

The first three games were far from masterpieces. Neither team reached the heights expected from the American and National League pennant winners. Arthur Daley, writing for the *New York Times*, gave negative reviews following each of the trio of games. After the initial contest in Yankee Stadium, which the Bronx Bombers won, 5–3, by scoring all five runs in the fifth inning on three of the game's four hits, Daley commented, "That vaunted Yankee power exploded with all of the force of a nickel firecracker in the opening game of the world series at the stadium yesterday. It was a mild little pfftt and it had an extremely low decibel content, but those four hits detonated just enough to blow the Dodgers out of the victory column and send the Bronx Bombers, main bombload still in the racks, winging off to a lead in the post-season classic."[2]

Game two was a romp for the Yankees, 10–3. The Dodger defense broke down, and the main culprit was the normally steady-fielding center fielder "Pistol Pete" Reiser. In the third inning he had difficulty corralling a ball that was hit by George "Snuffy" Stirnweiss. Later in the same Yankees' at bat, Reese missed making a diving catch on a drive by Johnny Lindell, and Stirnweiss scored on the play. In the bottom of the fourth, Reiser staggered and fell while tracking down Yankee third baseman Billy Johnson's towering fly ball that dropped for a triple. In the seventh inning, a single by Johnson slipped through

"Pistol Pete's" legs for a two-base error. Nearly fifty years later, Brooklyn coach Clyde Sukeforth would recall the Dodger center fielder's tough day: "[I] can see those two lazy fly balls that Reiser lost or never saw in the shadows, but the best of them have trouble in those October shadows in the Stadium."[3]

New York also helped its cause by banging out 15 hits off a quartet of Brooklyn pitchers. Daley, with tongue planted firmly in cheek, wrote:

> The world series represents baseball in its ultimate state, the attainment of the very pitch of perfection. The fine, clean limbed American boys, champions all, rise to the heights of superlative play with yeoman feats both afield and at bat. Oh yeah? ...The things which happened in the second game of the post-season classic (?) at the stadium occasionally defied credulity. There were errors of commission and omission by the Brooks in such profusion that their nickname of Beloved Bums seemed particularly fitting although the adjective didn't seem quite necessary.[4]

Down two games in the series, Brooklyn went home to Ebbets Field and won a slugfest, 9–8. The most notable fact about game three was that it took a World Series record of three hours and five minutes to complete. Employing a seldom-used prerogative, the official scorer awarded the victory to Casey, judging that the relief job turned in by Ralph Branca was not deserving of the decision.

Daley's commentary on the third game began: "The world series traveling circus moved into Brooklyn for a three-day show yesterday and it gets funnier with every performance. The dear old Dodgers, who are totally unused to prosperity, let a six run lead go to their heads, and quaffed too deeply of the elixir of success. As so frequently happens on such occasions, they soon developed a case of the blind staggers and barely reached home safely."[5]

Bobby Brown, a Yankee rookie who would later become president of the American League long after his playing days were over, remembered the game well:

> It was a memorable Series for me because I got 3 pinch hits and a walk which at the time broke a record. One of the hits [in the third game] was recorded as a double even though I hit the ball at least 15 feet over the fence. It hit the screen attached to the foul pole that extended above the fence. The screen was on the fair side of the pole, and a ground rule in vogue at the time called for the ball to be in "play" if it hit the screen. Later the rule was changed and all balls hit over the fence are automatically home runs. That would have been the first pinch hit home run in World Series history. Ironically Yogi hit a pinch hit home run a few [one] innings later.[6]

Had the aforementioned ground rule not been changed, the historic conclusion to the sixth game of the 1975 Fall Classic would never have occurred, and Carlton Fisk's memorable trot would have landed him at second base!

The pitching staffs of both teams were depleted for game four. Sore-armed Harry Taylor was the starter for Brooklyn but did not get out of the first inning. After walking in one run, he departed the game with the bases loaded and none out. The Bronx Bombers had an opportunity to blow the lid off. However, Hal Gregg came on for the Dodgers and retired the side without allowing another Yankee to cross the plate. He worked through the seventh inning, surrendering only one more tally.

New York countered with a 7–13 pitcher, Floyd Clifford "Bill" Bevens. Bevens pitched what probably was the strangest game in the history of October matchups. Through eight innings he gave up only one run. Brooklyn scored in the bottom of the fifth on two walks, a sacrifice, and a ground out.

Entering the bottom of the ninth inning, Bevens held a slim 2–1 lead, and the Yankees were about to move ahead, 3–1, in the series. He had given up eight bases on balls but had yet to yield a hit. Because a run had scored and so many Dodgers had been on base with free passes, some of the players were unaware that a no-hit game was in progress. Even Yankee manager Bucky Harris had not realized it until the top of the seventh, when a few of the Dodgers gave away the "secret," yelling at Bevens and promising to put an end to his masterpiece. No one had ever pitched a no-hit game in the Fall Classic, and Bill Bevens stood three outs away from achieving every pitcher's greatest dream.

The Dodger fans in Ebbets Field held their collective breath when Bevens took the mound in the bottom of the ninth. Their Bums did not need a no-hit game thrown into their caldron of October horrors. Meanwhile, the Bronx Bombers silently chanted "one, two, three" over and over again. The television audience felt a part of the action in a new and exciting way.

Mel Allen, the Yankees' legendary announcer, and Red Barber, the voice of the Dodgers, were airing the spectacle over the Mutual Broadcasting System. Allen had done the play-by-play for the first 4½ innings, never mentioning Brooklyn's lack of a hit. He commented, "I've always known that players on the bench don't mention a no hitter; they respect the dugout tradition. And I've always done the same. It's part of the romance of the game; it's one of the great things that separates it from other sports, like the seventh-inning stretch or 'Take Me Out to the Ball Game.'"[7]

Barber took over the microphone in the bottom of the fifth. "Granting himself the title of 'reporter, not dealer in superstition,' Barber gave his listening audience the Dodger line-score up to that point. They were 'one run, two errors, no hits.' Allen gasped. The Redhead shrugged."[8] From Allen's point of view, his partner in the booth had done the unspeakable. But up until the bottom of the ninth it had not made a difference.

Brooklyn's lead-off hitter, Bruce Edwards, flied out very deep to left field. Carl Furillo drew Beven's ninth walk. A harmless pop foul by John Jorgensen was grabbed by first baseman George McQuinn for the second out. Bevens was one out away from immortality.

Two baseball managerial minds strategized as Casey came to the plate. Shotton sent speedy Al Gionfriddo into the game to run for Furillo. Reiser, nursing a very sore ankle that was later diagnosed to be fractured, was called to pinch hit for the pitcher. Earlier in the afternoon, the Dodger outfielder had given up trying to take batting practice, unable to put any weight on his front foot. Shotton had sent Reiser back to the clubhouse where he removed his uniform and climbed into the whirlpool. When the game began, Reiser limped back to the dugout. After three innings, the pain was so great that he went back for another whirlpool treatment. Four innings later, Pete reappeared on the bench. Shotton's call for him to pinch hit came as somewhat of a surprise, although he was hoping desperately to get the chance.

With a three-and-one count on Reiser, Gionfriddo stole second base, sliding under the throw from Berra. The Yankee manager went against a cardinal rule of baseball, intentionally walking "Pistol Pete," who represented the winning run.

With the hobbled Dodger on first, Shotton sent Eddie Miksis in to run. Cookie Lavagetto, a right-handed batter, came to the plate to hit for Eddie Stanky. It was only the second time in '47 that the manager had used a pinch hitter for the Brooklyn second baseman. The only reason suggested for the switch was that Eddie was "semi-sick with a cold."[9] Lavagetto had expected to be called to be the pinch runner.

> "Go up and hit for Stanky," said Shotton. "Hit? He must have meant run. Did he say hit?" "G'wan up and hit," repeated Shotton, in that hayseed voice of his.[10]

Bevens threw two pitches to Lavagetto. The first was a swinging strike. Lavagetto's weakness, according to scouting reports, was a high and outside pitch. The second delivery was right there, but Cookie sliced it hard to the opposite field. The ball caromed high off the wooden right-field fence. Gionfriddo and Miksis sped around the bases and both scored. The ball game was over, and the Dodgers had won, 3–2.

At 3:51 P.M. on October 3, all Brooklyn went crazy and Bill Bevens entered the record books — as the pitcher who gave up ten bases on balls in a World Series game.

Lavagetto's hit made Casey the winning pitcher for the second day in a row. Casey had come into the game in the top of the ninth inning with one out and the bases loaded. He made just one pitch — a fastball to Henrich, producing a bouncer back to the mound. The Dodger reliever fielded it and threw home to force Rizzuto at the plate for the first out. Edwards pegged the ball to Robinson at first to get Henrich, completing the 1-2-3 double play.

In Peter Golenbock's book, *Bums*, Gionfriddo recalled Lavagetto's hit and the subsequent celebration:

Two outs, and so I'm running as soon as the ball is hit, and I scored the tying run, and when I crossed home plate I start waving like hell at Miksis because I can see Tommy Henrich in right having a hell of a time trying to pick the ball up, and I stood there at home whistling and hollering for Miksis to score, and all the way from first Miksis scored the winning run. Oh, Jesus, we went crazy. We tied up the Series, and we busted up his no-hitter, and we're jumping all over the place, everyone's throwing their hats around, grabbing Cookie, mobbing him, and with the fans swarming onto the field, it was all we could do to get into the clubhouse.[11]

When questioned about his managerial strategy, Harris refused to be second-guessed about having intentionally walked Reiser. Although he knew the Dodger outfielder's ankle was very painful, the manager countered, "He can still swing."[12]

The name "Lavagetto" would be forever memorialized; the name "Bevens" gained not immortality, but infamy.

New York Times writer Daley, commenting on Beven's misfortune, noted: "Floyd (Bill) Bevens is a Yankee pitcher who has been rebuffed so often by Lady Luck all during his major league career that it looked like a mismatch from the start. But the old gal really waited until the ninth inning yesterday to play on him the shabbiest trick of all. The strapping right-hander from Oregon was just about to step into the Hall of Fame when the prankish miss slyly stuck out her foot and tripped him."[13]

Dick Young of the *New York Daily News* put the event in perspective, writing, "Out of the mockery and ridicule of 'the worst World Series in history,' the greatest game ever played was born yesterday. They'll talk about it forever, those 33,443 fans who saw it."[14]

Years later, "Happy" Chandler, the retired commissioner, wrote, "My most outstanding memory of the world series was the day the Brooklyn [New York Yankee] pitcher Bevin [Bevens] lost his no-hitter in the 9th inning and the game, too. That was a spectacular occurrence."[15]

The 1947 Fall Classic was not over yet. The 2–2 deadlock was broken the next day when rookie Frank Shea pitched the Bronx Bombers to a 2–1 victory. Lavagetto went down swinging on a 3-2 pitch with the tying run at second base to end the game. For some, it was just reward for his dastardly act a day earlier. Bobby Brown commented a number of years later, writing, "Lavagetto's hit that broke up Bill Bevens' no hitter and won the game for the Dodgers is well described. What I distinctly remember was that he came up to bat as a pinch hitter in the 9th inning the next day in Game 5 with a chance to win the game and struck out."[16]

An interesting headline appeared in the *New York Times* the morning of game five, reporting the reaction to the memorable fourth game:

October 3, 1947: Yankee Floyd Bevens delivers the pitch that Dodger Cookie Lavagetto hit to break Bevin's no-hitter in game four of the World Series (National Baseball Library & Archive, Cooperstown, N.Y.).

Stunning Climax Sets Off Bedlam
As Elated Brooklyn Fans Go Wild

Rabid Rooters Hit New Peak of Frenzy—
Casey's One-Pitch Victory, Steal by
Gionfriddo Catch Fancy of Crowd[17]

The last line was an omen for the sixth contest, that was played in Yankee Stadium on October 5. The Yankees led the Series, 3–2.

With their backs to the wall, the Dodgers battled to stay alive. In the top of the sixth inning, Brooklyn scored four runs to go ahead, 8–5. When the Dodgers took the field in the bottom of the inning, Gionfriddo was sent to left as a defensive replacement. The shortest player in the majors at 5'4" was about to produce a giant memory for the Flatbush faithful.

To his teammates, Gionfriddo was known as "Satchel." The nickname was not a comment on his ability to catch long fly balls. It came from carrying money—$250,000 worth of it. Early in the '47 season, Al had been traded from the Pittsburgh Pirates along with a quarter million dollars for five Dodger players. Some hinted the only reason the little outfielder had been included in the deal was to serve as a courier for Branch Rickey, guaranteeing quick and safe delivery of the money.

With two out and two men on base, the "Yankee Clipper," Joe DiMaggio, hit a long fly towards the grandstand. Gionfriddo raced to the 415-foot mark in left field and made a leaping catch of the drive in front of the bullpen gate, preventing it from going over the railing for a three-run homer. The ball glistened as a white prize in the outfielder's glove.

It was one of the few occasions in the "Yankee Clipper's" lengthy career that he displayed outward emotion on the field. A *New York Times* account described his reaction: "It was a breathtaking catch for the third out of the inning. It stunned the proud Bombers and jarred even the imperturbable DiMaggio. Taking his position in center field with the start of the next inning, he was still walking inconsolably in circles, doubtless wondering whether he could believe his senses."[18]

Decades later, Phil Rizzuto, the New York shortstop, recalled Gionfriddo's grab, writing, "That catch by Al was one of the 10 most letdowns I've ever experienced — the only time Joe D showed any emotion — kicking the dirt at second base. We lost that game, but fortunately won the Series — [It is] amazing how a great defensive play turns the game around."[19]

October 6, 1974: Dodger Al Gionfriddo makes a one-handed catch of Joe DiMaggio's would-be homer (National Baseball Library & Archive, Cooperstown, N.Y.).

Brooklyn held on to win the sixth game by the score of 8–6, and the teams were even, 3–3. Amazingly, Gionfriddo's grab remains the second most memorable moment of the 1947 World Series but also remains among the greatest catches of all time.

New York won the finale, 5–2. Joe Page was the winning pitcher in relief of Shea and Bevens, and Rizzuto had a 3-hit game. The Yankees picked up their eleventh World Championship, and the Dodgers' October record fell to 0-4.

The 1947 Series went from uninspiring to exhilarating, from uneventful to unforgettable. As *Time* reported:

> It began lacklusterly, got worse before getting better, and ended in a nerve-twisting climax that practically stopped the normal pursuits of commerce in every U.S. city and town for three hours every afternoon. There were moments when it seemed as if the entire citizenry of the borough of Brooklyn might be carried off in one collective heart attack. For in losing, the Brooklyn Dodgers, the beloved Bums, had run the gamut from derring-do to derring-don't.[20]

The major contributors to the memories of 1947 — Bevens, Gionfriddo, and Lavagetto — each played his final major league game during that postseason. Casey appeared in a record six of the seven games, earning two victories and a save. The 219-pound reliever, who also ran the Dodgers' favorite beer parlor in Brooklyn, exhibited a tavern keeper's ability to quell disturbances. Game six took three hours and 19 minutes to complete, breaking the record set four days earlier in game two. And it wasn't the result of television's commercial breaks!

Two rookies, Robinson and Berra, hit .259 and .158 respectively. Both would display their Hall of Fame credentials during a number of Octobers to come.

As *Newsweek* summarized, "The final game of the 1947 World Series ended seven days of hysteria that engulfed Ebbets Field and Yankee Stadium and spread out to the rest of the country by radio and television. No series ever provided more shocks, or more color. Everything about the series was sensationally good, or sensationally bad."[21]

1948
World Series
Boston Braves and Cleveland Indians

First Game — October 6 at Boston

Cleveland	0	0	0	0	0	0	0	0	0		0	4	0
Boston	0	0	0	0	0	0	0	*1*	x		1	2	2

Feller

Sain

Both of the teams in the 1948 World Series were in their first Fall Classic in many years. The Boston Braves' most recent appearance had been in 1914. That season the "Miracle Braves," who rose to the pennant after being mired at the bottom of the league in mid–July, knocked off the Philadelphia Athletics in four straight games. The Cleveland Indians had last gained a postseason berth in 1920, subsequently defeating the Brooklyn Dodgers.

In the 1948 Fall Classic, the underdog Braves did better than many thought they could; consummate promoter and maverick, wooden-legged and sport-shirted Indians owner-president Bill Veeck crammed fans into every nook and cranny of Cleveland's Municipal Stadium; the Tribe's "boy-manager" Lou Boudreau gained the satisfaction of proving something to his boss; pitchers ruled the "dullest" of series; and a single play in the first game of the series was offered up for fans of future generations to remember.

The drama had actually begun a year earlier. In September 1947 Lou Boudreau, Cleveland's 30-year-old player-manager, said he would not continue at the helm of the Indians unless Veeck offered him a contract for more than one year.

Since becoming the Cleveland pilot in 1942 as a 24-year-old, an age when many ballplayers were still struggling to make it to the major leagues, Boudreau had been player-manager on a year-to-year basis. On September 13 Boudreau announced, "I'm not signing any more one-year contracts."[1] Three days later, Veeck, a former Marine, who was only a few years older than his boy-manager, reported to the press that he "probably would come to terms with Lou Boudreau, Cleveland manager, for next year."[2]

In *Veeck—As in Wreck*, the president of the club gave his evaluation of Boudreau as a manager: "My main objection to Lou was that he managed by hunch and desperation. You ask Casey Stengel why he made a certain move and he will tell you about a roommate he had in 1919 who had demonstrated some principle Casey was now putting into effect. You ask Lou and he will say, 'The way we're going, we had to do something.' If there is a better formula for making a situation worse, I have never heard of it."[3]

At the same time that Boudreau was seeking a multiyear contract, Veeck had plans to trade him, along with two other players and cash, to the St. Louis Browns. In return, Cleveland would obtain four players, including Vern Stephens, who would become the Indians' shortstop in 1948.

The trade was to be finalized in New York during the 1947 World Series between the Yankees and the Dodgers. Al Lopez, who was Veeck's choice to replace Boudreau, was in New York City waiting to be introduced as the new skipper. At the eleventh hour, Bill DeWitt, the Browns' president, insisted that the Indians pick up part of Boudreau's salary for the following three seasons. Veeck squelched the deal, unwilling to agree to DeWitt's new terms.

A monumental problem was developing for the Indians' owner. Reports of Boudreau's imminent departure had appeared in the Cleveland newspapers. A story in the October 4 edition of the *Boston Daily Globe* carried the headline: "Boudreau on Block! Veeck Dickering with St. Louis."[4] Cleveland faithful mounted a public outcry against Veeck's horrific plan to trade their popular boy-manager.

The *Cleveland News* printed a ballot on the first page of one of its editions, offering its readers the opportunity to express whether they wanted Veeck to trade Boudreau. More than 100,000 ballots flooded the newspaper's offices. The overwhelming majority of fans clearly wanted Lou to remain in Cleveland. They had sent a direct and unequivocal message to the Indians' management.

Bud Silverman, a close friend of Veeck, was attending the series in New York. A devoted Indians fan, he was a political reporter for the *Cleveland Plain Dealer* and had his finger on the pulse of the community. He urged Veeck to return to Cleveland with him in order to quell the public outcry and clear up the muddle involving Boudreau. Silverman advised the Cleveland owner: "Tonight you'll be able to accept defeat gracefully. Two days from now it will be too late."[5]

Veeck agreed to go to Cleveland, and they booked a flight that was scheduled to arrive there at 8 P.M. That allowed time for them to take in some of the fourth game of the Series. As fate would have it, that was the momentous contest in which Bill Bevens had a no-hitter in his grasp into the ninth inning. As flight time approached, the excitement in Ebbets Field intensified, and it became more and more difficult for Veeck to leave. As soon as Lavagetto's hit broke up Bevens's masterpiece and gave the Dodgers their stunning victory,

Veeck and Silverman rushed to catch a taxi. They arrived at the airport with only minutes to spare.

Veeck, whose right leg had been lost during World War II, spent the night pounding the pavements of Cleveland on his artificial limb, telling the citizenry that Boudreau would remain the manager: "After everybody had gone home ... I toured the taverns and discussed the trade with little knots of people at the bars. Early in the morning, I was still hitting joints in the back alleys, startling drunks in their maunderings so that I could listen to their voices and bow to their wills. The spirit of repentance was upon me, and nobody who strayed outdoors that night was safe from having his temper carefully surveyed and his will appeased."[6] Boudreau inked a two-year contract, assuring that he would return to the Indians' helm in 1948.

When the campaign began, the oddsmakers had posted the Indians at 20–1 to win the American League pennant. Reflecting on the team's success against those long-shot odds, Veeck commented: "In 1948, Lou had the greatest season any player ever had. It was an incredible year. When we needed a base hit, Louie gave it to us. If we needed an impossible play, Louie made it for us. He dominated the season so completely that most people, looking back, are under the impression he won the batting title. He didn't. Ted Williams beat him out. Lou, however, won all the awards. My opinion of his ability as a manager remained more or less unchanged. Lou is the best manager who ever hit .355."[7]

In addition to finishing runner-up to Williams, Boudreau scored 116 runs, drove in 106, and struck out a mere nine times in 506 plate appearances. He led the league in 12 offensive categories, tying the record set by St. Louis Cardinal Joe Medwick in 1937.

Both manager and player excelled in the one-game playoff for the pennant in which Cleveland beat the Boston Red Sox, 8–3. As reported in the *New York Times,* "Playing his own position at shortstop flawlessly, maneuvering his men hither and yon with rare judgement and watching like a hawk every pitch of his youthful moundsman, Lou still found time not only to larrup two homers over the left-field barrier, but added two singles, each of which figured in further scores."[8]

Boudreau had passed over his aces Bob Lemon and Bob Feller (Feller had pitched three innings the previous day) and went against the odds, starting left-hander Gene Bearden in Fenway Park. The southpaw became a 20-game winner, since playoff statistics were added to the regular-season totals.

The boy-manager stacked his lineup with right-handed hitters to take maximum advantage of Fenway Park's "Green Monster," an inviting target for any batter swinging from the right side of the plate. Included in Boudreau's game plan was putting utility infielder Allie Clark at first base, adding one more potential wall-banger to the lineup. Clark had never played first base in the major leagues. Was this another "hunch" or a cleverly devised plan? Not much, in fact, ever came of the move, and Clark's presence in the game had little effect on its outcome. He was the only Indian starter to go hitless, and not a single ball was hit near enough to him to test his mettle as a first-sacker.

Traditionally, the postseason had been scheduled without travel days only when teams from the same section of the country were facing each other. The games of the 1945 Series between the Detroit Tigers and the Chicago Cubs were planned for consecutive days. The same was true two years later when the New York Yankees and the Brooklyn Dodgers played for the championship. On the other hand, in 1946 the Boston Red Sox and the St. Louis Cardinals met in an intersectional matchup, and days off were provided to help the teams who had to take the long train ride from one city to the other. Veeck tried to influence the scheduling of the 1948 World Series because he wanted to play without the travel days. He claimed it would save the participating clubs money on hotel accommodations and meals. He also believed, self servingly, that Cleveland's pitching staff had more depth than Boston's, and the days off would favor the Braves. The schedule makers complied with Veeck's wishes, and the series took place without a break.

Game one of the 1948 World Series featured an outstanding pitchers' duel between Johnny Sain of the Braves and Bob Feller of the Indians. The 40,135 fans in Braves Field were treated to a variety of crackling curve balls from Sain's repertoire and to the "heat" generated by "Rapid Robert" Feller's exploding fastball.

Going into the bottom of the eighth inning, with the Braves coming to bat, neither team had scored. Feller had limited Boston to a single in the fifth, and Sain had scattered four harmless hits. The Indians' fireballer issued a walk to Bill Salkeld to put the leadoff man on base. Phil Masi was sent in to run for Salkeld. Masi took second on a sacrifice bunt, and Eddie Stanky, batting eighth in the order, was given an intentional pass. Because of the eventual outcome of the inning and the game, much would be made of this questionable decision. Sibby Sisti came into the game as a pinch runner for Stanky. The next batter, Sain, drove a ball to right field, and it was gathered in for the second out.

Tommy Holmes, the Braves' leading hitter in 1948, came to the plate. Before the first pitch was delivered, Boudreau signaled for a timed pickoff play at second base. On the precise count, the shortstop sneaked in behind Masi, and Feller wheeled and fired a strike to Boudreau — a strike similar to the ones he had delivered to the shortstop on seven successful pickoff plays during the regular season. Lou put a tag on the sliding Masi, and the umpire made the call. Bill Stewart gave the palms down signal — SAFE! The Indians argued vehemently but to no avail.

Holmes, with a one-and-one count, grounded the next pitch between the third baseman and the bag for a single. Masi scored from second base for the game's only run in the Braves' 1–0 victory. Later, Holmes wrote, "It gave me the thrill of a lifetime because I drove in the winning run."[9]

October 6, 1948: Cleveland's Lou Boudreau puts the tag on Boston's Phil Masi — or does he? Despite the Indians' vehement arguments, umpire Bill Stewart called it safe (AP/Wide World).

Boudreau and his Indian teammates were sure that Masi had been out at second. The manager put the play in perspective, saying, "I had him all right. But Umpire Bill Stewart had his opinion. I know that those men are the best in the business. But it was too bad that such a masterful pitching performance had to be ruined by one decision."[10]

The *Cleveland News* was not as forgiving. A headline in the October 7 edition stated its opinion clearly: "Ump Said 'Safe'; Camera Says 'Out.'"[11]

The sequence camera that filmed the play showed Boudreau tagging Masi on the shoulder before he reached the bag. It was clear he hadn't totally missed the baserunner as the umpire had claimed.

Lucien Thayer, the *Boston Globe*'s picture editor, entered the debate, giving an erudite lesson about the limits of photographic interpretation: "The picture shows Boudreau APPARENTLY putting the ball on Masi before he slid in. The fundamental point is that the camera cannot possibly show whether Boudreau ACTUALLY had the ball on Masi. Even the eye of the camera can deceive under the angular and distance conditions under which the photograph was made."[12]

American League president William Harridge, when shown the picture, merely smiled and said, "Officially he's safe."[13]

Each of the game's pitchers had a reaction. The loser, Feller, seemed most upset about having walked Salkeld, who became the winning run. As reported in the *Cleveland News*, Feller recalled, "It seems every time I walk a man it beats me."[14] The winning hurler, Sain, commented years later, saying, "When I saw Boudreau tag him with the ball, I thought at first, 'Oh, oh, he's out.' It was one of those plays where you hope your man is safe if you are on the bench and you holler loud that he is out if you are on the other bench. I thought the pictures never really showed whether he was safe or out, but he looked out from where we sat."[15]

Mel Harder, a Cleveland coach at the time, said, "The Indians had a very good pick off play and Boudreau put it on. Masi slid head first into the bag but Boudreau tagged him on the shoulder when his hand was a foot from the base, but the umpire called Masi safe."[16]

Harder saw Boudreau's tag from the Indians' point of view. No doubt about it. Masi was out! Interestingly, Sisti, the Braves' baserunner, saw it the same way. Forty years later, he noted, "I was on 1st running for Eddie Stanky. Johnny Cooney was coaching 1st base. We both had a good look of the play at 2nd and we both agreed that Phil Masi was out."[17] Another Brave, Earl Torgeson concurred: "It was a bad call at second base on Masi. He was definitely OUT!!"[18]

The umpire had made his call — SAFE! Holmes had driven in Masi, and game one of the 1948 Fall Classic was over. Once this reality struck home, the eye of the storm shifted from Stewart to Boudreau and his eighth-inning decision to intentionally walk Stanky, putting runners at first and second base.

Boudreau had his reasons. He was aware of the competitive spirit Stanky had exhibited throughout his career. The Braves second baseman had hit .315 during the regular season but had done very little offensively since returning to the lineup after recovering from a broken leg. The Indians' manager was hoping to set up a double play. Boudreau's strategy, however, conflicted with the scouting report indicating that Sain, even though he was a pitcher, rarely hit the ball on the ground. If Sain had struck out, Feller still would have had to face Holmes and his team-leading average.

The manager explained his reasoning (or his "hunch"?) to Ed McAuley of the *Cleveland News*: "I knew that if we missed the double play, we'd have to pitch to Holmes. But Stanky has the reputation of being one of the greatest clutch hitters in the business and Holmes, for all his .325 average, would not be leading off if he were a star in the runs-batted-in department. Unfortunately, he made a hit this time and it cost us the ball game. So I'm a lousy manager. I didn't have to wait until today to find out that strategy is wonderful or terrible depending on whether or not it works."[19]

The Boston Braves had captured game one and they looked forward to the next day's clash. A new theme song had become popular at Braves Field during the summer of 1948. It was the rhyme that had been penned that summer by John Gillooly of the *Boston Record*: "Sain and Spahn / Spahn and Sain / Then we hope / For two days of rain."[20]

From September 6 through the pennant-clinching victory on the 26th, the two Braves pitchers started 11 of the team's 16 games. Because of rainouts and open dates on the schedule, manager Billy Southworth had been able to make maximum use of his pair of aces, the right-handed Sain and the left-handed Warren Spahn. In the stretch drive during which Boston beat back the Brooklyn Dodgers and the St. Louis Cardinals to clinch the pennant, Sain went 5–1 and Spahn chipped in with a 4–1 mark. Each went the distance in those victories. During one part of the season, Sain had nine complete games in a 29-day period. He ended the season with a 24–15 record, and Spahn finished at 15–12.

The second contest was a matchup of future Hall of Famers. Lemon beat Spahn, 4–1, to even the World Series games at one game apiece. In the bottom of the first inning, Boston scored a run and had runners at first and second with one out. Marvin Rickert was at the plate. Before the pitch was delivered, Boudreau signaled for a timed pickoff play at second base. On the precise count, the shortstop sneaked in behind Torgeson, and Lemon wheeled and threw a strike to Boudreau. Lou put a tag on the sliding Torgeson, and umpire Bill Grieve made the call — OUT! The pickoff helped get the Indians out of the inning. The Braves did not score the rest of the day.

Commenting on the successful pickoff in game two, Boudreau noted that an American League umpire made the call. A National League arbiter had been at second base in game one. He went on to explain: "It's a funny thing … but the umpires in the American League not only know enough to watch for it but I've given them our signals for the play so that they can see it coming. I'd have preferred to do the same thing with the National League umpires but the only time I was with them was at Commissioner Chandler's conference. And I couldn't do it then because Billy Southworth also was present."[21]

Without a day for travel, the setting for the next three games switched from the Charles River to Lake Erie. Comparison of the sizes of those two bodies of water served as a measure of the difference between the seating capacities of the stadiums in which the World Series was being played.

Crowds of about 40,000 had squeezed into Braves Field for the first two contests. Cavernous Municipal Stadium in Cleveland, the new full-time home of the Indians, held over 80,000 spectators. Prior to 1947, the first year of Veeck's club presidency, the Indians had only played their weekend games at Municipal Stadium. Cleveland's weekday contests had taken place in (National) League Park at Lexington Avenue and East Sixty-Sixth Street, a much smaller ballyard.

Veeck wanted to cram more bodies into Municipal Stadium for a baseball game than had been in any ballpark before. The third game of the Series would not be that occasion. Morning rain kept attendance down, and Bearden's left arm kept the Braves off the scoreboard in the 2–0 Cleveland victory.

Over 81,000 people did show up for game four and saw Cleveland's Steve Gromek face Sain, who went to the mound with two days' rest. The Indians won, 2–1, to take a 3–1 lead in the Series. Larry Doby's four-bagger in the bottom of the third inning provided the margin of victory.

Pitchers had been in control through the first four games. Even though the Indians held a commanding lead, the statistics were amazingly even. Each team had 21 hits of which 17 were singles, four were doubles, and one was a home run. Cleveland and Boston had divided equally the 26 strikeouts and the 14 walks. *Time* magazine conveyed the tone of those games, reporting, "The 1948 World Series was in danger of being remembered only for precision pitching. Grantland Rice called it the Series of silent bats. Disgusted fans and sportswriters complained that it was the dullest World Series in memory. What many wanted were baseballs rattling off the fences."[22]

If the games were boring and dull, the fans did not have to suffer long. Three of the first four matchups were completed quickly, lasting between 91 and 102 minutes.

Fans attending the third and final game played in Municipal Stadium watched 16 men cross the plate. The Braves' 11 runs matched the total number scored by both clubs to that point. Cleveland's five runs, their largest output, were not enough. In the midst of defeat, Veeck achieved his own personal victory. On October 10, 86,288 fans passed through the turnstiles, becoming the largest crowd in baseball history.

The Indians went back to Boston the next day and wrapped up the championship with a 4–3 victory behind the pitching of two of their ace starters, Lemon and Bearden. Cleveland, under the tutelage of player-manager Boudreau, had combined outstanding pitching with an anemic .199 team batting average in becoming the 1948 World Champions. *Time* pointed to Boudreau's contributions: "What they [the Braves] lacked, among other things, was someone like tireless Lou Boudreau, the Indians' manager and shortstop, the man who would be most remembered in the 1948 Series. He was not only the brain of Cleveland's keyed-up baseball organism, he was also the heart of it. Boudreau's pick-off play (catching a runner off base) was easily the Series' most spectacular play, and an example of his drill-order perfectionism."[23]

Following the final game, Arthur Daley of the *New York Times* gave his critique of the job that Boudreau had done: "Manager Lou Boudreau did some of his muscular master-minding when he doubled home the first run in the third but he also gave with the high-powered thought waves when he derricked Bob Lemon in favor of Gene Bearden in the eighth. That was a most daring gamble because he was using tomorrow's pitcher, thus putting all his eggs in one basket. In that strategic move he was following Leo Durocher's philosophy. The Lip always has barked, "So what? It might rain tomorrow.""[24]

1951
National League Playoff
Brooklyn Dodgers and New York Giants

Third Game — October 3 at New York

Brooklyn	1	0	0	0	0	0	0	3	0		4	8	0
New York	0	0	0	0	0	0	1	0	*4*		5	8	0

Newcombe, Branca[9]

Maglie, Jansen[9]

Few teams entering the 1951 season had experienced as much postseason frustration as the Brooklyn Dodgers had in the five previous years. Brooklyn had participated in the first-ever, best-of-three playoff in 1946, losing two straight games to the eventual World Champion St. Louis Cardinals. They made it to the Series the following year but lost to the New York Yankees, four games to three. In 1949 the Dodgers captured the National League flag on the final day of the season with a 10-inning victory over the Philadelphia Phillies, but they lost in the World Series in five games to the Bronx Bombers. In 1950, on the last day of the regular season, the Phillies' Dick Sisler hit an extra-inning, game-winning home run to defeat the Dodgers and claim the pennant. It was a heartbreaking defeat for the team from Flatbush, whose blistering charge to catch the front-running Whiz Kids fell short.

From 1946 through 1950 the Brooklyn Dodgers could have gone to the World Series as the National League champs four times if they had been blessed with a break here or there in a couple of key games over that five-year span.

In 1951 the National League season was again extended beyond the normal 154-game schedule. For only the second time in its long history, the Senior Circuit required a best-out-of-three-games playoff to determine which team would capture the flag and become its representative in the World Series. The New York Giants and the Dodgers battled to the very end. Then, in a instant, "The Shot Heard Round the World" destroyed the dreams of the Flatbush faithful and etched the vision of a momentous home run in the memories of fans of the Great American Pastime.

The Dodgers had been the early season pacesetters in 1951, and the other teams had scrambled and chased them. The New York Giants, their rivals from the Polo Grounds, caught them down the stretch. The Bums held on for dear life and finished in a flat-footed tie with the "Jints."

Early in the campaign, a race to the finish had seemed unlikely. Brooklyn broke from the gate with an 8–4 record, whereas the Giants failed to win any of their first 11 contests. Five of those losses were to the Dodgers. The Polo Grounders continued to struggle through May and sat in fifth place, 4½ games behind Brooklyn, at the end of the month. With the season in jeopardy, the Giants looked for help from their farm system and called up a youngster named Willie Mays, who was hitting .477 for Minneapolis of the American Association. Outfielder Monte Irvin recalled the move: "We were in 5th place in May of 1951. Willie Mays reported to us in Phila. During the 3 game Series he got no hits but caught everything in the outfield, [and] threw out everybody that tried to score. After winning all three games we moved to the Polo Grounds that Friday nite and the first time up against Warren Spahn he hit a tremendous home run off the left-center-field facade — he was on his way."[1]

As a result of taking all three games played against New York over the July 4 holiday, the Dodgers stretched their league lead to 7½ games. And a little over a month later, they held a commanding 13-game bulge over second-place New York.

But on August 12, the Giants began one of the "maddest dashes" to the title that the game of baseball had ever seen. A key to their newfound success, as they ran off a string of 16 straight victories, was their 21-year-old rookie, Mays. Both offensively and defensively, he provided a magic spark that had been missing earlier in the season.

From the start of the streak, which began with a double-header sweep over Philadelphia, until the final game of the season the New York Giants compiled an amazing 36–7 record. Catcher Wes Westrum remembered the head-to-head meetings with Brooklyn, saying, "Of course [we] had to beat the Dodgers when we met them and did beat them six out of seven games in the drive to cut the lead.... Beat them when you meet them was our 'Battle Cry.'"[2] During that same span, Brooklyn played only three games over .500 at 25–22, leaving the Dodgers and the Giants deadlocked at 95–58 with one game to go.

Manager Leo Durocher led his Giants into Braves Field, Boston, where they ended their amazing 50-day counterattack by winning, 3–2. Once again, the Dodgers were finishing the season against the Phillies. Charlie Dressen, pilot of the gang from Flatbush, had seen Don Newcombe shut out the Phillies, 5–0, and pick up his twentieth win in a night game on the next-to-last day of the campaign. On the season-ending Sunday afternoon, the Dodgers fell behind the Phils early, 6–1. They had closed the gap to 8–5, when they received word the Giants had won in Boston. A Dodger loss would send another pennant flying out the window. Having led most of the campaign, it would have been a bitter pill for the players and the fans to swallow.

The Giants were celebrating on the train back to New York, aware that their adversaries from Ebbets Field were trailing the Phillies. Late in the trip the bad news reached the Giants. Brooklyn had scored three times in the top of the eighth inning to knot the contest, 8–8.

Dressen went to his bullpen and found Newcombe ready to come back, with less than 24 hours' rest, and try to shut down the Whiz Kids. Eddie Sawyer summoned his ace Robin Roberts, who had pitched eight innings the previous day, and asked him to do the same to the Dodgers. During those years, it would not have seemed right had Newk and Robin not faced each other in both the season's opener and finale.

The game moved into the bottom of the twelfth inning, and Jackie Robinson took control. He robbed Eddie Waitkus of a two-out, bases-loaded single, diving headlong and grabbing a whistling line-drive. In the top of the fourteenth, Robinson came to bat and hit a game-winning homer to assure Brooklyn of a tie for the crown. Newcombe yielded one hit in 5⅔ innings of relief. Roberts was the loser, pitching 6⅔ innings.

A flip of the coin awarded game one of the playoff to Brooklyn and Ebbets Field. It was a day when home runs were decisive — and a preview to a final and momentous memory. Andy Pafko gave the Bums a lead in the second when he connected off Jim Hearn. Bobby Thomson hit a two-run homer off Ralph Branca in the top of the fourth inning to put New York ahead to stay. Irvin provided an insurance run off Branca in the eighth to make the score 3–1, and Durocher's team took a 1–0 lead in the series.

Some years later, Larry Jansen of the Giants wrote about the pitching strategy for the remainder of the playoff, saying, "Leo [Durocher] called [Sal] Maglie & myself into his office before the second game and we talked about taking a chance with [Sheldon] Jones pitching and give Maglie the extra day of rest and relieve with me in the 3rd game if Sal got in trouble. Sal & I had pitched a lot the last two weeks of the season and were tired."[3]

The manager's strategy did not work. Jones went to the mound in the Polo Grounds for game two. He would be the first of three Giant hurlers to be battered by the Dodgers in their 10–0 barrage. Six weeks of Brooklyn's downhill struggle seemed to have turned around in that one-game onslaught, which featured four Dodger home runs and 13 hits in all.

The long National League campaign came down to a one-game playoff that would take place on October 3 in the Polo Grounds. Russ Hodges and Al Hirshberg in *My Giants* described the setting: "The crowd was big, but far from a sellout. The Polo Grounds capacity of fifty-six thousand was hardly taxed by the thirty-four thousand who showed up, but I guess a lot of people figured the Giants didn't have a chance after that 10–0 debacle the day before. In the years since, I've run into about a million who claim they saw the ball game. Maybe they were there in spirit."[4]

Sal Maglie was the Giants' starting pitcher. He was in search of his twenty-fourth and most important victory of the season. Newcombe was on the hill for the Dodgers.

Brooklyn's "Beautiful Bums" continued their scoring ways of the previous day. In the top of the first inning they jumped out to a 1–0 lead, when Robinson drove home "Pee Wee" Reese, who had walked. Newcombe protected the slim margin until the bottom of the seventh when Irvin tagged up and scored from third after Thomson's fly out to center field.

The Dodgers quickly retaliated in the top of the eighth. Reese singled and went to third on a hit by Duke Snider. A Maglie wild pitch allowed Reese to cross the plate with the go-ahead run, giving Brooklyn a 2–1 edge. Two more Dodgers scored before Maglie and the Giants could get the third out.

The Giants went out in order in the bottom of the eighth. In the top of the ninth Jansen replaced Maglie, and three Dodgers went down quietly.

With a three-run lead and three outs to go, Newcombe went to the mound to hoist the pennant flag for the Dodgers. The Bums' faithful followers began to smell victory. Giants fans were slowly losing hope of catching their arch rivals and perennial adversaries. Durocher, who had tasted defeat as the manager of the Dodgers in the 1946 National League playoff, sensed that he was about to taste that same agony as skipper of the Polo Grounders.

Alvin Dark and Don Mueller led off the bottom half of the ninth with singles. Aroused Giants fans groaned when Irvin popped out. Two outs to go. It was then that those in the press box were given the following information: "Attention: Press World Series Credentials for Ebbets Field can be picked up at 6 o'clock tonight at the Biltmore Hotel."[5]

Whitey Lockman slammed a double to left, driving in Dark. The score was 4–2, and runners were at second and third base. Lockman described the situation, writing, "Don Mueller had sprained his ankle on going into 3rd base. During the time out, I recall that Freddie Fitzsimmons, our 1st base coach, walked down to 2nd base and said two prayers, one for Mueller and the other for Bobby to get a hit."[6]

Manager Dressen came to the mound. Newcombe had given him 8⅓ strong innings that Wednesday afternoon, after having pitched 14⅔ innings the previous Saturday and Sunday in Philadelphia. Brooklyn hurler Carl Erskine later recalled some of the details of the final inning, saying, "Dressen fearing that he [Newcombe] might be tiring, got the bullpen going when the Giants got a man on. Branca and I were up throwing. When a second Giant reached base, Dressen called the bullpen and asked if we were ready. Clyde Sukeforth, the bullpen coach and catcher said, 'They're both ready but Erskine is bouncing his curve sometimes.' 'Let me have Branca,' said Charlie."[7]

Erskine, recalling Dressen's choice of Branca, added, "I do think that the pitching change was influenced by the fact that Campy was hurt and not catching."[8]

Branca, who had been the losing pitcher in the opener, walked from the pen to the mound. If he could retire two Giants he would deliver the pennant to Ebbets Field. With first base open, Dressen decided against walking the next batter, Thomson, who represented the winning run.

Hodges, "The Voice of the Giants," provided the audio of the next few, amazing moments of baseball history. He told the listening audience, "So don't go away.... Light up that Chesterfield.... Stay right with us and we'll see how Ralph Branca will fare against Bobby Thomson.... Thomson against the Brooklyn club has hit a lot of long ones this year.... He has seven home runs."[9]

Branca's first pitch was a called strike. Thomson swung at the second delivery and sent the ball on its momentous journey. The long fly gave birth to Hodges's historic words:

> It's gonna be ... I believe ... the Giants win the pennant ... the Giants win the pennant ... the Giants win the pennant ... the Giants win the pennant ... Bobby Thomson hit it into the lower deck of the left-field stands ...The Giants win the pennant and they're going crazy. They're going crazy ... I don't believe it ... I don't believe it ... I will not believe it ... Bobby Thomson hit a line drive into the lower deck of the left-field stands and the place is going crazy ...The Giants — Horace Stoneham has got a winner ...The Giants win it by a score of 5–4 and they're picking up Bobby Thomson and carrying him off the field.[10]

Erskine, recalling the memorable at bat, wrote, "The pitch Thomson hit was up and in — just where the pitch should have been. The pitch he took for a strike was a low fastball — right in his power. All of this [is] to say that destiny was siding with the Giants."[11]

The three-run homer gave the New York Giants a 5–4 victory and catapulted them to the top of the National League standing — blasting the Brooklyn Dodgers out of the World Series. "Delirium broke loose below Coogan's Bluff. Men wept with joy. Women wept too."[12] The resurrected Giants had come back from the dead again. That had been the story of the regular season, and it had just become the glory of the playoff as well.

Shortly after the game, Thomson described the rush of feelings that were pounding within him:

> I didn't run around the bases — I rode around 'em on a cloud.
> Wow, I still don't know what time it is or where I am! Frankly, I don't care.
> Going around those bases in the ninth inning, I just couldn't believe what was happening to me. It felt as if I was actually living one of those middle-of-the-night dreams. You know, everything was hazy.

I heard yells ... I saw paper flying ... I noticed people jumping in the air but through it all I just kept riding high on that cloud.[13]

Years later he reflected again on the miraculous moment, saying, "It boils down to a great rivalry between the Giants and the Dodgers — and rivalries are what create interest and excitement among the players and fans and media. The Dodgers were razzing us from the dugout. It looked hopeless and I felt dejected. A few hits and suddenly the stage is set. I stayed loose, but determined and got lucky and hit one."[14]

It was a home run that came with such impact that the memory of it was burned deeply into the minds of fans throughout the baseball world. "For it was at that moment, on October 3, 1951, at the Polo Grounds, that the name of Bobby Thomson would be etched and associated forever with a swing of the bat so stunning and incredible as to make believers of dreamers everywhere."[15]

Thomson's teammate Irvin characterized the event: "Recently Hank Aaron's 715th home run was selected as the most memorable moment in baseball history. Well, we knew after Hank Aaron had hit his 714th home run that it was just a matter of time before he hit the record breaker. But Bobby's feat was totally unexpected, it was sudden and stunning, came under the greatest pressure imaginable, and was the most unbelievable experience for everyone connected with it."[16]

Branca's fateful pitch brought him a notoriety that would stay with him forever. Following the loss, his pain was evident. "Amid a scene of silent despair brief moments after the game, Branca sat on a staircase in the center of the Dodger dressing room, still in uniform, with his dark curly-haired head sunk between his knees. He was not crying, for he was beyond tears."[17] Years later he mentioned the eternal nature of one pitch: "A guy commits murder and he gets pardoned after 20 years. I didn't get pardoned.... It's just like an alcoholic. You're going to have to live with this until they put you in the ground."[18]

As the years passed, Thomson and Branca built a solid friendship and often appeared together at gatherings, recalling their memories of that 1951 moment. Thomson would recreate his mood as he stood at the plate that October afternoon. Branca would sometimes tell how his second delivery to Thomson was intended to be a waste pitch to set up his curve ball — a ball he never got to throw.

At one of those gatherings, in New York in June 1991, each spoke about the result of what had transpired on a ball field forty years earlier. "'Ralph,' said Thomson, 'didn't run away and hide.'" "'I lost a game,' Branca said, 'but I made a friend.'"[19]

The World Series began in Yankee Stadium on October 4, the day after the playoff. The Bronx Bombers would become the World Champions, defeating the Giants four games to two.

The season was over for the men of Leo Durocher. It could have ended one week earlier had it not been for Thomson's historic blast. In *The October Heroes* Irvin recalled the waning moments of the Giants' final game against the Yankees, a 4–3 loss to the Bronx Bombers. The Giants had scored twice in the top of the ninth, cutting the Yanks' margin to one run. With a man on third and two out, Durocher called on Sal Yvars to pinch-hit for Henry Thompson. Irvin said, "We were sitting on the bench wondering if we had any more miracles left in our bag. And for a second we thought we did. Sal really ripped one. He sent a screaming line drive out to right field. Hank Bauer went rushing for it and as he did he lost his footing. He slipped and fell, but some how he caught the ball and held on to it. It was a hell of a catch."[20]

That was the last out. The Yankees had captured the 1951 Fall Classic. Irvin added a final thought: "But I'll tell you the truth, as much as we wanted to win the Series we didn't feel that badly let down. We were still thinking about the play-off against the Dodgers. That was our year, right there, when Bobby hit that ball."[21]

1954

World Series

Cleveland Indians and New York Giants

First Game — September 29 at New York

Cleveland	2	0	0	0	0	0	0	0	0	0	2	8	0
New York	0	0	2	0	0	0	0	0	0	3	5	9	3

Lemon

Maglie, Liddle[8], Grissom[8]

In the working-class neighborhoods of the Bronx and Cleveland, "8 to 5" was the familiar refrain for the weekday working hours. In late September 1954, it came to stand for much more: "8 to 5" elicited optimism for those who supported the Indians in the midwestern city, and it angered those who resided near Coogan's Bluff. For those numbers represented the odds favoring the Indians over the Giants in the upcoming World Series.

Cleveland was participating in the series for the first time since 1948, when they had beaten the Boston Braves, four games to two. The Giants had been there most recently in 1951, courtesy of Bobby Thomson's "Shot Heard Round the World." The New York Yankees had gone on to capture the championship in six games.

During the 1954 season the Indians set a major-league record, winning 111 times and outdistancing the Yankees, whose 103 wins were only good enough for a second-place finish. The Tribe, under the steady leadership of manager Al Lopez, featured a pitching staff that established a record-setting American League mark for earned run average at 2.78. The trio of Bob Lemon, Early Wynn, and Mike Garcia combined for 65 of the Tribe's victories. The accomplishments of Bobby Avila and Larry Doby put them at the top of the league in a number of offensive categories. Avila led the Junior Circuit in hitting with a .341 average, and Doby captured the home run and RBI titles with 32 round-trippers and 126 runs driven in.

Based on their impressive statistics, oddsmakers, believing the Tribe were the major league's best, christened them "8 to 5" favorites to win the crown.

New Yorkers had a different opinion. Throughout the season, their Giants had battled a very competitive group of National League teams and had won the pennant. Brooklyn had been their closest competitor throughout the season, and New York had finished five games in front of them. Two days before the opener, over a million fans came out to cheer their conquering heroes during a festive ticker-tape parade up Broadway from Battery Park to City Hall.

The New York press built a hopeful case for the hometown favorites. In a two-part series prior to game one, John Drebinger, of the *New York Times* searched for some chink in the Indians' armor.

With regard to pitching, Drebinger reminded his readers that although Cleveland had its "big three," the Giants would counter with quality pitching of their own. Sal Maglie, Ruben Gomez, and lefty John Antonelli would hurl a legitimate challenge at the Indians batters. In summary, he wrote, "For the long 154-game haul, depth is of utmost importance. In a world series it is less essential. Hence the mound superiority which at first appears to weigh heavily in the Indians' favor looms less formidable when applied to the brief whirl of a series."[1]

In a position-by-position evaluation of the defenses, Drebinger gave the overall edge to the Polo Grounders. He deemed the quality of the Giants' infield superior to that of the Indians. And when discussion turned to the outfield, one name was invoked: Mays. "As for the outfield, well, here you already must know what's coming. There is only one Willie Mays, and the Giants have him. Willie unquestionably is one of the great center fielders of our time."[2]

Part two of Drebinger's report focused on the offenses and the managers. The Giants had a batting champion: Mays. They also had the runner-up: Don Mueller, who had been beaten out by "The Say-Hey Kid" on the final day of the campaign. Willie's .345 average bettered Mueller's by three points. After examining various aspects of the teams' offenses, the reporter added, "Behind Doby, Avila and Rosen, however, the Tribe's attack is not quite as varied, nor does it carry the depth of the Giant battle array. As a result, the offensive advantage must be granted to the Polo Grounders."[3]

Finally, the focus was on the men making the decisions. Lopez was depicted as "the sound, orthodox leader who plays it close to the vest and according to the book, which he knows very well."[4] In the Giants' dugout would be Leo "The Lip" Durocher, managing in his third World Series. Drebinger speculated that the outcome of the series might well depend on him: "If Leo's magic hunch plays click, the Giants could well win this series in six games. Might even make it in five. But if they backfire, the steadier hand of Alphonse Lopez could pilot the Tribe home a winner in seven."[5]

New Yorkers garnered additional hope against the "8 to 5" odds by examining the quality of the eight teams in the American League that season. The Junior Circuit was a very strange battleground in 1954. Only three clubs — the Indians, the Yankees, and the White Sox — posted winning records. The fourth-place Red

Sox staggered to a 69–85 mark, a full 42 games behind Cleveland — while the final four clubs disappeared from the radar screen. The Indians split 44 games in head-to-head meetings with the Yankees and the White Sox. They had beaten up on the five lesser lights in the league to forge their championship. New Yorkers were savvy enough to see something significant in that pattern.

The 1954 World Series began in New York on September 29. On a hot and steamy afternoon, 52,751 baseball aficionados streamed through the gates of the Polo Grounds. It was the largest crowd to attend a game in a National League park in postseason history.

Lopez sent 23-game–winner Bob Lemon to the mound against the Giants. Durocher countered with 37-year-old Sal "The Barber" Maglie, owner of a 14–6 record. Cleveland played to form, putting two tallies on the board in the top of the first inning. The usually "razor sharp" Maglie hit the leadoff batter, Al Smith, sending him to first base. Avila followed with a single to right, moving Smith to third. Maglie retired the next two batters on routine pop flies in the infield. Before the Giants right-hander could escape, Vic Wertz hit a line drive to right field for a triple, driving in the first two runs of the game.

The Giants, who had threatened in the bottom of the first but did not score, tied the game, 2–2, on three singles, a walk, and an infield out in the bottom of the third inning.

The contest remained deadlocked until the final blow was struck seven innings later. But, before arriving at that dramatic juncture, the record number of fans in the Polo Grounds and a television audience numbering in the millions witnessed one of the great spectacles in all of sport's history — a spectacle that lasted only a few seconds from beginning to end. It was one of those defensive gems that all serious baseball fans can forever visualize.

In the top of the eighth, Maglie walked Doby. Al Rosen banged a single off the Giants shortstop's hand, putting runners at first and second with no one out. Durocher removed Maglie and brought in left-hander Don Liddle. Liddle's job was to retire Wertz, who already had three hits, including the triple in the first inning, which had plated the Indians' only runs.

Durocher, Liddle, and catcher Wes Westrum huddled at the mound. The manager wanted Wertz to see high fastballs. Liddle's curve was his most effective pitch, and Wertz was considered a low fastball hitter. The pitcher recalled his feelings at the time, saying, "I had a very good curve ball and very good control of it, so I felt that Leo had pulled the rug from under me."[6] He went on to describe the sequence of pitches to the Indians' left-handed slugger:

> First pitch — Fast ball high over the middle [of the plate]. Call strike one. Now the great catcher Westrum came half way to the mound and said, he'll bunt.
>
> Second pitch — Fast ball high & tight. Attempted bunt. Foul ball strike two.

Third pitch — Curve ball way outside. Ball one.

Fourth pitch — Fast ball high and away. A strike, but Willie had to go deep into center field and make the greatest catch in baseball. (1 out)[7]

With the crack of Wertz's bat, Mays had turned his back and set sail for the deepest part of the Polo Grounds. Throughout the game, the wind had been blowing from third base toward first and had made it especially difficult to hit a ball deep to center field. That enabled Mays to play the hitters shallower than usual. Wertz had driven the ball on a line, and only Willie's great instinct enabled him to hone in on the shot. In his book, *A Day in the Bleachers*, Arnold Hano recreated the scene as he witnessed it: "Then I looked at Willie, and alarm raced through me, peril flaring against my heart. To my utter astonishment, the young Giant center fielder — the inimitable Mays, most skilled of outfielders, unique in his ability to scent the length and direction of any drive and then turn and move to the final destination of the ball — Mays was turned full around, head down, running as hard as he could, straight toward the runway between the two bleacher sections."[8]

The flight of the ball carried it to the farthest reaches of center field, toward that part of the field that led to the "old Club House." With his back to home plate, Mays raced to catch up with the descending drive. The welcoming hand of the fully extended outfielder cradled it, robbing Wertz and the Indians of a critical extra-base hit.

It was not solely the catch that brought the crowd to its feet and started a roar of excitement throughout the Polo Grounds. For, in seemingly one motion, Mays, with his cap flying off his head, whirled and threw the ball back to the infield, a split instant before he would be lying prone on the ground.

The throw was not just an empty prayer; it had a mission, and quickly reached second baseman Davey Williams. Doby, himself a center fielder, sensed that Mays might be able to catch Wertz's blast and remained close enough to second to tag up and make it to third, but no farther. Rosen, who did not have as much faith in Willie's chances of catching up with the drive, was hanging around second base when the ball was caught and had to scamper back to first to avoid becoming a memorable piece of trivia in one of baseball's great moments. Had Mays fallen down before throwing the ball, or had the throw been weak and off-target, Doby easily could have scored from second base with what would have been the winning run.

There have been varying reports as to how far the ball traveled. Some accounts said Mays caught the ball 450 feet from home plate; others said 480 feet. The latter cannot be accurate, since the sign on the Club House wall just above the Eddie Grant Memorial in the deepest part of center field read "483." Mays didn't make the catch in front of the Club House wall but at the base of the fence in front of the bleachers. Liddle suggested another distance: "It is 425 to the bottom of the fence & Willie was half a step from

September 29, 1954: In one of the greatest catches in baseball history, Willie Mays robs Vic Wertz and the Indians of a critical extra-base hit (AP/Wide World).

the warning track. He caught the ball 415 ft from Home Plate. It's still a very long fly ball."[9]

In a letter recalling the play, Williams made an amusing comment: "Funny you should ask. For all these years I have jokingly ask[ed] everyone I heard discussing the play — just who Willie threw the ball to. If they would follow the play on re-runs I would have been on TV more than Milton Berle."[10]

Wertz told a reporter for the *Cleveland Plain Dealer,* "'I never hit a ball harder in my life,' he muttered of the blast to the bleachers wall that Willie Mays pulled down. 'I know this sounds funny, but I actually thought that thing was going to carry into the bleachers. When I smacked the ball, it felt so good and I was so sure of how hard I tagged it that all the details were erased from my mind. I can't even tell you what [pitch] I hit.'"[11]

Mays's comments about the catch appeared the following day: "'Ah knew, ah had that baby all the way,' said Say-Hey. 'That was a long ball and ah just said, Willie, it's time you moved those feet. Ah just got the jump on it and beat it to the wall.'"[12]

It would not be long before comparisons were made between Mays's catch and others' and between Mays and other center fielders. The following note appeared the next day in the *Cleveland Plain Dealer*: "For years, baseball writers have marveled at Al Gionfriddo's great catch on Joe DiMaggio at the Yankee Stadium in the 1947 World Series, but Willie Mays' effort today topped that fine play."[13]

Manager Lopez agreed: "Best catch I've ever seen in a World Series.... Better than the one Gionfriddo made off of Joe DiMaggio in the stadium."[14]

DiMaggio saw the play while working as a special correspondent for a news syndicate. He offered a different opinion, stating, "I think that the catch Al Gionfriddo made on the ball I hit in 1947 series with the Dodgers was greater than Mays' catch."[15]

Years later, Cleveland outfielder Dave Philley registered a minority opinion, writing, "Ninety % of centerfielders would have made that catch facing the infield. All Baseball People knew that he dressed it up. Show-boated, we called it."[16] Teammate Wally Westlake disagreed, saying, "Willie made a great catch — he just cranked up the afterburner and out ran the ball! ... Only one centerfielder would have made the catch and his name is Willie Mays. You sure as hell don't have the time to showboat a ball that was hit damned near 500 feet!"[17]

Comparisons between some of the premier center fielders of all time were also generated by "The Catch." Tris Speaker, considered by many to be baseball's greatest at that position, was photographed with Mays before the start of the third game of the Series. Arthur Daley described the meeting: "'Cup your hand as if you're giving Willie advice,' shouted a lens snapper. 'No, siree,' laughed Tris. 'I can't give this boy any advice. He knows all the answers already.'"[18]

In a book written some years later, Monte Irvin compared "The Yankee Clipper" and "The Say-Hey Kid":

> Their styles out there were so dissimilar. Joe was smooth, Willie was always running out from under his cap, making basket catches, diving after balls. He may not have looked as graceful as Joe, but he made every

play, and a lot of them were plays that nobody ever expected him to make. Like that catch on Vic Wertz in the 1954 Series. It was one of the greatest catches I've ever seen. He'd tried to play that one down. I didn't think he had a chance in the world to get even near that ball, but yet he told me he had it all the way. His judgment was that precise.[19]

"The Catch" had been made, and the game moved into extra innings. However, Willie was not finished with Wertz. In the top of the tenth inning, the Indians' first baseman blasted a leadoff shot to left–center field for his fourth hit of the day. Mays made another phenomenal play, cutting off the ball and holding Wertz to a double. After being sacrificed to third, Wertz was stranded there.

New York came to bat in the bottom of the tenth with the score deadlocked at two apiece. Lemon was still pitching for the Indians. With one out, he walked Mays. "The Say-Hey Kid" was the type of baserunner who could distract a pitcher and change the focus of his concentration from the batter's box to first base — or whichever base Willie happened to occupy.

Mays was about to have a direct offensive effect on the outcome of game one. As he would recall, "'When Grasso came in to catch in place of Hegan,' he said shyly, 'I noticed that he don't take no warm-up throw to second. There are some catchers who don't need no warm-up. But he does. So I flashed the sign to Leo, asking if I could steal. Go ahead, if you want, he signals. So I stole second.'"[20] Following the game, Durocher offered a slightly different version, saying Willie had gone on his own. But he couldn't quarrel with the result.

With Mays on second, Lopez opted to walk Henry Thompson to set up a possible double play with Irvin coming to bat. Durocher had other plans. James "Dusty" Rhodes sat in the dugout waiting for such a moment. He was a "free spirit" from Rock Hill, S.C., and a pinch hitter par excellence. During the season Durocher had called Dusty to come off the bench and hit 45 times, and he had delivered on 15 occasions. Overall that season he had a .341 average with 15 homers and 48 RBIs in 164 official at bats. Leo sent Rhodes to the plate to bat for Irvin.

Commenting on Lemon's first pitch (a high curveball), Rhodes said, "I liked the looks of it real fine. So I went after it. The next thing I knew the ball was sailing out toward the promised land."[21] "The promised land" was barely 270 feet away. The Polo Grounds offered the shortest trip to "Canaan" in the major leagues, and Dusty had taken that route. Mays and Thompson were not sure that the "shot" would make it to the stands, and they hung around their bases. When it landed in the first row, seven feet inside the right-field foul line, they scampered home ahead of Rhodes to climax the 5–2 win for the Giants. When asked for his immediate thoughts about his homer, Dusty replied, "The minute I hit it I knew it was going to drop in or be caught."[22]

Game one was history. The Giants and their fans were ecstatic, having secured victory, as well as an eternal memory.

Sportswriters in Cleveland questioned the "justice" of a sport in which a 450-foot blast could be an out, and a 270-foot pop fly could be a game-winning, three-run homer. As Geoffrey Fisher reported in the *Cleveland News*, "They'll be talking about Dusty Rhodes' Fu Manchu home run as long as chop suey is served with rice and bean cakes. It was as oriental as a chop stick and as painful as an infected bunion."[23] Those in the losers' camp also realized that "When historians delve into the musty archives a century hence and note that a home run by James Rhodes ended a World Series game on September 29, 1954, they will have no way of knowing it was a pop fly which traveled, at a generous estimate, 270 feet."[24]

With the passage of time, the details of that home run — and perhaps even the home run itself — would be forgotten by many. What would not be forgotten about that game and about that World Series would be "The Catch" and the names of Mays and Wertz.

It had been Willie Mays's game. His stunning robbery of Wertz in the eighth inning and the throw — as well as his defensive play against the same Wertz two innings later — had kept his team in the contest. His steal of second base had set up Rhodes's game-winning at bat.

Part of the mission of the Cleveland newspapers the day after game one was to remind the Indians' fans that all had not been lost. After all, their team had dropped the first game in 1948 to the Boston Braves and had come back to win the championship. That October, game two had been the turning point.

In 1954 game two was not the turning point for Cleveland. The hometown Polo Grounders won that one also. The score was 3–1, with Antonelli going the distance and pitching an eight-hitter. Rhodes was called to pinch-hit in the fifth inning, and he delivered a "dying quail" single to center field, tying the contest, 1–1. The Giants' go-ahead run scored later in the same inning. Dusty remained in the game, and in the seventh inning he hit a mammoth home run that bounced off the right-field roof. His second homer was far from the "Chinese" variety.

A change of scenery did not change Cleveland's plight. When the teams moved to Municipal Stadium, Garcia got the starting nod for the Indians against Gomez of the Giants. New York went ahead early in the game and stayed on top for a 6–2 win, taking a 3–0 series lead. Rhodes appeared in the third inning and singled to drive in two runs, which set a World Series record of three consecutive pinch hits. Later he struck out twice, proving his mortality. Mays contributed his first three hits in the Giants' victory.

The Polo Grounders completed their sweep the next day, beating the Indians, 7–4. Durocher never went to the bench for Rhodes. In the eighth inning he did go to the bullpen for his ace, Antonelli.

That move provided grist for a story about Hank Greenberg, the Indians' vice president. After he had become reconciled to the fact that his team would probably lose the World Series, he hoped Cleveland would, at the very least, come from behind and pull out game four. That would necessitate a fifth game, and the "take" from the 80,000 people in attendance at Municipal Stadium would help pay for a new air conditioning system in the club's offices.

The Giants built an early 7–0 lead before Cleveland rebounded with three runs in the fifth. Greenberg had renewed hope, if not for the Series at least for the air conditioning. "But then Greenberg looked down at the Giants' bullpen and saw the Giants' ace left-hander, Johnny Antonelli, warming up. Greenberg gasped, 'He wouldn't! Leo wouldn't do that to us, would he?' Leo not only would, but did, bringing in Antonelli to shut the door on the Indians. And supply the last bit of cider to what had once been the Indians' 'sure thing.'"[25]

The Indians, who had won 111 of their first 154 games, could not win any of its final four — the four most important in 1954. In a short series anything can happen. What was it that happened in that Fall Classic? What turned the oddsmakers' predictions upside down? Perhaps Cleveland manager Al Lopez said it best: "I guess losing the first game at the Polo Grounds hurt us the most. We had so many chances when a hit or a long fly would have scored someone. Willie Mays made that great catch on Wertz's drive and after that we never were the same."[26]

Two of the Indians echoed the same sentiment. Westlake wrote, "We got our fannies kicked royal but it was still fun. If we had won the first game which we could have won as easy as we lost it, I think it would have been a great Series."[27] Third baseman Al Rosen was more specific, referring to Willie's grab. He reflected, "An unbelievable catch. Actually in retrospect, [it] was the turning point in the Series."[28]

1955
World Series
Brooklyn Dodgers and New York Yankees

Seventh Game — October 4 at New York

Brooklyn	0	0	0		1	0	1		0	0	0	2 5 0
New York	0	0	0		0	0	*0*		0	0	0	0 8 1

Podres

Byrne, Grim[6], Turley[8]

Zero and seven and counting.... Hope can be fragile; it can be easily destroyed. No one knew that better than the baseball fans along Flatbush Avenue in Brooklyn. Seven times their Beloved Bums had fought their way to the Fall Classic, and seven times they had broken the hearts of the faithful. There were the series in which the Dodgers died of "natural causes," finding themselves outclassed by the opposition's talents. On other occasions, however, the Bums had been the victims of bad luck or self-destruction at inopportune moments. Memories of Wambsganss, Casey, Owen, and Henrich come quickly to mind.

Five times, Brooklyn's opponent had been the despised Bronx Bombers from the other side of the city. Those years, 1941, 1947, 1949, 1952, and 1953, were draped in black, and for each a bell tolled in the heart of every Dodger fan.

New York was returning to the 1955 series after a one-year hiatus, having been beaten in '54 by the Cleveland Indians. That unbelievable occurrence had halted a string of five successive league crowns by the Bronx Bombers. From 1949 through 1953, they had also gone on to win the World Series Championship, under the tutelage of the "Ol' Professor," Charles Dillon "Casey" Stengel. Seven and zero and counting.... The Yankees had won their last seven Fall Classics against the National League pennant winners. Hope can be powerful; it can last for a long time.

The Brooklyn Dodgers were hoping 1955 would bring them their first crown. The New York Yankees were planning to capture their seventeenth trophy and place it on the mantle alongside all of the others they had won throughout the club's legendary and colorful history. And Stengel was hoping to manage his club to victory for the sixth time in as many attempts.

Walter "Smokey" Alston, the second-year manager of the Dodgers, had led his team to the pennant in an impressive manner. His pitching staff had carried Brooklyn early in the season, with Don Newcombe taking a 17–1 record into the month of August. "The Boys of Summer"—1955 version—had exploded to a 10–0 start to the season, en route to an early 22–2 record. Featuring a strong right-handed hitting lineup, including Gil Hodges, Roy Campanella, Jackie Robinson, Carl Furillo, and Captain "Pee Wee" Reese, it had been over a year since a left-hander had gone the distance and beaten the Dodgers.

However, Brooklyn's masterful mound corps had broken down toward the end of the season. During the second half of the campaign, arm and shoulder miseries nagged Newcombe, Carl Erskine, Billy Loes, and Johnny Podres for varying lengths of time. Newcombe picked up only three wins in August and September, finishing with a 20–5 record. Nevertheless, the National League champs rode home with a comfortable 13½-game bulge over the Milwaukee Braves. When Alston was asked if he thought the Dodgers feared the mighty Yankees, he answered, "I certainly don't [fear them]. I don't see any reason why they should be [feared]."[1]

New York had won the American League title by three games, but they did not have an easy time doing it. The Bronx Bombers didn't scare the opposition as much as they once had. Joe DiMaggio's retirement a couple of years earlier had signaled the end of an era, and the Mickey Mantle regime had not yet reached maturity. At the start of the '55 Series, "The Mick" was suffering from a strained muscle, and his availability was in question.

The "Big Three," Allie Reynolds, Vic Raschi, and Ed Lopat, who had accounted for numerous regular and postseason victories, had retired. Their places on the roster had been filled by Edward "Whitey" Ford, Tommy Byrne, Bob Turley, and Don Larsen. Not one member of the 1955 staff had beaten the Dodgers in a World Series game.

In 1955 there were times when the Yankees had done the unthinkable. Throughout their long and storied history, the Bronx Bombers had regularly pressured their opponents into making the big mistake. During their drive to the '55 pennant, there were times when the Yanks had beaten themselves.

Arthur Daley, writing in the *New York Times*, previewed the Bronx Bombers:

> Too many folks have a misconception of the type of team that was represented by two baseball generations of Murderers' Row. The thunder of Yankee bats drowned out two other factors the Yanks had going for them. The Ruth teams and the DiMaggio teams also had the slickest fielders in the business, defenses that were airtight. What's more, they also had superlative pitching.
>
> The 1955 model of the Yankees can't begin to compare with their diamond ancestors.[2]

The 1955 Fall Classic went seven games, with the home team winning each of the first six. With the outcome of the climactic seventh contest hanging precariously in the balance, a brash rookie left-hander made good on his promised shutout, leading his team to their long-awaited championship. The victory was sealed with another outstanding postseason catch, providing a joyous and beautiful memory for the fans of the hard-luck Brooklyn Dodgers.

Yankee Stadium was the site of the opener on September 28. Newcombe carried the hopes of the Dodgers and their optimistic supporters on his broad shoulders against left-hander Ford and the Yankees.

Newcombe could not stifle the Bronx Bombers' bats. The Yanks blasted him for six runs and eight hits, including three round-trippers, before he was relieved by Don Bessent in the sixth inning. New York won the game, 6–5, with Ford hurling eight innings. Two home runs by Joe Collins and another by Elston Howard highlighted the victory. The only excitement for the Dodgers came on homers by Furillo and Duke Snider and on Robinson's steal of home in the eighth inning.

Stengel sent Byrne, a 35-year-old southpaw, against Brooklyn in game two. Loes was Alston's choice to rekindle the fires of hope for the Bums. The Yankees won again, 4–2. All of their runs crossed the plate in the bottom of the fourth, with Byrne, the winning and route-going pitcher, driving in the final two.

As the clubs headed across town to Ebbets Field, many of the 2,848,000 residents of the borough of Brooklyn were experiencing that sinking feeling again. No team had ever come back to win a seven-game World Series after losing the first two. And that was the Dodgers' challenge as they looked ahead to game three.

In their first two victories, the Bronx Bombers had achieved something many thought was nearly impossible. Not once, but twice, Stengel sent lefties after the Dodgers' right-handed power, and both times his gamble paid off in wins. Prior to those World Series games, it had been over a year since a southpaw had gone the distance and beaten the Dodgers. Only one left-hander had pitched a full game against Brooklyn during the 1955 season. Luis Arroyo of the Cardinals had weathered the Dodgers' awesome attack for nine innings, but even he had lost the game. For Ford and Byrne to have accomplished the feat on successive days sounded a screeching alarm for the Flatbush faithful.

Game three took place on September 30 in Ebbets Field. That day Arthur Daley examined the Dodgers' pitching in his column, "Sports of the Times." After extolling the work of Newcombe and ace reliever Clem Labine, he wondered about the remainder of the Bums' staff: "There have been some recent flash returns to form by the intelligent Carl Erskine and the eccentric Billy Loes. But how permanent are they? It's to be doubted that the Brooks can win without their help. Karl Spooner, the fireballing lefty, almost was sent back to the minors in midseason to recover from the miseries in his arm. Since then he's been impressive at times. So have Sandy Koufax, Don Bessent and Roger Craig. But does a manager entrust world series assignments to such kids?"[3] Daley failed to mention another one of the "kids," the young lefty whom Alston sent out in the third game to attempt to apply the brakes to the Yankees' championship ride.

Johnny Podres had pitched a complete game for the Dodgers on June 14, but then had failed to go the route in 13 straight starts. He had experienced arm trouble and, like Spooner, was almost sent back to the minors for rehabilitation. He ended the regular season with a 9–10 record, one of only two Dodger pitchers under .500.

Podres started against the Yankees on his twenty-third birthday, and he brought the presents with him. Johnny packaged and delivered a stay of execution to his teammates and to the hometown fans in Ebbets Field who were living on borrowed time. While he was holding the Bronx Bombers to seven hits, Campanella was smacking a two-run homer, and Robinson was frustrating the Yankees' defense with his aggressive base running. The "birthday boy" pitched nine strong innings, and the Dodgers won the crucial third tilt, 8–3.

Buoyed by Podres's outing, the Dodgers went on to win games four and five as well, with right-handers Erskine, Bessent, Craig, and Labine contributing to the cause in the 8–5 and 5–3 victories. Snider, who had blasted his second series home run in game three, connected twice the following day. Campanella homered in the Bums' second win, and Sandy Amoros contributed a two-run blast in game five.

Hope had been restored! The genie was out of the bottle! What the slender 6 foot, 170 pound southpaw from tiny Witherbee, N.Y., had begun in the first game in Ebbets Field, the big bats had continued during the duration of their stay in the comfortable confines of Flatbush. The once-again "Beautiful Bums" were taking a 3–2 lead to Yankee Stadium, needing just one more victory to rewrite their story.

Back in the Bronx, Stengel had his pair of left-handed "Dodger killers" rested and ready for games six and seven. Alston was not so fortunate. Newcombe's strong right arm was throbbing with pain, and he was declared out of action for the remainder of the series.

In game six, Ford followed the script and pitched the Yankees to a 5–1 victory. New York scored all of their runs in the first inning, three coming on "Moose" Skowron's opposite-field home run.

Two more "portsiders" were waiting in the wings for the final contest — Byrne vs. Podres, veteran vs. rookie. On October 4, each would seek his second victory and the World Championship for his team.

The people of Brooklyn, who had ridden a roller coaster the entire week, were hoping in the wings. Symbolic of the Dodgers' World Series woes down

October 4, 1955: Dodger left fielder Sandy Amos gloves Yogi Berra's powerhouse drive (AP/Wide World).

Amoros relays to Pee Wee Reese, who throws to Gil Hodges to double off Gil McDougald (AP/Wide World).

through the years, the Bums' fans in 1955 had gone from the depths of despair to the heights of elation. Would their team soar one more time, or would the mystique of the Bronx Bombers in fabled Yankee Stadium plunge their "Boys of Summer" into a pit of defeat? No one took a poll on that question, but it was not hard to imagine what the answer from the honest, tortured souls along Flatbush Avenue might have been.

After the sixth game, Johnny Podres assured captain "Pee Wee" Reese, saying, "Don't worry, Pee Wee, I'll shut them out tomorrow."[4] On game day, while warming up, he told the bullpen catcher Dixie Howell, "Dixie, there's no way that line-up can beat me today."[5] That was the bravado of a confident young man preparing to do something no Dodger pitcher had ever done — win game seven of the World Series.

Through the first three innings both pitchers held the opposition scoreless. New York had men in scoring position twice, but could not score. The Dodgers were limited to two meaningless singles by Byrne.

In the top of the fourth the Bums broke through when Hodges singled home Campanella for a 1–0 lead. A second Dodger run crossed the plate in the top of the sixth, the product of a very peculiar inning. Reese led off with a single. Snider bunted him to second, and was safe himself when Skowron dropped the ball making the tag at first. It was ruled a sacrifice and an error. Campanella moved the runners along with another sacrifice bunt for the first out of the inning. Furillo was intentionally walked to load the bases. Then Hodges sent Bob Cerv deep in center to grab a run-scoring sacrifice fly. Don

Hoak followed with another intentional walk. The final Dodger batter in the inning was George "Shotgun" Shuba, who pinch-hit for Don Zimmer. Shuba grounded out to first base. Statistics on that half-inning showed that although seven men came to the plate, there were only two official at bats.

In the bottom of the frame Alston made defensive adjustments. He moved Junior Gilliam from left field to second base, taking Zimmer's spot. Alston inserted Edmundo Isasi Amoros, a Spanish speaking left-hander from Mantanzas, Cuba, into left field.

Trailing 2–0, the Yankees' Billy Martin worked Podres for a walk, and Gil McDougald bunted safely for a hit. With runners at first and second, left-hander Yogi Berra — a dead pull–hitter — came to bat. Dodger outfielders Amoros, Snider, and Furillo shifted dramatically toward right field. Alston had Labine ready in the bullpen, but he was allowing his young pitcher to face one more batter.

Podres's offering was high and hard and on the outside part of the plate. Berra went with the pitch and hit a slicing fly ball the opposite way. The unexpected path of the ball took it down the left-field line, into what had become a cavernous no-man's land. Baserunners were off as soon as they saw the direction of Berra's drive. A double into the corner would have scored both men, tying the game. Berra, representing the go-ahead run, would be at second base with no one out. And Podres would be on the bench, responsible for the go-ahead run standing halfway home.

But as Daley reported, "That was when a penitent Lady Luck, conscience stricken by the many shabby tricks she'd played on the Brooks throughout the years, put wings on the feet of Sandy Amoros and glue in his glove. He made an electrifying catch of Yogi's wrong-field wallop and turned it into a double play."[6]

After Amoros's catch, his momentum carried him perilously close to the left-field stands. Sandy pulled up, turned and threw the ball to Reese, who gunned it to Hodges to double-up a dumbfounded McDougald at first base. Reese later explained the play, saying, "It just developed.... Sandy's throw was high and as I reached for it with my glove, I caught sight of McDougald scurrying back to first. I just fired it, that's all."[7]

McDougald, years later, shared his thoughts about his part in the twin-killing:

> I've looked at the film shot of Sandy Amoros' catch many times since I was the one who got doubled up at first base on his play. I still feel that my baserunning at that time was justified because no one commented on how he caught the ball. Sandy was running toward the left field wall and if he had kept running could have made the catch easy, but might have made contact with the fence and in that case I would've never been doubled up. Instead he pulled up abruptly and as he did this I took off for third as I represented the winning [tying] run. The film does show him leaning back from the ball and he made the stab for the ball and found the Easter egg which won the Series for Brooklyn.[8]

Now, with two outs and a runner at second, Podres got Hank Bauer to ground out. The Dodgers were still ahead, 2–0.

The Beautiful Bums took their lead into the top of the seventh inning, a lead they would not relinquish on the way to a 2–0 victory and their first World Championship. Their 39 years of frustration had ended. Spontaneous celebrations erupted in Brooklyn, N.Y., and in a number of Adirondack communities where the Witherbee native and series hero, Johnny Podres, had learned to play the game on sandlots — towns such as Mineville, Port Henry, Ticonderoga, Moriah, and Elizabethtown.

In some quarters, "The Catch" that had occurred just over a year earlier in the Polo Grounds was being given second billing to "THE CATCH" of 1955. The glove on the right hand of the speedster Amoros had made the difference. Had Gilliam still been patrolling left field, there most likely would have been a far different outcome in the 1955 World Series.

Peter Golenbock, in his oral history of the Dodgers, *Bums*, recounted: "Of all the possible Dodger heroes, Amoros was among the most unlikely. He was virtually invisible to the public, for he spoke no English and was unusually diffident for a professional athlete. Reporters didn't ask him questions, because they knew he couldn't answer. Sometimes they would wave, and he would smile and nod. Sandy lived like a gypsy while on the Dodgers. He never rented an apartment, but most of the time lived on Roy Campanella's yacht. Roy had learned to speak Spanish playing winter ball in the Caribbean."[9]

John Lardner, in *Newsweek*, recounted Amoros's description of the catch. It was a description limited by the language, but not by the result:

> "You ran a long way, Sandy," one of the boys in the clubhouse said.
> "Sí, long way," said Amoros.
> "Made mucho, catcho," continued the interpreter, in pidgin.
> "Made catch," said Sandy, lighting his cigar.
> There are better ways of saying it. At any rate, it was thanks to a man who plays in Spanish that the Dodgers have their primer compeonato mundial. It was a long time coming.[10]

Both the local and national press reported the importance and the impact of the Dodgers' "primer compeonato mundial." In the *New York Times*, on the day following the great triumph, these words welcomed all Brooklynites to the "Promised Land":

> If the good burghers are pinching themselves with unaccustomed violence this morning, they need to do so no longer. It wasn't a dream, folks. Implausible though it may seem, the Dodgers won the world championship for the first time in their history yesterday. Honest, injun. It really did happen.
> It wasn't a mirage, an oasis that parched Brooklynites had seen vanish

before their eyes so often in the past. This was real, an oasis of rich green foliage, which felt suspiciously like dollar bills, and of clear water, which tasted like champagne.[11]

Many years later, Podres recalled the series and his part in it: "The 1955 World Series was no doubt my greatest thrill in baseball.... Sandy Amoros made the catch of the year. Otherwise the Dodgers may still have been looking for that 1st World Series win. Duke Snider, although I was selected MVP in '55, probably should have gotten that honor. He had a great Series hitting four home runs."[12]

The October 17 edition of *Time* magazine put it succinctly: "Everest had been scaled, man had run the four minute mile and last week the Brooklyn Dodgers won the World Series."[13] It was the first, the last, the only Fall Classic victory in Flatbush.

1956
World Series
Brooklyn Dodgers and New York Yankees

Fifth Game — October 8 at New York

Brooklyn	0	0	0	0	0	0	0	0	0	*0*	*0*	*0*
New York	0	0	0	1	0	1	0	0	x	2	5	0

Maglie
Larsen

In 1956, as postseason excitement began to build, something new and different stirred in the hearts of Brooklyn Dodger fans. The Flatbush faithful were anticipating the Fall Classic with the knowledge, born from their experience in 1955, that their team could win a World Series. The club that had struggled for so long against the odds, the fates, and the misfortunes had come out victorious the previous October, defeating the New York Yankees four games to three. They were prepared to do it again.

The Yankees were also back, seeking revenge for their ignominious loss the previous October. By the end of the season the Bronx Bombers had stretched their July 4 lead of three and a half games to nine lengths over the Cleveland Indians. Mickey Mantle anchored the offense, winning the coveted Triple Crown, by leading the league in hitting (.358), home runs (52), and runs batted in (130). Whitey Ford was the ace of the pitching staff, compiling a 19–6 record to go with a stingy 2.47 earned run average.

Don Larsen's "perfecto" in the 1956 World Series would add one more powerful memory to the list of the New York Yankees' legendary accomplishments and one more unceremonious distinction to the story of the Brooklyn Dodgers.

Brooklyn had done battle in the highly competitive National League. In early May they were in fourth place but only 1½ games out of first. By late July the Bums had fallen six games behind the front runners. From that point on they began closing the gap, and as the season neared its conclusion, the Dodgers joined a nip-and-tuck pennant battle with the Milwaukee Braves and the Cincinnati Reds. The Reds were the first to fall off the pace. Brooklyn and

Milwaukee went down to the wire, and the defending World Champions defeated the Pittsburgh Pirates on the final day of the campaign, staving off a playoff with the Braves.

During the 1956 season a new name was used to describe the Dodgers. It was not an appellation of endearment such as the "Beautiful, Beloved Bums." It was a statement of fact — they were being called the "old" Dodgers.

An article in the *New York Times* mentioned the harsh reality, commenting, "So speculation starts anew. Yankee fans had studied the three National League contenders down the homestretch. They agreed that Milwaukee had the best pitching, but that Cincinnati had both the best hitting and the best defense. The only superlative for the Dodgers was that of oldest."[1]

Indeed, Brooklyn had grown "long in the tooth." Thirty-four-year-old catcher Roy Campanella had accumulated the bumps and bruises of his special trade. Jackie Robinson, 37, had become somewhat "thick in the middle," and captain "Pee Wee" Reese was holding down shortstop in his thirty-seventh summer.

The Dodgers' elder statesman, 39-year-old Sal "The Barber" Maglie pitched the opener for Brooklyn. An ex–Giant, he had joined the Dodgers through a trade with the Cleveland Indians early in the season and had been a vital cog in the team's late-season drive to the pennant. The sensation of the previous fall, 24-year-old Johnny Podres, was wearing a sailor's suit. During 1956 he split his pitching between the Bainbridge Naval Training Station squad in Maryland and the Norfolk, Virginia, base team. (He went to the mound against military base teams and college clubs during his season away from the Dodgers.[2]) He was not available to add his left-handed talent to Brooklyn's pitching corps that summer.

New York manager Casey Stengel, at age 66, was in search of his sixth championship, having led the Yanks to their seventh flag in his eight years at the helm. He nominated Ford to face the Dodgers in Ebbets Field in game one. Casey was not worried about breaking the "cardinal rule" that advised against using lefties against Brooklyn, especially in their cozy home ball yard.

What had worked so well for "the Professor" in the first two games the year before backfired on October 3, 1956. Ford was hammered from the hill after a three-inning struggle in which he surrendered five runs. Brooklyn went on to win, 6–3. Two of their right-handed power hitters, Robinson and Gil Hodges, slammed home runs. The Yankees also had their "geriatric" contributor. Enos "Country" Slaughter, 40 years young, had a three-for-five day at the plate.

The second contest was probably the worst game the New York Yankees had ever played in a World Series. Don Larsen was the Bronx Bombers' first pitcher. He was staked to a six-run lead as his teammates clubbed Don Newcombe from the mound in the second inning. "Newk," who had led the majors with a record of 27–7, continued his pattern of futility in October. Later that afternoon as he was leaving Ebbets Field, the frustrated pitcher "popped" a heckling parking-lot attendant.

Brooklyn also "popped" Larsen, along with John Kucks and Tommy Byrne, for six runs in the bottom of the second, tying the contest. Two other "Toms," Sturdivant and Morgan, pitched for the Yankees in the third inning, surrendering two more runs. After three hours and 26 ugly minutes — and 11 bases on balls by seven Yankee pitchers — the Dodgers had their second victory, 13–8.

In 1956 the Yanks had stumbled into the same hole the Dodgers had found themselves in one year earlier. They had dropped the first two games and were going home for the next three. Only one team had ever climbed out of that particular pit and won a seven-game series, and the Bronx Bombers were playing that team.

Although Stengel had made nine pitching changes in the first two games at Ebbets Field, the struggling, embattled New York pitching staff came together after the 13–8 debacle and regrouped.

At home in Yankee Stadium, Stengel recalled Ford, who already had a loss under his belt, to hurl the third contest. Whitey went the distance in a 5–3 New York win. Slaughter belted a three-run homer in the sixth and ended the day hitting .583. "'I'd be fibbing if I didn't own up that the homer meant something a little special to me,' Slaughter said. 'You know, I'm getting toward the second half of my career, and you like to prove you can still do it.'"[3]

The next day, Sturdivant, who had surrendered two hits and two walks in less than an inning in game two, followed the pattern of rejuvenation started by Ford. Sturdivant also went the distance, holding the Dodgers to six hits in the Yankees' 6–2 victory.

Brooklyn and New York were tied at two wins apiece. Yankee Stadium was the site of a very special game five, which was held on the afternoon of October 8. The Dodger skipper Walter Alston brought back Maglie, and the right-hander pitched nine outstanding innings, allowing the Bronx Bombers only two runs and five hits.

New York countered with Larsen, who had started game two, and had given up four runs in only 1⅔ innings of work. The 6'4", 220-pound, strong-armed right-hander had put together an 11–5 record in his first full season in the Bronx. As a rookie in 1953 he had played for the St. Louis Browns and compiled a record of 7–12. Larsen became an Oriole when the franchise was moved to Baltimore for the 1954 season. He proceeded to lead the league in losses, compiling an underwhelming 3–21 mark, with two of his wins coming against the Yankees. Casey and the other Yankee masterminds saw something they liked in the 20-game loser. On November 18, 1954, New York traded for a pitcher with tremendous potential.

Along with unlimited pitching potential, the young man the Yankees had acquired also had a taste for the night life and all it had to offer. One incident in particular during spring training in 1956 caused the Yankees management great consternation. After a night on the town, Larsen wrapped his car around a pole while returning to his hotel at 5 A.M. Stengel, searching for a way to get through to Larsen and redirect his energy, chose not to fine his errant right-hander. Later, the manager said, "That big feller can be one of the greatest if he wants to be."[4]

The *New York Times* summed up Larsen's 11–5 campaign in 1956:

> Although he received plenty of chances, Don did not produce early in the season. Apparently, however, he stayed reasonably close to the line off the field, for Stengel turned back to him toward the end of the campaign. Again Larsen proved a tower of strength.
>
> His strong finish earned Larsen the starting assignment in the second game of the series in Ebbets Field last Friday. It proved to be a debacle.[5]

Interestingly, in an article written by Arthur Daley one year earlier, there had been another summation of Larsen's ability. It also mentioned Bob Turley, a fireballing righty. Daley observed, "The top Yankee right-handers, Bob Turley and Don Larsen, are likely to fashion no-hitters or get their ears pinned back in the first inning."[6]

In game five, Larsen retired the Dodgers "one, two, three" in the top half of the first. After going two and two on the leadoff hitter Jim Gilliam, Larsen struck him out. He had walked Gilliam twice in his brief stint in game two. Reese worked the right-hander to a three ball and two strike count before he also fanned. Reese would be the only Brooklyn hitter to have a three-ball count that afternoon. The final batter of the first inning, Duke Snider, lined out to right field.

Through two outs in the bottom of the fourth inning, both pitchers had set down every batter they faced. Larsen had a scare in the second when Robinson hit a hot smash off third baseman Andy Carey's glove. The ball caromed toward shortstop Gil McDougald, who pounced on it and threw to first to beat Robinson and complete the strange 5–6–3 infield out.

Mantle came to bat with two outs in the fourth. Maglie gave up the first hit and the first run when Mickey sent a two-and-two pitch into the right-field stands for his third Series homer. "The Barber," who had shaved the Phillies clean in a no-hit game two weeks earlier, held New York to one more run. Carey scored in the bottom of the sixth, staking the Yankees to a 2–0 lead.

What Larsen had done through four, he continued to do through seven. Twenty-one Dodgers had come to the plate, and twenty-one had returned to the bench without solving Larsen's assortment of fastballs, curves, and change-ups. Each was delivered from the new "no wind-up" delivery that he had begun to develop and use late in the season. The credit for the switch to the unorthodox style was given to Del Baker, a coach for the Boston Red Sox. "'All the time I was using the wind-up I was tipping off my pitches,' he [Larsen] said. 'No matter what I threw, Baker knew in advance what was coming. So I went to Jim Turner [Yankee pitching coach] and asked his permission to drop the wind-up. He gave me the okay and I've pitched without a wind-up ever since. I like it, too.'"[7] Larsen believed the delivery helped him with his control and served to keep the hitters off balance, while not taking anything away from his blazing fastball.

Whatever it was that day, the Dodgers were not doing anything against the big, powerful right-hander. To go along with Robinson's ground out via third and short, there had been a few more "what ifs." What if Mantle had not made a spectacular running backhand catch on Hodges's drive to center in the fifth inning? And, what if the next batter, Sandy Amoros, had pulled the ball a little less and it had landed in the right-field stands to the left of the foul pole rather than just to the right of it?

Through seven innings, Larsen had a perfect game brewing. Fans agonized with each pitch, cheering loudly on every Dodger out. In comparison the Yankees' dugout stood quiet. No one dared address what was happening on the field. Yogi Berra, the Yankees' catcher, commented on times like that, saying, "In the dugout you sometimes talk about a no-hitter when a guy has one going, and we might have if the score had been 8–0 or something like that. But a walk and a home run could've tied the game in the ninth and we could've lost it so nobody said nothing."[8] Berra had been there before — nine years earlier — when Bill Bevens was on the mound in the late innings for the Yankees against the Dodgers in another World Series.

By the top of the eighth inning, Yankee fans were on their feet, anticipating either a great spectacle or a terrible letdown. *The United Press* reported the final six outs:

> Dodger Eighth — Robinson, with a 0-2 count, was out, Larsen to Collins. Hodges lined to Carey. Amoros flied to Mantle and Larsen had retired 24 Dodgers in a row....
> Dodger Ninth — Furillo up. Foul, strike one. Foul, strike two. Ball one. Foul. Foul. Furillo flied to Bauer. Campanella up. Foul, strike one. Martin threw out Campanella. Mitchell batted for Maglie. Ball one. Strike one, called. Strike two, swinging. Strike three, called.[9]

When Larsen delivered his ninety-seventh pitch for a called third strike, pinch hitter Dale Mitchell looked quizzically at umpire Babe Pinelli, believing the ball was inches outside. Pinelli's raised right hand signaled the end. Twenty-seven had gone up to hit; twenty-seven had gone down. It was the World Series' first no-hit game, and a perfect one to boot. The Yankees had won, 2–0.

At that point, on a bright and clear October afternoon, there were very few partisan fans among the throng of 64,519 in Yankee Stadium. Many had worked hard, willing Larsen to perfection. Everyone knew they had witnessed an historic event. And even though it was a bit strange to believe Don Larsen had been the one to do it, his name was forever etched in the record books.

It was an accomplishment that, years later, Major League Baseball would officially designate as "the most memorable moment" in World Series and All-Star Game history.

As Shirley Povich reported:

> It was over. Automatically, the massive 226-pounder from San Diego started walking from the mound toward the dugout, as pitchers are supposed to do at the finish.
>
> But this time there was a woodenness in his steps and his stride was that of a man in a daze. The spell was broken for Larsen when Yogi Berra ran onto the field to embrace him.
>
> It was not Larsen jumping for joy. It was the more demonstrative Berra. His battery mate leaped full tilt at the big guy. In self-defense, Larsen caught Berra in mid-air as one would catch a frolicking child, and that's how they made their way toward the Yankee bench, Larsen carrying Berra.[10]

That poignant picture was etched in the memories of fans throughout the baseball world, and it remains a treasured image from one of the most phenomenal performances in sports history.

Povich's wonderfully descriptive words provided a summary of the day. He wrote, "The million-to-one shot came in. Hell froze over. A month of Sundays hit the calendar. Don Larsen today pitched a no-hitter, no-run, no-man-reach-first game in a World Series."[11]

Following the game, Pinelli, the veteran National League umpire, said, "I've seen everything and I've got to say that this gave me the biggest thrill of my 29 years of umpiring, even though it was an American Leaguer who pitched the game.... I was starting to cry when Mitchell came up in the ninth inning."[12]

In a letter written over 30 years later, McDougald, the Yankees' shortstop, recalled that Mitchell's strikeout was his main recollection from the game. He said, "The reason being he was one of the few ball players who never struck out much at all and could still get down the line quick.... He took the third strike call but in my mind it was a very questionable call but sometimes things work in your favor in certain situations."[13]

The Yankees held the lead, three games to two. So far, the pattern had been a replication of what had happened a year earlier. The loser of the first two games had rallied to win three in their home ballpark. Heading across the city to Ebbets Field, the Yankees needed to win one more game to become the World Champions. They had lost the last five games they had played in Flatbush, so that task was hardly an automatic assignment for the Bronx Bombers.

Clem Labine, who had pitched in short relief in game three, went to the hill for the Dodgers. Turley, who had thrown a scoreless inning in the first game and then had been battered around in his brief appearance in the second contest, was Stengel's choice to nail down the championship.

October 8, 1956: Yogi Berra jumps for joy into the arms of pitcher Don Larsen to celebrate the Yankee's 2–0 win (Bettman).

For the second straight day, both pitchers turned in exceptional performances. Robinson came to the plate in the bottom of the tenth and delivered a single off the left-field wall to score Gilliam with the day's only run, putting the victory in the Dodgers' column.

Turley was the tough-luck loser. He couldn't have pitched much better, giving up only four hits. He was in his second season with the Yanks, having been a part of the massive 18-player trade that also had brought Larsen to the team. In many quarters, Turley was considered the key player in the deal for New York. During the 1956 season he had put together an 8–4 record with an earned run average close to five. Turley's loss, coming on the heals of Larsen's masterpiece, raised an issue that had perplexed Stengel for some time. Referring to the loser of the sixth game, Casey had made an incisive comment in formal "Stengelese" during the most recent spring training: "I can't figger out that feller. He don't smoke. He don't drink. He don't chase around none. But he can't win as good as that misbehavin' feller which you know about."[14]

Clearly, Casey felt there was an injustice being done. On one hand he saw the clean living, hard working Turley not getting all he deserved; and on the other hand he saw Larsen's less consistent effort gaining more rewards. Stengel wouldn't give up on either one of the pitchers, and he had great hopes for each. The enigma, however, was Larsen, about whom he said, "See that big feller out there: He can throw, he can hit, he can field, he can run. He can be one of baseball's greatest pitchers any time he puts his mind to it."[15]

Game seven was won handily by the Yanks, 9–0. Berra hit two homers in the first three innings, and Kucks cruised home with the victory for the World Champion New York Yankees. Once again, Newcombe tried and failed to be the same pitcher in October that he had been during the other six months of the season. Stengel's staff, which had been mercilessly rocked in the first two battles, ended with five consecutive complete games, a feat they had not accomplished during the entire regular season.

When the Beautiful Bums became the World Champions in 1955, the players and fans of Brooklyn hoped Lady Luck would shine on them for years to come. After Wambsganss's unassisted triple play, Owen's passed ball, and Bevens's flirtation with no-hit fame for 8⅔ innings against them, the Dodgers did not want, nor deserve, any more World Series notoriety. Now they would live for all time with the ultimate feat of failure. They had been the team that was unable to get even a single man on base in a World Series game — the game played in Yankee Stadium, the Bronx, New York, on October 8, 1956.

1960
World Series
New York Yankees and Pittsburgh Pirates

Seventh Game — October 13 at Pittsburgh

New York   0   0   0   0   1   4   0   2   2   9 13 1
Pittsburgh   2   2   0   0   0   0   0   5 *1*   10 11 0
Turley, Stafford[2], Shantz[3], Coates[8], Terry[9]
Law, Face[6], Friend[9], Haddix[9]

The 1960 World Series between the Pittsburgh Pirates and the New York Yankees was a set of seven amazing games. After six contests, the teams were tied with three wins apiece. Pittsburgh's trio of victories served as a reminder of Yogi Berra's immortal words: "The game isn't over till it's over."[1] Pirate wins came in the first, fourth, and fifth contests when both of the teams were in the game until the final out. In the other three games, which went to the Yankees, New York pummeled Pittsburgh with a fusillade of hits and runs, pounding the Pirates unmercifully.

Game seven combined the flavors of the previous six contests. It offered occasions for seat-squirming, which only close and hotly contested ball games generate. It also included an onslaught of runs. And the Series' last hurrah was a magical, memorable moment that became a powerful vision for baseball fans to savor.

It is reasonable to treat the 1960 Fall Classic as two separate series. The content of each was interesting, and the contrast was amazing.

Consider the "Pirate Series" first. The Bucs were the new kids on the block. It was their first World Series since the era of "Pie" Traynor, "Kiki" Cuyler, and the Waner brothers — Paul and Lloyd. Pittsburgh was looking to win its first postseason game since 1925, when they had beaten Washington for the championship, four games to three. In 1927 they had been swept by the Yankees, 4–0.

The 1960 Pirates were managed by Danny Murtaugh, who had taken over at the helm in 1957. Prior to that change in leadership, Pittsburgh had customarily finished at or near the bottom of the National League. In 1958 they rose into the rarefied air of second place, only to fall back to fourth the following year.

During the final two months of their pennant-winning season, the Bucs staged a number of exciting comebacks and finished at the head of the pack. The "Steel City" was alive with cautious enthusiasm.

Murtaugh blended a few outstanding players with a group of experienced and solid veterans. Dick Groat led the league with a .325 average. Roberto Clemente, in his sixth year and hitting at a .314 clip, had his highest mark to date. Vernon Law with a 20–9 record, Bob Friend, Harvey Haddix, and the forkball-reliever El Roy Face led the mound corps.

The first game was played in Pittsburgh's Forbes Field on October 5. Casey Stengel decided to save ace Whitey Ford for game three in Yankee Stadium, since each of his prized left-hander's five World Series victories had come in the home park. "The Professor" started right-hander Art Ditmar against the Pirates, and Murtaugh countered with Law.

Roger Maris touched Law for a bases-empty home run in the top of the first inning. In the bottom half Ditmar faced only six batters, all but one of them reaching base. Stengel made an early call to the bullpen for Jim Coates. Before the reliever could extinguish the flames, Pittsburgh had tallied three times for a 3–1 lead. The Bucs scored twice in the fourth on Bill Mazeroski's home run and added another in the sixth. Face relieved Law in the eighth inning. He surrendered two runs in the ninth but preserved Pittsburgh's 6–4 series-opening victory.

In game four in Yankee Stadium, the Pirates picked up their second win. Once again Law went to the mound and was opposed by Ralph Terry. Bill Skowron's home run in the fourth gave the Yanks a 1–0 lead, and Terry held the Pirates hitless through four. In the fifth, Pittsburgh ended the Yankee hurler's string, with three hits and three runs to take a 3–1 lead.

The Yankees pushed across a run in their half of the seventh and had two men on base with no one out. With Bob Cerv coming to the plate, Murtaugh again replaced Law with Face. Cerv greeted El Roy with a 400-foot line drive to center field. Bill Virdon, off with the crack of the bat, ran the ball down and caught it at the base of the right-center-field fence, crashing into the barrier. It proved to be a game-saving grab. The little right-handed reliever retired seven more Yankees and picked up his second save as Law registered his second win. With the 3–2 Buc victory, the Fall Classic was deadlocked, 2–2, with one more contest to be played in the legendary "House that Ruth Built."

That game also went to the Pirates. Stengel chose Ditmar to be his starting pitcher, and he retired only four batters in his second Series appearance. Pittsburgh hung three runs on the board during Ditmar's abbreviated outing. Bill Stafford pitched strong relief for the Yankees, but the home team could not overtake the Pirates. Haddix kept the Bronx Bombers in check, allowing single tallies in the second and third. Once again, Face got Murtaugh's call from the pen to protect the lead. For the third time, Face obliged, and Pittsburgh was victorious, 5–2. With a 3–2 lead, the men of Murtaugh headed home to "Steel City" and to the welcoming refrain of "Beat 'em Bucs." In the "Pirate Series" they had captured games one, four, and five by the scores of 6–4, 3–2 and 5–2.

The "Yankee Series" began in Pittsburgh on October 6, with the Bronx Bombers trailing in games, 1–0. According to the rumor mill, Stengel was managing his final season with the Yanks. It was being advertised as the "last hurrah" of a magnificent managerial career. Throughout most of the campaign, his team had been in a tight battle with the Baltimore Orioles and the Chicago White Sox. Not until the final two weeks of the season were the Yankees able to pull away and capture their tenth American League pennant in the 12-year reign of Charles Dillon "Casey" Stengel. A win in the 1960 series would bring Stengel his eighth ring, breaking the tie with Joe McCarthy for managing the most World Champions.

Yankee offensive prowess had been the major ingredient in their race to the pennant. John Drebinger, writing in the *New York Times*, outlined the nature of the Bronx Bombers' strength:

> Mind, this is not an overpowering, crushing attack such as other Yankee teams brought into the series in the days of the Babe Ruth–Lou Gehrig era and the latter-day sluggers such as Joe DiMaggio, Bill Dickey, Charles Keller and Johnny Mize.
>
> Yet, in some respects, it is even more imposing by reason of its tremendous depth and balance of hitting power from either side of the plate. Casey Stengel will have fellows sitting on the bench who are fully a match for anything the other side has to offer in long-ball hitting.[2]

Stengel tapped Bob Turley to pitch game two. Mixing fastballs and curves, Turley allowed three runs through 8⅓ innings before the diminutive one, 5' 6½", 140-pound Bobby Shantz, came to his relief and retired the final two Pirates. The Yankees surrendered 13 hits but were never in trouble. Keyed by a seven-run sixth inning, the Bombers sent 16 men across the plate. Six Pittsburgh hurlers bore the brunt of the 19-hit attack in the Yanks' 16–3 romp. Mickey Mantle contributed two home runs and five RBIs to the Bronx Bombers' totals.

Stengel sent Ford after the Bucs in game three in Yankee Stadium. He hurled a masterful four-hit shutout, beginning a personal 33⅔ inning scoreless "October streak" that would place his name in the record books. Because of Ford's outstanding performance, the Yankees needed only one run. They got that — and nine more — waltzing to a 10–0 drubbing of the Bucs. Mantle homered again, as did Bobby Richardson — in grand-slam fashion. The New York second baseman drove in six runs in the game, as the Yankees took the series lead, 2–1.

The fourth and fifth contests went to Pittsburgh in a more ordinary manner. When Ford led his team onto the field in "Steel City" for game six, the Yankees were trailing three games to two. Friend, who had been hammered by the Yanks in his earlier start, was battered again. Five other members of the Bucs' staff were also victims of the assault, as the Bronx Bombers banged out 17 hits and scored 12 runs. Richardson, batting from his customary eighth position in the lineup, drove in three more runs to give him 12, a World Series record. And if that weren't enough, Ford threw nine more goose eggs at the Pirates. The final score was New York 12–Pittsburgh 0. Never had there been a World Series shutout of that magnitude.

That signaled the end of the "Yankee Series." They had won three times by the combined score of 38–3!

The decisive seventh game took place on October 13 in Pittsburgh. The 1960 World Series, which had produced the extremes of the pitchers' duel and the blowout and not much in between, would also provide a magical moment for the 36,683 fans in Forbes Field on a warm, hazy Thursday afternoon — a moment that would live as part of the timeless lore of baseball.

Turley pitched for Stengel's Yanks. Perhaps "the Professor" wished that he had saved his ace, Ford, for the final game and had used Turley a day earlier — at least with the previous day's outcome being such a blowout. The skipper explained his decision in his unique style:

> "In a few innings I kin tell if Ford's good," he intoned. "There's his age with three days' rest and Turley has always won the sixth game, which you can look it up."
> That clarified everything. So Stengel droned on. "There are two things when you start Ford," he said. "How many men will steal?"
> Presumably he was referring to Whitey's knack of keeping potential base stealers honest. But the Ol' Perfessor neither expanded on that topic nor bothered to supply the second item.[3]

Turley, who had pitched well in the Yankees' first win, received the message that he would be the starter by signal rather than by word. He recalled, "When I reached my locker in the clubhouse, I saw a baseball in one of my spiked shoes. It was a brand new ball and was the tip-off that I was to be the starter. Sure, I had an idea I would be it, but you never can tell with Casey."[4]

Law, with two victories already in the bag, was seeking number three for the World Championship. Remembering his pregame jitters, he wrote, "Knowing that I was pitching the final game I didn't sleep too well realizing that if I did poorly it would cause us to lose the series as pitching is about 70–80% of the game — So there was a lot of pressure to perform well."[5] He settled the butterflies in his stomach quickly, retiring the Yankees without a run in their first at bat.

In the bottom half of the inning, Turley retired the first two Pirates. He followed with a walk to Bob Skinner, after going to a full count. Rocky Nelson, who had replaced a struggling Dick Stuart in the lineup, picked out a Turley pitch and lined it into the lower right-field stands, giving Pittsburgh a 2–0 lead. When Smokey Burgess led off the bottom of the second with a single, Stengel, without hesitating, went to the bullpen for Coates. Before Jim could get things in order, he allowed the Bucs two more runs. Pittsburgh held a 4–0 bulge.

During the first five innings in their three victories, the Yankees had scored 21 runs. When "Moose" Skowron homered for New York in the top of the fifth frame of the seventh game, it was the Yanks' first tally. With a 4–1 lead, the Pirates and their fans had reason for optimism. It looked like it was going to be a "Pirate Series" game.

Before the chants of "Beat 'em Bucs" could resound through Forbes Field, the Bronx Bombers rallied. In the top of the sixth, Face relieved Law with two on base. Law said, "I was disappointed being taken out of the game with a 4–2 [4–1] lead but El Roy had done a fantastic job up till then but it wasn't his day."[6] The Yanks forged ahead on a single by Mantle, and a three-run "fly ball" by Berra that landed in the upper deck in right field just inside the foul pole and 300 feet from home plate.

That afternoon "the reliable one," who had held New York in check in each of his three previous relief appearances, was unable to work his magic. New York led, 5–4, and Buc optimism became Buc concern. When the Bronx Bombers added two more insurance runs off Face in the top of the eighth, stretching the lead to 7–4, there was reason to expect that Stengel soon would be wearing his tie-breaking World Series ring.

Events in the last inning and a half of the final game defy complete understanding. There was a freak bounce, an uncovered base, instinctive reactions and four-ply wallops. It may well have been designed by whoever creates the scripts that keep all of the "what-if" games going at full steam during baseball's "hot-stove league" season.

Gino Cimoli, pinch-hitting for Face, started the Pirates' half of the eighth with a single. Virdon hit a routine hopper toward shortstop Tony Kubek, but before Kubek could catch the ball and start a probable double-play, it took an unexpected bounce and struck him in his Adam's apple. In agonizing pain, he was removed from the game and taken to the hospital. With no one out — rather than two out — the Bucs were very much alive. Shantz remembered the unfortunate event and said, "The turning point of that series was the bad hop double play ball to Kubek. We certainly outplayed them but that's the breaks of the game."[7]

Groat singled to left field, scoring Cimoli to draw Pittsburgh within two runs of the Yankees, 7–5. Coates relieved Shantz on the mound and faced Skinner who sacrificed the base runners to second and third. Nelson hit a medium fly ball to Maris in right field, not deep enough to score Virdon from third base. Two were out.

New York was almost out of the inning. Clemente hit a slow chopper to Skowron, wide of first base. Coates, reacting slowly, did not get to the bag in time to make the critical third out. "Coates was probably so busy trying to figure out what his share of the winners' purse would be that he forgot to cover the bag. It was a rock (baseball parlance for a bone-head play) that was to grow bigger than Gibraltar. It should have ended the inning."[8] A run scored, and it was now a 7–6 ballgame. Hal Smith ignited the crowd in the next at bat, belting a three-run homer over the left-field wall and propelling the Pirates to an astounding 9–7 lead.

New York came to bat in the top of the ninth inning. Perhaps it was safe to envision the World Series flag flapping in the breeze high above Forbes Field. The Pirates were only three outs away.

Murtaugh sent Friend out to finish the job. The first two Yankees singled, putting the tying runs on base. Haddix replaced Friend. With lefty against lefty, Maris popped out weakly to the catcher. Mantle continued his torrid hitting, delivering a run-scoring single to right–center field. Berra stood in the batter's box, with Gil McDougald on third base and Mantle on first. There was one out and the Yankees were a run behind.

What happened next was the amazing result of a player's pure instinct. Berra slapped a hard grounder to Nelson at first, who fielded the ball cleanly and stepped on the bag to retire Yogi. Then he wheeled to fire the ball to second to double-up Mantle, end the game, and take the season's prize. Mantle, realizing that his only chance for safety was to return to first base, deftly slid back under Nelson's tag. That heady reaction allowed McDougald to score the tying run and extend the game.

In the bottom of the ninth, Terry climbed the hill for New York in the 9–9 thriller. The first batter was the Pittsburgh second baseman and number eight hitter, Bill Mazeroski. In an instant, Buc boosters realized their long-awaited dream. The Pirates' last at bat ended at almost the same moment it began. On Terry's second delivery, the batter and the pitcher were united in a unique bond for all time. Mazeroski swung and delivered the home run that brought the Pirates a sudden and startling 10–9 victory and a World Series Championship.

Friend, who had been battered in each of his three outings during the Series, said, "Maz's Home-Run in the 9th was a sight to see. A 440' blast over the left-center-field wall."[9]

Newsweek described the scene:

> There stood Ralph Terry, a handsome New York Yankee pitcher, praying in vain that it hadn't happened, that he hadn't thrown the high fastball straight over the heart of the plate....
>
> On the base paths, Bill Mazeroski, the Pittsburgh Pirate who had hit the ball, rounded first base and looked up in time to see the ball clear the left-center-field fence. He jumped in the air, whipped off his plastic helmet, and began whirling his right arm, like a cheerleader gone berserk, cheering for a victory that was already won.[10]

October 13, 1960: Bill Mazeroski delivers the championship (AP/Wide World).

When asked what his "immortal" pitch had been, Terry replied, "The wrong one."[11]

There have been a number of different stories about the ball Mazeroski blasted for the historic home run. One account, which appeared in the *New York Times* the following day, mentioned a 14-year-old schoolboy retrieving it and going to the Pirate dressing room to give it to the day's hero. Rather than taking the memento, it was reported that Mazeroski autographed the ball and gave it to the boy, saying, "'You keep it son, ... The memory is good enough for me.'"[12]

Haddix, who had relieved Friend in the top of the ninth, was the winning pitcher in the fantastic finale. The author of 12 consecutive innings of perfect baseball in one game during the 1959 season, he called his two victories in the 1960 World Series "the supreme moment"[13] of his career. He described his response to Mazeroski's home run, writing, "I ran to home plate. I was the first guy there. The umpire said, 'Now you've got to let him touch home.' With that everybody else was out there on top of me. Afterwards I looked down, and my shoestrings were all split and sticking out of my shoes from all the guys spiking them. I never did shake Mazeroski's hand at home plate."[14]

Virdon, commenting a number of years later, shared his recall of the game-winner: "Bill is a good friend of mine and I couldn't have been more pleased if I had hit the home run myself. It was hit high and far and it seemed like minutes before it cleared the fence. We kept watching the ball and Yogi who was playing left. When he gave up the effort to catch the ball, we knew it had a chance. I think we all jumped several feet in the air when it cleared the brick wall. That home run ended the most exciting season of my career and ignited a very fun filled evening."[15]

Mickey Vernon, a coach for the victorious Bucs, offered his thoughts: "There were so many things that happened in that game and in the Series that just another 'great hit' was bound to happen and for 'Maz' to be the one to hit the winning home run — it couldn't happen to a nicer guy and a great player to boot."[16]

"Steel City" blew its stack at 3:36 P.M. October 13, 1960, a second after Bill Mazeroski forged his dramatic home run. The World Series flag flew proudly in Forbes Field.

On Mazeroski's crushing blow, Stengel ended his memorable reign as the Yankees' manager. He had not won the ring to break the deadlock with his predecessor Joe McCarthy.

The lasting significance of Mazeroski's home run was recalled in a 1988 newspaper account, which brought it to the public's attention again. When the ball left the bat, there was confusion about who had made the historic pitch. Chuck Thompson, the play-by-play announcer, had erroneously reported that Ditmar had served up Maz's game-winner. A beer commercial, incorporating the original account of the Mazeroski homer, was aired during the 1985 World Series. Ditmar sued both the beer company and the producer of the commercial. The retired Yankee pitcher charged that the mistaken account held him up to "undeserved ridicule, humiliation and contempt."[17] He went on to say that it may have cost him appearance money for playing in Old-Timers games and charity golf tournaments. On October 11, 1988, it was reported that the ex-pitcher had "lost a Supreme Court bid to revive his suit."[18]

1962
World Series
New York Yankees and San Francisco Giants

Seventh Game — October 16 at San Francisco

New York	0	0	0		0	1	0		0	0	0	1	7	0
San Francisco	0	0	0		0	0	0		0	0	*0*	0	4	1

Terry
Sanford, O'Dell[8]

The 1962 major-league baseball season set a record for being the longest in the history of the Great American Pastime. It began on April 9 in two traditional big-league locales — Cincinnati, Ohio, and Washington, D.C. — and concluded on the afternoon of October 16 at Candlestick Park in "Johnny-come-lately" San Francisco, California. The final pitch was hit on the line toward the Yankee second baseman, who made a World Series–saving grab with the tying run at third base and the winning run on second.

It was a year when the great traditions of the past were renewed in all of their glory in new surroundings. In postseason play, the time-honored battles of the boroughs of New York were partially transported to the West Coast. Once again, newspapers reported the successes and the failures of the Dodgers, Giants, and Yankees and the accomplishments of Willie, Mickey, and the Duke.

Before the World Series began, the Los Angeles Dodgers and the San Francisco Giants met to determine who would wear the National League crown. The two teams played to a 101–61 flat-footed tie in the first season of the major leagues' expanded 162-game schedule.

Los Angeles and San Francisco faced each other in the National League's fourth playoff. The Dodgers had been in each of the previous three: 1946, 1951, and 1959. The Giants had been there only once, the memorable 1951 three-game set. A short subway ride had separated the teams 11 years earlier, but in 1962 there was a 400-mile divide between them. It was a different era and different ballparks, but for many it was still a royal backyard battle between the "Bums" and the "Jints."

San Francisco captured the opener in Candlestick Park, 8–0, with Willie

85

Mays slamming two home runs. Including the games at the close of the regular season, this was the third consecutive contest in which the Dodgers had failed to score.

The second and third playoff games took place in Dodger Stadium, Los Angeles, the team's shining new home. Prior to 1962 they had played in the L.A. Coliseum, which had been built for the 1932 Olympics. It was a misshapen oddity that made the baseball games an adventure. Down the left-field line, the wall was a mere 251 feet from home plate. To add a degree of difficulty to the inviting home-run heaven, a 42-foot-high screen stretched from the left-field corner to left–center field.

In 1962 the Dodgers had drawn nearly 2,700,000 fans to their new stadium. For the first home game with the Giants, a sparse gathering of 25,231 perplexed followers were scattered throughout the ballpark. And when San Francisco jumped off to a 5–0 lead, most in "the crowd" probably wondered why they had bothered coming at all. But Los Angeles put an end to their 35-inning scoring drought, scoring eight times in the game's later stages for an 8–7 victory, tying the playoff. The teams used 42 players in the 4-hour 18-minute affair, the longest nine-inning game in major league history.

On October 3, 11 years to the day of Bobby Thomson's "Shot Heard Round the World," the Dodgers and the Giants would decide the National League pennant in another "one-game season." And once again, the game hung in the balance until the final inning.

When the Giants came to bat in the top of the ninth, the score was 4–2 in favor of the Dodgers. San Francisco manager Alvin Dark, who 11 years earlier had led off that final inning with a hit, sent pinch hitter Matty Alou to the plate to do the same — and he delivered. Moments later he was erased by Harvey Kuenn's fielder's choice grounder. Two walks by Ed Roebuck loaded the bases and brought Mays to the plate. He promptly lashed an infield single off the pitcher's leg, driving home the third run. After a sacrifice fly, a wild pitch, a couple of walks and an error, the Giants had taken the lead, 6–4. The go-ahead run scored when Los Angeles pitcher Stan Williams issued a free pass with the bases loaded. That bit of agony was immediately added to the Dodger franchise's collection of frustrating finishes. In 1962 there had not been the shock of a mighty home run, but rather the disappointment of a decisive Giant comeback, built piece by painful piece.

Billy Pierce, who had authored the three-hit shutout in the opener, came in to quell the Dodgers in the bottom of the ninth. He did it in "one-two-three" fashion.

The National League season was over. San Francisco's Giants were going to the World Series to face the American League's best, the New York Yankees.

October 1962 featured a jet-age renewal of one of the great subway rivalries. The chartered flight was the method of travel over the 3,000-mile expanse between the homes of the Yankees and the Giants. Distance did not dim the powerful recall of other ages. The Fall Classic brought back magical memories of managers Huggins and McGraw, McCarthy and Terry, and Stengel and Durocher. In '62, there were Houk and Dark. It resurrected visions of Ruth and Frisch, of Dickey and Hubbell, of DiMaggio and Irvin. New York and San Francisco offered Mantle and Mays.

The Yankees had won the Junior Circuit by five games over Minnesota, despite having played only .500 ball from early August until they clinched the pennant. They brought an offensive band of bombers into San Francisco for the opener on October 4. The bats of Elston Howard, Bill Skowron, Bobby Richardson, Tom Tresh, Clete Boyer, Tony Kubek, and Yogi Berra joined the "M and M Boys," Mickey Mantle and Roger Maris.

Whitey Ford and Billy O'Dell opposed each other in the opener. New York struck early, scoring twice in the top of the first inning on a double by Maris, which Alou had swiped from the stands and saved from becoming a three-run homer. Jose Pagan's two-out squeeze bunt in the second scored Mays, cutting the Yankees' lead to 2–1. It represented the Giants' greatest accomplishment of the day, ending Ford's amazing World Series consecutive scoreless streak at 33⅔ innings. San Francisco came back to tie the contest, 2–2, but Boyer's homer in the seventh provided the game-winning run as the Yankees went on to a 6–2 win.

In a back-and-forth pattern that came to symbolize the series, the Giants won game two. Jack Sanford, with a season's record of 24–7 — including 16 consecutive victories — bested 23-game–winner Ralph Terry, 2–0. The Yankees collected only three hits for the day. Terry's doom was sealed in the bottom of the first when Chuck Hiller scored the only run San Francisco needed. Willie McCovey provided some insurance with a seventh-inning lead off homer.

Two days later the teams played game three in Yankee Stadium. Again the pitchers excelled with the first six innings producing nothing but goose eggs. Pierce, a Giants lefty, was touched for successive singles by Tresh, Mantle, and Maris in the home half of the seventh. With the aid of some errant fielding by San Francisco, two runs were home. Later in the inning a force out accounted for the third and deciding run. The Giants scrambled back in the top of the ninth, but only tallied twice and fell short. The game ended in the Yankees' favor, 3–2, propelling them to a 2–1 series advantage.

The relentless Giants came back and won game four, evening the Series at two apiece. With the game deadlocked, 2–2, in the seventh, Hiller hit the first-ever World Series grand slam by a National Leaguer, leading San Francisco to a 7–3 victory. Defense played a key role in the game. Mays and Jose Pagan made outstanding plays to thwart the Yankees. Willie came within a whisker of recreating his 1954 catch off the bat of Vic Wertz. He sped toward the monuments in the deepest part of center field in an attempt to outrun a drive by Skowron. He went flying out from under his cap, but the ball dropped just beyond his reach for a mighty triple.

A day of rain interrupted the proceedings, but the teams were back at it the following afternoon. Terry, the tough-luck loser in game two, went the distance for a 5–3 victory. Tresh won the game in the eighth with a timely three-run clout off Sanford.

Through the fifth game, the offensive muscle of both the Yankees and Giants had been blunted. Pitching had kept the games close, with both teams staying in contention until late into the contests. That had been the Giants' game plan and their only hope for victory. Their advance scout, Tom "Clancy" Sheehan, had the task of assessing the Bronx Bombers' major strengths and weaknesses. Sheehan had followed the Yankees during the latter part of the season, making extensive notes about what it would take to beat them. "Sheehan and manager Alvin Dark spent many pre–Series hours poring over Clancy's little treasure. Often southpaw pitcher Billy Pierce, who while in the American League knew the Yankee hitters as few men did, joined the brain sessions. Out of these conspiratorial rendezvous came a 'Yankee book' that was startlingly effective."[1]

What the Giants had planned for the Yankees, they were also experiencing themselves. The lack of offense was examined in the *New York Times*:

> This has been a deftly played World Series for the most part and has been packed with high drama by two excellently managed ball clubs. What has lifted it a mite out of the ordinary is that the supposed stars of the production have contributed so little. They should be ashamed to pick up their World Series checks.
>
> Roger Maris has collected three hits and Mickey Mantle two, none of them home runs. If you take away from Willie Mays — and the suggestion is offered that no one try — the hits he made off his private patsy, Whitey Ford, he winds up with a single safety. The other San Francisco muscle man, Orlando Cepeda, hasn't even one. He has been so dreadful he has been benched.[2]

A travel day and three days of soaking California rain from the tail end of a typhoon gave the teams ample opportunity to contemplate games six and seven. On the third rainy day they journeyed to Modesto, in the dry country, for workouts and tension relief.

The field was made playable with the help of clearing skies and three helicopters stirring up breezes in Candlestick Park, and the sixth game was played on October 15. In the "win-lose-win-lose" pattern of the series, it was the Giants' turn to rebound, and they played to form. Pierce continued to muffle the Bronx Bombers' potentially powerful bats, fashioning a three-hitter. Ford took the loss in the 5–2 Giants victory, and the count stood New York 3–San Francisco 3.

In game seven, the 43,948 fans got exactly what they had come to expect: strong pitching, poor hitting, good defense, and teams trading victories.

First was the pitching. Terry and Sanford had already hooked up twice, and each had one well-pitched win. Their final matchup proved to be the best of the three. Next was the hitting. It had taken second place to the hurling during the previous six contests. In the seventh game only one run scored and 11 hits were distributed between the clubs. The Giants ended the series hitting .226, and the Bronx Bombers were an anemic .199. Third was the fielding. Outstanding plays highlighted the defenses. Jim Davenport, at the "hot-corner," made two outstanding catches early in the game to boost Sanford and the Giants. The Yanks' Tresh robbed Mays of at least a double, just before Willie McCovey lashed a mighty triple to center. Finally, there was this postseason's unrelenting pattern. It was the Yankees' turn to win, and they did. And as an added benefit, the fans at the "Stick" and those watching on television witnessed one of baseball's magical moments.

Terry pitched a perfect game for 5⅔ innings and yielded only four hits on the day. The Yankees' offense produced the contest's only run in the fifth. Skowron led off the inning with a single through shortstop, and Boyer followed with a hit to center. Then, Sanford did the unthinkable, walking his opposite number, Terry, on a three-and-two pitch. Adding insult to injury, Sanford had fanned Terry in six of their seven previous confrontations. Tony Kubek followed with the key offensive blow of the game, grounding into a run-scoring double-play.

The Giants' last chance in the bottom of the ninth produced excitement and jitters. Pinch hitter Matty Alou reached first on a drag-bunt single. Terry reached back and threw third strikes past Alou and Hiller. That brought Mays to bat, with one out to go: "Terry blazed one to the outside and the magnificent Mays attacked it. The ball, a screaming blur of white, flashed out toward the right-field corner. A base hit! Alou, amid the bedlam, was off with the drive. He rounded second base under a full head of steam and with that head tucked deep between his shoulders as he strained for speed, speed, speed!"[3]

Maris, whose fine defensive play was often overlooked by fans because of his prowess as a home-run hitter, got a good jump on the ball and quickly reached it in the right-field corner. Third-base coach Whitey Lockman, respecting Maris's strong and accurate throwing arm, held up Alou at third base. Mays was standing at second. Kubek wrote about Lockman's decision: "He [Lockman] said he was second guessed a lot for not sending Alou on the double Mays hit down the R F line with 2 outs and trailing 1–0. Remember, McCovey was up next, 1st base open, and Cepeda on deck — Whitey L [Lockman] said he went after the game to our catcher Elston Howard & asked 'What would have happened had he sent Alou?' Ellie told him, 'The game would have been over w/o McCovey coming to the plate.'"[4]

McCovey, who had homered off Terry in game two and had hit a 410-foot triple to center field in his previous at bat, stepped to the plate. Ralph Houk went to the mound to talk with his pitcher:

HOUK: How's your control?
TERRY: Good.
HOUK: Do you want to put him on base and try for a force?
TERRY: I'd just as soon pitch to this fellow.
HOUK: Pitch to him.[5]

A single would score the tying and, probably, the winning runs. The pitcher contemplated the "wrong pitch" he had thrown to Mazeroski two years before and the resulting catastrophic World Series loss.

Terry stared in and sized up the Giants' powerful left-handed batter. He stretched and threw. The 6'4" slugger swung and hit a tremendous drive that curved foul down the right-field line. McCovey took a cut at the next pitch, "and for an instant it looked like a payoff for San Francisco. But second baseman Richardson froze to the ball as it landed in his glove with a thud and in the next instant the jubilant Yanks were smothering and pounding Terry on the back."[6] The 1–0 victory brought the New York Yankees the 1962 World Championship, the twentieth in the history of their franchise.

The most significant aspect of the play and its outcome was the second baseman's positioning before the swing of the bat. Richardson commented on how he played McCovey: "Manager Houk had motioned to him from the dugout to move over, but 'some strange sense told me to play him more toward the first base side. I guess I was really out of position. A yard to one side or another and I couldn't have had a chance at that ball.'"[7]

Mays, who was on second base at the time, also noticed that Richardson had adjusted for McCovey. He remembered: "That was a base hit that McCovey hit. Richardson never would have caught that ball except he was playing out of position. He was playing on the outfield grass in short right field. If he'd been where a second baseman should have been, it would have gone through for a hit."[8]

Richardson, at that instant, had been the player in the right place at the right time. In a discussion between former teammates on the NBC *Game of the Week* in July 1988, Kubek said, "You are remembered for the great catch in the 1962 World Series." Richardson replied, "Yes I am. It wasn't a difficult catch, but it is getting to be greater all the time."[9]

Certain World Series images and memories have become magnified over the years. The '62 moment exemplifies that phenomenon. Richardson had characterized the catch in a similar fashion a few years before his comments on NBC. "I know a lot of people picture me leaping up to catch the ball — but actually, though it was hit hard, it had a lot of backspin on it and when the ball came down, I caught it chest high. I didn't even have to jump."[10]

McCovey came within a whisker of becoming a World Series hero. No one could have been happier with the outcome than Terry. It would have been devastating to have lost another critical game, especially after having thrown so well. When it was all over, Joe DiMaggio said, "This ... was the best-pitched World Series game I've ever seen, and I was the man hired to hit the ball."[11]

The final confrontation between Terry and McCovey represented something very special. Terry had known what it was to be the "goat." His fatal pitch to Mazeroski in 1960 was indelibly stamped in his memory and in the memories of baseball fans everywhere. About his 1962 test Terry said, "I am a very lucky fellow and I certainly thank God for a second opportunity.... You don't often get another chance to prove yourself, in baseball or in life."[12] He went on to remind the listener that baseball is a game that often determines its heroes and its villains by small strokes of luck or misfortune: "'I'm the luckiest man in the world,' said the grateful Ralph Terry. 'A foot more to the right and I lose the game.'"[13] In an interview years later, he remarked, "I was looking at this as a chance to redeem myself. Otherwise, I might have been remembered as one of the great losers of all time."[14]

The New York Yankees won the grand prize — the 1962 World Championship and their twentieth title in 40 years. Terry, after a 23-victory regular season, realized his ultimate goal when the final out of the seventh game was securely nestled in Richardson's glove.

Even in defeat, the San Francisco Giants gained a prize of great value. They had won the respect of the hometown fans.

> Instead of bitterness and frustration in the wake of defeat, there was a sense of something having been won; the respect of a city that had jeered at their team's slumps, and taken their successes for granted, and never believed until the last game of the longest series that the Giants had the stuff that makes champions.
>
> The Giants lost with classic dignity and there were no tears. No laughter either, but pride and relief. The Giants had lost forever the tag "immigrants"; they had become San Franciscans and they did it the hard way, fighting and losing a brave fight.[15]

1969

World Series

Baltimore Orioles and New York Mets

Third Game — October 14 at New York

Baltimore	0	0	0	*0*	0	0	*0*	0	0	0	4	1
New York	1	2	0	0	0	1	0	1	x	5	6	0

Palmer, Leonhard[7]
Gentry, Ryan[7]

Fourth Game — October 15 at New York

Baltimore	0	0	0	0	0	0	0	0	*1*	0	1	6	1
New York	0	1	0	0	0	0	0	0	0	1	2	10	1

Cuellar, Watt[8], Hall[10], Richert[10]
Seaver

When the New York Mets departed from La Guardia Airport en route to Baltimore, Maryland, for the first game of the 1969 World Series, everyone knew they were the heavy underdogs in the upcoming battle. The Orioles were the runaway pennant winners in the American League. The October 10 edition of the *New York Times* noted, Met chances of winning the World Series are about the same as their preseason chances of winning the pennant. Let that be a comfort to you."[1]

The Mets' long climb to the pinnacle of the National League began in 1962, when the New York "Metropolitans" played their first game. Walter O'Malley and Horace C. Stoneham had moved the Dodgers and the Giants west following the 1957 season. After three-quarters of a century of providing some of baseball's greatest thrills, the National League had abandoned New York. The loyal fans who had cheered Jackie Robinson, Gil Hodges, Leo Durocher, Duke Snider, Willie Mays, and "Pee Wee" Reese were left without a team. And the Yankees were unable to win vast numbers of them over to their "house" in the Bronx. In 1958, with a single team for all of New York City and its environs, attendance at Yankee Stadium dropped by nearly 70,000. Many baseball lovers in New York could never accept the history, tradition, and success of the Yankees. They hoped for something more.

New York mayor Robert F. Wagner also wanted more. He wanted to find a Senior Circuit franchise for his city. Enlisting the aid of William A. Shea, a sports-minded lawyer, the process began. At first, Shea attempted to lure an existing franchise to the Big Apple, concentrating his attention on the Cincinnati Reds and the Philadelphia Phillies. When that approach failed he initiated plans for a third major league — the Continental League — which would include a New York team playing in a new stadium in Flushing. Others from across the country and Canada brought similar excitement to the project. Early in 1960 it appeared that there would be a Continental League. However, financial restraints and other realities were impossible to overcome, and on August 2, 1960, plans for the new league were put to rest.

From this aborted plan came four new major-league franchises. One of them was a National League team for New York, which fulfilled Shea's dream of having everyday baseball in his city again. On October 17, 1960, the New York "Metropolitans" were born.

The early Mets gave their followers some of the worst exhibitions the game had ever known, and the dream became a living nightmare. From the drafting of Hobie Landrith as "the first Met" until the completion of the roster with names such as Jay Hook, Elio Chacon, Bob Miller, and "Roadblock" Jones, the Mets were destined to strike fear in the hearts of no one. There were many unknowns and some known has-beens in camp for their inaugural spring training. Gus Bell, Frank Thomas, and Richie Ashburn manned the first Met outfield. Marvelous Marvin Throneberry joined the club later in their initial season, coming over from the Baltimore Orioles in a trade for Landrith. In that move "the first Met" was replaced by "the all-time Met of the early 1960s."

The New York Mets built links with the city's legendary sporting past. The Polo Grounds, with its storied traditions from the long history of the Giants, was the new team's home for their first two years of life. Hodges, a Beautiful Bum for 11 years before he flew west with the Dodgers, was taken in the player draft and came "home." The club drew organizational leadership from the Yankees. George M. Weiss, the Bronx Bombers' long-time general manager, became the fledgling club's president and G.M. And the one and only Charles Dillon "Casey" Stengel climbed back into uniform and took charge on the field. The "Ol Professor" had managed Brooklyn, the Boston Braves, and most recently had completed an outstanding 12-year stint with the Yanks. Joseph Durso in *Casey* reminded his readers: "It was the fifth time in nearly 50 years that Stengel had marched on New York: In 1912, eagerly, to join the Dodgers; in 1921, jubilantly, to become a Giant; in 1932, gratefully, to coach the Dodgers; in 1948, solemnly, to take over the Yankees, and now in October 1961, apprehensively, to direct the Mets."[2]

After a rain-out on opening day, 1962, the Mets played their inaugural game the following night in St. Louis. In the first inning, Roger Craig committed a balk with the Cardinals' Bill White on third base. Quickly, the Mets were behind, 1–0. The final score of their first contest was St. Louis 11–New York 4. On Friday the thirteenth of April, before a small crowd of 12,447 fans on a cool, drizzly afternoon, the Mets faced the Pittsburgh Pirates in their opener in the Polo Grounds. Three wild pitches helped the Pirates score two runs on the way to their 4–3 victory.

New York lost nine straight games before picking up the franchise's first victory. Those humble beginnings would mark their fortunes for some time to come.

Durso wrote, "The idea was that the Mets would entertain the public with a kind of Circus Maximus. The aim: to keep the people docile until times grew better. The ringleader: Casey Stengel, who would run the show by doing what had come naturally since his days of mischief-making at Western Dental College."[3]

The "Amazin' Mets," who often had trouble catching in the field, did catch on with the fans. A tradition was in the making, and they drew 922,530 to the Polo Grounds in their initial season. The club passed the 1,000,000 mark in 1963 and shortly thereafter moved toward an annual paid attendance of over 2,000,000 fans.

On the field, however, progress was slower. It was a long, winding, rugged, uphill road from "notoriety" to "respectability." In 1963 the Mets lost 111 games. A year later they registered 109 defeats, with 20 of them belonging to Tracy Stallard in a disheartening 10–20 campaign.

Stengel was able to bide time for the organization while it went through the painful period of development and growth. Durso commented, "He [Stengel] emphasized the fact that the Yankees had 'fired' him and that he had now been reincarnated as the Great White Father of the Amazing Mets, who were everything the Yankees weren't — warm, lovable, comically unpredictable, splendidly unsuccessful Sad Sacks."[4]

On April 17, 1964, the Mets played their first game in brand new Shea Stadium. A sparkling, modern, five-tier ballpark in Flushing with a symmetrical playing field, a huge electronic scoreboard, and a 1500-seat restaurant symbolized the Mets' new image.

At the dedication there was an attempt to blend the historic past with the hope for an exciting future. Shea, the moving force behind the founding of the Mets, filled one empty champagne bottle with water from Brooklyn's Gowanus Canal and another with water from the Harlem River near the site of the Polo Grounds. He poured the waters together to symbolize the melding of the Dodgers' and the Giants' traditions into the new Mets.

Even though attendance continued to increase, many fans still mourned the passing of the Dodgers and the Giants, New York's "true" National League teams.

Wes Westrum climbed into the manager's seat in 1965 when Stengel retired after breaking his hip on July 25, five days before his seventy-fifth birthday. Under Westrum, the team finished dead-last again—15 games out of the ninth spot. During Westrum's years at the helm, new names began to appear on the lineup cards. In 1965 Ron Swoboda and Tug McGraw put on Met uniforms for the first time. Ed Kranepool and Jerry Grote joined the club in 1966, and the team climbed out of the cellar, finishing in ninth place with a record of 66–95. The next year, Tom Seaver and Cleon Jones were added, but New York descended back to the basement. In 1968 Gil Hodges became the manager, and he "penciled in" the names Bud Harrelson, Jerry Koosman, and Nolan Ryan. The Mets were a ninth-place team, ending up with a 73–89 record. They also finished without their manager. On September 24, Hodges suffered a heart attack, and his future with the team was in question.

The "Amazin' Mets" entered the 1969 season as a 100–1 shot to win the National League pennant. Hodges had recovered and was back managing the team, but only time would tell how much stress and strain he could take and how much frustration his club would give him.

For 1969 each of the leagues had been divided into two six-team divisions. New York was assured of finishing no lower than sixth place!

At times during the summer of '69, the Mets were much closer to the pack than many thought they had any right to be. At other points along the way, they could be found as many as 9½ games behind the front-running Chicago Cubs. Riding the strong pitching of Koosman (17–9) and Seaver (25–7), New York put on an amazing late-season rush. Early in September they moved to within ½ game of the Cubs after sweeping a series from them. The Mets took over first place on September 10 with a victory over Montreal that was coupled with a Cubs loss to Philadelphia. Chicago had fallen from the lead after 155 consecutive days at the top. New York continued to win, building an eight-game cushion. Their high point came on September 24, the monumental day when they clinched the Eastern Division of the National League.

New York's top two pitchers, Koosman and Seaver, a lefty and a righty, were being cast in the mold of Spahn and Sain and of Koufax and Drysdale. The moundsmen and Mets magic had been the basic ingredients in the miracle.

The club brought an anemic .242 team batting average into the National League Championship Series to face the Atlanta Braves who, despite geography, had won the West. Once again the Mets were the underdogs, but the miracles continued during the Mets' march to the pennant. When the pitching faltered, New York's bats came alive just in time to rescue the club. They captured the NLCS, beating the Braves in three straight games by the scores of 9–5, 11–6 and 7–4.

The American League Champion Baltimore Orioles were waiting to take on the Mets. They had decimated the American League East, romping to a 19-length win over the field. They followed their regular season success by handling the Minnesota Twins in three games. The Orioles needed 12 innings to win the first, 4–3, and 11 innings to capture the second, 1–0. The final game was more in Baltimore's style. They pounded Minnesota 11–2.

During the regular season, the Orioles won 109 times. Mike Cuellar (23–11), Dave McNally (20–7) and Jim Palmer (16–4) were the nucleus of Baltimore's strong staff. The Orioles also had an outstanding offense built around the two Robinsons — Frank and Brooks — Elrod Hendricks, Mark Belanger, Paul Blair, Boog Powell, and Don Buford. That blend of personnel, under second-year manager Earl Weaver, led Arthur Daley to write in the *New York Times*, "It's somewhat obvious that Baltimore is the best team in baseball. It has the same beautiful balance of the old-time Yankees of the Ruthian era — explosive hitting, slick defense and overpowering pitching."[5]

Baltimore was one of the most talented teams of the modern era. No one was quite sure what to make of New York. Many were not even convinced that the Mets were the best team in the National League in 1969. But no one could deny that they were there to play in the World Series. The Mets, after their season of magic and wonder, believed they were on their way to the championship and no one could stop them — not even the Baltimore Orioles. Their fans, including New York Mayor John Lindsay, who had expressed unabashed optimism, felt the same way, however unreasonable it may have seemed.

Baltimore's fans came to Memorial Stadium in large numbers to cheer the Orioles, but at times their attention was distracted by their beloved Colts. For Baltimore was, first and foremost, a football city. They came out "to watch" the Orioles, but they "lived for" the Colts. On January 12, 1969, the Colts and John Unitas had been in the World Championship game. The powerful National League Champions lost, 16–7. They were beaten by a band of American League upstarts, the New York Jets, with a brash young quarterback named Joe Namath leading them to the miraculous upset.

When the 1969 World Series was over, major league baseball had a new team to add to its list of champions. The unbelievable happened, and the Mets claimed equality with the rest of the baseball world. And tucked in the midst of the franchise's fondest memories were a number of spectacular moments from that Fall Classic. There was the power and excitement of a diving Ron Swoboda making his miracle catch in game four. And then, perhaps the most vivid memory, the "double-vision" of a fleet and acrobatic Tommy Agee grabbing two drives out of the sky to help bring the Mets a victory in game three.

The opener was played on October 11 in Memorial Stadium, and a pair of 20-game winners, Seaver and Cuellar, faced each other. Buford led off the bottom of the first inning with a home run, giving the Orioles a quick 1–0 advantage. He also contributed a run-scoring double in the fourth to support Cuellar in the 4–1 victory.

The Mets' stellar pitching had lost some of its luster. Seaver tired in the early innings, continuing the pattern that had appeared unexpectedly against the Braves. Baltimore's victory delivered "reality" to New York's doorstep. "The Mets' propensity for amazing everyone with their endless supply of miracles was halted with disconcerting abruptness."[6]

Koosman went to the mound the next day and attempted to regain momentum for the Mets. He held Baltimore hitless through six innings. In the next 2⅔ frames he surrendered two hits and a run before being relieved by Ron Taylor. Koosman left the game with a 2–1 lead, and Taylor retired Brooks Robinson on a roller, leaving the series even at one game apiece.

The Mets returned home to friendly Shea Stadium, to "Magic Land," in Flushing for game three on October 14. From the middle of August through the NLCS, they had won 23 of the 28 games played there. On an overcast afternoon, Gary Gentry, with relief help from Ryan, shut out the Orioles on four hits, 5–0. The continuing resurgence of New York's pitching was a major factor in the victory.

The rest of the third game was owned by Tommie Agee. As Buford had done in Baltimore in game one, Agee led off the bottom of the first inning with a home run over the fence in left–center field. That might have been expected from the first batter for the "Amazin' Mets" in their inaugural World Series home opener. Agee's offense was only part of the story. It was on defense that the game belonged to the 27-year-old center fielder.

In the fourth inning, after Gentry had fanned Blair, Frank Robinson lined a shot to left field, and Jones made a diving trap of the ball. It was ruled a single. Powell singled to right, moving Robinson to third. Brooks Robinson was Gentry's second strikeout victim in the inning. Then Hendricks tagged an opposite-field liner to left center. Agee sprinted across the grass and, with his glove stretched across his body, made an outstanding grab for the final out.

The catch would stir memories of some of the other great ones from the past — Mays of the Giants, Gionfriddo and Amoros of the Dodgers. Agee of the Mets was added to that group, and he was not finished yet. In the opinion of many, the best was still to come.

Hendricks opened the seventh with a long fly to Agee. Dave Johnson, the Oriole infielder who would become the manager of the Mets in 1984, also flied out to center. With two away, Gentry walked three straight Orioles: Belanger, Dave May, and Buford. Hodges brought in Ryan to replace Gentry. The first batter, Blair, drove the ball on a line to the right-center-field gap:

> Agee tore after it with his peculiar rolling gait, much like a sailor too long at sea on an old-fashioned clipper ship. What added to his difficulties was that the wind pushed down on the ball. Tommie had to dive for it. So he skidded on his profile, glove stretched out in front of him as three runners spun around the bases.
>
> Kerplunk! Into that outstretched glove dropped the ball for one of the great catches of World Series history.[7]

The pair of amazing catches were instrumental in the Mets' 5–0 win. Weaver, the Orioles' manager, credited Agee with the victory, stating, "He batted in one run for them, and took five away from us."[8]

Comparisons were made between Agee's two outstanding grabs, as well as between those and other memorable postseason catches.

Commenting on Hendricks's fourth-inning liner, Agee said, "I saw the ball well because the sky was cloudy, not bright, but I wasn't sure I could reach it. I figure, if I can touch a ball I can hold it.... I knew it would be tough because it was away from my glove side — and it almost went through my webbing."[9]

Contrary to the opinions of many of the onlookers, Agee thought his second catch was not as difficult as the first. "It's an easier play because it was on my glove side ... and I didn't have as far to go, but the wind kept taking it away and I had to dive."[10]

Joe Pignatano, a Mets coach in the bullpen, described the second play from his vantage point, saying, "Any time you make a catch on your feet and then make one on the ground, the second has to be harder.... I got a good look at Tommie's face as he started after the ball and he had an expression that said he didn't think he could get it. Then, as he got closer, the expression changed — and he got it."[11]

Agee had arrived in New York in 1968, after being traded from the Chicago White Sox, and he became the twenty-eighth player to patrol center field in the short history of the Mets. In the personal experiences of Agee, which included years of struggle and development as a ballplayer, one could trace — in microcosm — the development of the New York Mets from early frustration to eventual fulfillment. He was beaned by a Bob Gibson fastball in his first at bat for his new team in spring training, and his car was stolen from the Shea Stadium parking lot shortly after the regular season began. And after his first 34 at bats as a Met, he was zero for the season. He ended his first campaign in Flushing with a meager .217 batting average.

Agee's career improved as the Mets improved. The high point for him during the '69 season, when he hit .271 and led the team in home runs and runs batted in, had occurred in the third game of the World Series. The World Championship would be added to that accomplishment two games later.

Buoyed by Agee's heroics, the Mets took a 2–1 lead into the fourth game. It was a lead they wouldn't relinquish in their rush to their first championship.

Game four went ten innings before Seaver picked up the 2–1 victory. Swoboda provided the special memory in that contest. The Mets went into the top of the ninth, holding a 1–0 lead. With one away Frank Robinson singled to left for the Orioles. Boog Powell followed with a single to right field, with Robinson sliding into third base. That set the stage for Swoboda's heroics. Brooks Robinson lashed a sinking line drive to right, in front of the New York outfielder. Without a moment's hesitation, the acrobatic muscleman of the Mets raced in and made a diving, tumbling grab. Robinson scored from third, tying the game, 1–1.

That catch also looms large in the memories of Mets fans, and some who saw it ranked it above Agee's. Baltimore players "were unanimous in their opinion that Ron Swoboda's game saving catch in the ninth inning yesterday was better than the two defensive gems turned in by Tommie Agee on Tuesday."[12]

The vision of the right fielder diving headlong across the outfield grass and catching the ball is a lasting picture of both grace and desperation. Although a run scored to tie the game, it could have been much worse. Had Swoboda played it safe and taken it on the bounce, the Orioles' rally would have continued in full force. Worse yet, had the ball gotten by him and rolled to the fence, the lead run certainly would have crossed the plate. Still, the Mets broke the tie in the bottom of the tenth and picked up a 2–1 victory.

After the game, Swoboda commented on the ninth-inning dilemma — which turned out for him to be no dilemma at all: "You just have to take the chance you can reach the ball.... So I just go as far as I can and pray. If there's even one chance in a thousand to catch it, I'm going to try."[13] Some 20 years later, in answer to a question about the catch, he remarked philosophically, "Just imagine a game you played as a child becoming the vehicle to your wildest adult dreams!"[14]

In game five, Baltimore broke on top, 3–0. Swoboda's sliding save had been instrumental in delivering defeat to the Orioles the previous day. Shoe polish and a home run by a player who had hit only three others in the two previous seasons brought doom to Baltimore in the final game of the World Series.

In the bottom of the sixth, Jones argued that he had been hit by a pitch from McNally. At the batter's request, the umpire examined the baseball and found shoe polish on it. Compelled by the evidence, the arbiter awarded first base to Jones. Donn Clendenon immediately followed with his third round-tripper of the series, closing the gap to 3–2. Later, Al Weis hit a dramatic two-run homer to break a 3–3 tie, only his fourth round-tripper over a two-year span.

The impossible dream came true at 3:17 P.M. on a sunny and cool fall afternoon when Cleon Jones caught a fly ball off the bat of Dave Johnson. The final score of the series-clinching fifth game was 5–3.

Statistics revealed some of the reasons why the Mets had won the championship. Buford, Blair, Johnson, and Brooks Robinson hit a combined .080. Five of the Orioles' 23 hits came from batters in the ninth spot in the order, and pitchers had driven in three of the losers' nine runs. During one stretch in the series, Baltimore went 19 innings without scoring.

But the "Amazin' Mets" had a bit of the miraculous working for them throughout those five October games. "When the Mets finally clinched the championship, a blizzard of ticker tape settled over Manhattan; and at Shea Stadium fans pulled up chunks of turf, festooning themselves with the magic sod as if its newly-established healing qualities could cure all their fears and ills as merely walking upon it had cured those of their heroes."[15]

The New York Mets had made their home in ninth or tenth place in each of the previous seven years of the team's existence. In 1969 they climbed to the top rung of baseball's ladder.

The Mets had been "Amazin'" since their inaugural season. The term was used to describe the way they butchered and betrayed the Great American Pastime. Sometime during the 1969 season, when many were looking the other way, a magic transformation had taken place. The team came to believe, the fans came to believe, and then in October, the baseball world believed. And "Amazin'" came to mean miraculous, unbeatable, unbelievable, and World Champion.

Daley, in an article entitled "Defying Belief," put a final touch on the story for 1969: "The Mets won. Ah, those Mets! They are amazing, fantastic, preposterous, stupendous, colossal, inconceivable and wonderful. Take your pick, one adjective or all."[16]

1970

World Series

Baltimore Orioles and Cincinnati Reds

When fans of the Great American Pastime think about the 1970 World Series, some focus on the outstanding quality of the teams that participated in those five games. One club had established itself as a dominant force; the other had begun to display the style and character that promised to make it a power for years to come.

Many people, however, don't remember much about either of the teams. What they recall is the player who took the series into his glove and turned it into his own Fall Classic highlight film.

The Baltimore Orioles and the Cincinnati Reds faced each other that October. "Dynasty" was being used to describe the Orioles, for this was their third World Series appearance in five years. They had beaten the Los Angeles Dodgers in four straight games to become the champions in 1966. In 1969 they ran up against the "Amazin' Mets," losing to them in a five-game set. Logic had been overwhelmed by an unbeatable magic. Baltimore viewed 1970 as the opportunity to atone for their crushing defeat.

The Cincinnati Reds had been dubbed "the Big Red Machine." They were a young team featuring power, pitching, and defense. The nucleus of the club had been assembled since the Reds' last postseason series appearance, which had been in 1961.

Each of the managers was in the dawn of his major league managerial career, and each had a promising future in the trade.

For the second straight season, Earl Weaver and his Orioles had wreaked havoc on the American League East, winning 108 times (one less than the previous year) and capturing their division by 15 games. Three pitchers accounted for 68 of the victories — Mike Cuellar (24), Dave McNally (24) and Jim Palmer (20). The Robinsons — Brooks and Frank — Boog Powell, Paul Blair, Don Buford, and Mark Belanger were back to avenge their surprising and painful finish in the 1969 Fall Classic.

After clinching the pennant, Baltimore refused to coast into the American League Championship Series. Following a September 19 defeat by the

Cleveland Indians, the Orioles won their final 11 games of the regular season. Then they marched through the ALCS, dominating the Minnesota Twins 10–6, 11–3 and 6–1. The Orioles entered the World Series riding the crest of a 14-game winning streak.

George "Sparky" Anderson was in his rookie year as a major league manager and had the Reds sitting at the top of the National League West for all but one day during the campaign. They finished with a 102–60 record and a 14½-game bulge over the Los Angeles Dodgers. In the National League Championship Series, they disposed of the Pittsburgh Pirates in three close contests, 3–0, 3–1 and 3–2. Pete Rose, Johnny Bench, Tony Perez, and Lee May were four of the spark plugs that ignited "the Big Red Machine." Jim Merritt won 20 games, but a tender elbow had made him ineffective during the final stretch of the season. Although it wasn't evident in the sweep of the Pirates, other Cincinnati pitchers were weakened by nagging injuries. As a result, the staff was not at full strength to face the Orioles.

The 1970 October matchup did not produce either a memorable moment that fans would recall as the turning point or the singular event when they thought their eyes had deceived them. The five games offered a collage of actions that blended into one graceful movement. Although they occurred at a number of isolated moments, it was as if they had happened as a unity at one point in time. The "great play" that third baseman Brooks Robinson made — or at least as "it" is remembered by some — was a mosaic of dives, jumps, sprawls, and throws. With the passage of time, that collection of defensive gems has been shaped into a single jewel of excellence.

Of the nine putouts and 14 assists credited to Robinson, at least seven lay in the "great to phenomenal" range. Some were critical to the outcome of a particular game; others derived their significance from the pure power of the artist's athletic grace and ability. Seldom does an outstanding defensive play gain immortality equal to that afforded the mighty offensive accomplishment. The composite vision of Brooks Calbert Robinson, Jr., vintage 1970, was a spectacular exception to the rule and became the special memory of that World Series.

The opener took place on October 10 in three-month-old Riverfront Stadium, Cincinnati. It was the first World Series game ever played on Astro-Turf. Weaver tapped Palmer to go to the mound for Baltimore. The Orioles manager was hesitant about sending either of his two 24-game–winning left-handers against "the Big Red Machine." Many National League portsiders had been run over and crushed by the Reds as they steamrolled through the regular season and the NLCS. From the home dugout, Anderson countered with Gary Nolan.

To the delight of most of the 51,531 fans, Cincinnati scored in the bottom of the first inning, when Bench singled home Bobby Tolan. With two out Brooks Robinson "collared" a Bernie Carbo line drive toward third, robbing the Cincinnati outfielder of a run-scoring hit. It would be recorded in the memory bank as "Catch Number One." Few who saw this series would remember that Robinson booted a grounder early in the opener.

In the bottom of the third, the Reds went ahead, 3–0, on a Tolan walk off Palmer and May's home run down the left-field line. Nolan retired the first ten Orioles he faced before Blair beat out a chopper with one away in the fourth. Left-hander Boog Powell stroked an 0-2 pitch to the opposite field for a home run, making the score 3–2. In the following inning Baltimore's Elrod Hendricks evened things up, depositing one of Nolan's pitches into the right-field seats.

The sixth inning contained two plays that have been widely discussed. One was Robinson's "Catch Number Two"; the other was an umpire's decision.

May, leading off for the Reds tested Brooks at third, drilling a scorcher barely inside the bag. "But Brooksie the magician backhanded the ball in foul territory and made an unbelievable acrobatic throw for a one-bounce out at first, the big skip that AstroTurf provided helping the completion."[1]

After the game, Harry Dalton, the Orioles' general manager, told Weaver, "'That's got to be one of the 10 best plays Brooks ever made, Earl.' Weaver disagreed. 'I'd put it in his top 100 plays.' Then he corrected himself. 'Those hundred,' he said, 'are only since I've been here.'"[2]

The next batter, Carbo, walked, and Tommy Helms singled him to third base. Carbo tried to score when Ty Cline pounded a vintage "Baltimore Chop" directly in front of home. O's catcher Hendricks pounced on the ball and lunged for Carbo as he was sliding across the plate. Umpire Ken Burkhart, who had gotten himself out of position, was spilled in the melee. Still trapped in the traffic jam, he thumbed Carbo out. An argument ensued, with Anderson claiming if Hendricks had tagged the base runner at all it had been with his glove. The ball, Anderson correctly noted, was in Hendricks' other hand.

Arthur Daley of the *New York Times* assessed Carbo's reaction: "'The catcher must have tagged the umpire,' he was quoted as saying. 'The only way he could have gotten at me was through the umpire.' This play can't miss being immortalized as an 'instant replay special.'"[3]

The Reds' potential big inning had ended dramatically as the result of "Catch Number Two" and "the call." The Cincinnati media referred to the latter as "The Big Blue Blunder that broke the Big Red Machine."[4]

In the top of the seventh, Robinson exchanged his glove for his bat and cleared the left-field wall for the winning run in the 4–3 game. Brooks had already contributed more offensively to the Orioles' cause than he had done the previous October when he had struggled, hitting .053 (one hit in 19 at bats).

A crowd of 51,131 came to Riverfront Stadium for the second game. Cuellar and Jim McGlothlin were the opposing pitchers. Weaver was sending one of his ace left-handers against the Reds, and any apprehension he might have had about this move became reality the first time they came to bat. May's two-run double sparked Cincinnati to a 3–0 getaway. Two innings later, Tolan added another run with a shot into the right-field mezzanine. The Reds were firing on all nine cylinders, and it looked like the Orioles' 15-game winning streak was nearing its end. Bench followed Tolan's homer with a walk. With the Cincinnati catcher on first base, May hit a shot down the third base line. It became "Catch Number Three." Brooks speared the smash labeled "double" and flipped it to second to begin a rally-ending twin-killing.

From then on the game belonged to Baltimore. In their next two at bats they scored the six runs needed for a 6–5 victory. A home run by Powell in the fourth, and RBI hits in the fifth by Blair, Powell, Brooks, and Hendricks gave the Orioles their come-from-behind win. Baltimore had jumped ahead in the Fall Classic, 2–0.

After two defeats at home, the Reds' manager put it in perspective, saying, "Brooks Robinson of the Baltimore Orioles is beating our club single-handedly.... After you talk about everybody else, if Robinson isn't there, we have two victories and they have none."[5]

And a disappointed but admiring Rose added, "You sort of expect it, don't you? It's a thrill to see baseball plays made like that, even when they hurt you. I'd pay to watch him."[6]

McNally, Baltimore's other left-handed, 24-game winner, was the starter in game three. In the bottom half of the first inning, the Orioles scored two quick runs and were on their way to win number three and consecutive victory number 17. McNally led the O's to a lopsided 9–3 decision. He became the first pitcher in World Series history to hit a grand slam, clearing the bases with a drive off Wayne Granger. Other offensive highlights for "the Birds" were Buford's home run, Frank Robinson and Blair with three hits apiece, and Brooks's two doubles that drove in two runs.

Also, Robinson cashed in with "Catches Four, Five and Six." Before a crowd of 51,773 in Memorial Stadium, Brooks showed the hometowners what he had been doing to the Reds on the synthetic surface in Cincinnati.

Baltimore fans didn't have to wait long to see the magic show. Rose and Tolan led off the game with singles, and Perez, with a two ball and no strike count, hit a high hopper behind third base. Brooks grabbed it, stepped on third, and fired to first for a twin-killing. His fourth gem was in the bag. With two down, Bench hit a line drive toward left field. "No. 5" of the Orioles leaped and snared the shot for his fifth phenomenal defensive play and the third out of the inning.

"Catch Number Six" came in the sixth inning. Robinson made a head-long dive to his left and caught Bench's line drive. Commenting on the play, Robinson said, "It was just a reflex action. He hit it so hard it was curving back towards me."[7]

When the Oriole third baseman came to bat in the bottom of the inning, Bench, the frustrated Cincinnati catcher, barked, "I'm gonna hit the next one over your head."[8]

With the Fall Classic standing at 3–0 in favor of the Orioles, the Most Valuable Player had already been chosen, or so it seemed. The automobile presented by Chevrolet would, no doubt, be in Brooks's garage. Rose, searching for a remedy for the Reds' woes, told a reporter, "You know, me and Johnny Bench got an automobile distributorship. If we knew Robinson wanted a car so badly we'd have given him one before this thing started. I've never seen anything like him in my life."[9]

When Robinson was asked if he could recall a collection of defensive plays equal to the ones he had made in the first three games, he responded, "This is the best Series I've had, but I don't know of any best play I've ever made."[10]

First-game pitchers Palmer and Nolan returned for the fourth contest. With the Orioles leading, 5–3, in the eighth, May hit a 430-foot drive into the bleacher seats in left–center field for a three-run homer. That gave the Reds a 6–5 victory and brought an end to Baltimore's winning streak.

All of Brooks's plays that day were of the garden variety. However, he helped his healthy batting average with a four-for-four afternoon.

The last game was played on the afternoon of October 15. Baltimore, behind Cuellar, ended Cincinnati's faint hopes with a 9–3 win. The Reds scored first, as they had done in three of the first four matchups, taking a 3–0 lead. Three innings later the Orioles were on top for good, 6–3. Merv Rettenmund and Frank Robinson homered for "the Birds." Brooks singled in the fifth inning, finishing with a .428 batting average. Blair also had an outstanding turn-around from the previous World Series when he had hit .100. Against the Reds, he led all players with a gaudy .474 average.

Robinson saved his final spectacular play for the ninth inning. "Catch Number Seven," which was perhaps his most acrobatic, came against none other than Bench, who pulled a low liner past third. Brooks made a diving backhand catch in the dirt, sliding into foul territory.

As was fitting and proper, Pat Corrales, the final Reds' batter, hit a routine grounder Robinson's way. Brooks scooped it up and threw to first, retiring Corrales for the final out of the 1970 World Series.

The set of five games, with three one-run decisions, home runs aplenty, and spectacular defense, provided a wonderful sporting experience for fans along the Ohio River and around the Chesapeake Bay, as well as for the television audience across the country. A vision of the 33-year-old third sacker, with burned cork under his eyes, dirt on his uniform, and number "5" on his back, making miraculous play after miraculous play was etched into the memories of millions. Robinson, commenting on his extraordinary series, said, "I knew that Bench and Tony Perez would be pulling a lot of pitches down the line no matter how good our pitching was. They are too good a pair of hitters to stop all the time. I felt it was going to happen. But this is the odd thing: In baseball what you expect to happen often doesn't happen. But it did happen.

October 13, 1970: A diving catch by Baltimore third baseman Brooks Robinson robs the Reds' Johnny Bench of a line drive (AP/Wide World).

I don't think it will ever happen to me again — that I will get that many opportunities to make plays like that, not day after day, the way it was. It was amazing, so many chances."[11]

Years later, he added another reflection, writing, "I never had 5 games in a row like that in any of the 23 years that I played. It was once in a lifetime."[12]

The Cincinnati Reds' experience was similar to the one that the victorious Baltimore Orioles had endured the year before. Rose, Bench, Tolan, and Perez, the spark of "the Big Red Machine," managed only 14 hits in 76 times at bat for a miserable .184 average. The pitching staff also struggled, surrendering 6.69 earned runs per game.

The following account from the New York Times summed up Cincinnati's disappointing Fall Classic: "Moments after the fifth and final game was over, reported the Associated Press, a woman walked into the Memorial Stadium offices of the Oriole management with a small jar of assorted nuts and bolts. The jar was labeled 'The Big Red Machine.' And a few minutes after that, Boog Powell, the Baltimore first baseman, said, 'It's the big dead machine now.'"[13]

The 1970 Fall Classic was history, but the Hall of Fame in Cooperstown, New York, could not have Brooks Robinson quite yet. However, they did take the glove that had been on the receiving end of seven Series miracles and many others during its lifetime of faithful service.

> And Brooks? He is 33, but like some things — say, the replica of the flag that was still there that waved in center field during the Series — he will stay around Baltimore as long as people appreciate third basemen who can snub out bombs bursting in air. Or run the National League all the way back to Cincinnati with only a bat and a glove.[14]

1972
World Series
Cincinnati Reds and Oakland Athletics

Second Game — October 15 at Cincinnati

Oakland	0	1	1	0	0	0	0	0	0	2	9	2
Cincinnati	0	0	0	0	0	0	0	0	*1*	1	6	0

Hunter, Fingers[9]
Grimsley, Borbon[6], Hall[8]

The 1972 American and National League pennant winners represented the extremes in the spectrum of major-league baseball. The collision of "red-and-white" and the "kelly green-and-gold-and-white" brought some of the issues of an embattled society front and center on the World Series stage. Struggles during the 1960s, which had focused on civil rights and America's involvement in Vietnam, had instigated debates and demonstrations about values and personal lifestyles. The climax of the 1972 edition of the Great American Pastime made it clear that baseball had not escaped the effects of the social turmoil.

The Cincinnati Reds defeated the Pittsburgh Pirates three games to two in the League Championship Series to claim their spot in the World Series. During the regular season, the Reds' 15-game-winner Gary Nolan led an adequate but unspectacular pitching staff, with the nucleus comprising Ross Grimsley, Jack Billingham, Don Gullett, and Clay Carroll.

Bats and speed made "the Big Red Machine" go. The top three men in the order, Pete Rose, Joe Morgan, and Bobby Tolan, set the table for the muscle of Johnny Bench and Tony Perez. That combination rode to 95 victories in the western division of the Senior Circuit.

Cincinnati represented the traditional values of baseball and American society. Ideals of hard work and dedication were epitomized in the play of "Charlie Hustle," Pete Rose. As Roger Angell described, "Rose is unmistakable on a ball field. He is ardent, entertaining, and unquenchable. He burns by day and by night. He sprints to first base on walks, dives on his belly on the base paths or chasing line drives in the outfield, and pulls in fly balls in left field with a slicing, downward motion that says 'There!'"[1]

While an increasing number of America's young people — and some of her elders as well — were choosing the popular longer hairstyles, directives came from Cincinnati's front office making it clear that the Reds players were to be appropriately shorn and shaved. And "appropriate" for hairstyles was defined as "short." The "red and white" stood staunchly for the ideals of America — the flag, motherhood, and apple pie.

Their opponents from the American League were the Oakland Athletics, a new-breed team represented by other-worldly colors — kelly green, gold, and white. The A's had won their five-game set against the Detroit Tigers to claim the Junior Circuit's pennant. Unlike the Reds, Oakland's pitching staff was its strong suit. It was a nicely balanced group of starters — with two right-handers and two left-handers — backed up by one of the game's premier relief pitchers. The Athletics would throw "Catfish" Hunter, "Blue Moon" Odom, Ken Holtzman, Vida Blue, and Rollie Fingers at the Reds' power-packed lineup. Joe Rudi, the team's leading hitter at .305, and Reggie Jackson had delivered the brunt of the A's offensive attack. Unfortunately for the A's, Jackson suffered a hamstring injury in the playoff against the Tigers, and crutches would be the only wood he would carry during the '72 World Series.

Charles Oscar Finley, a 54-year-old insurance executive, had purchased the club in 1961 when they were the Kansas City Athletics. He moved them to Oakland and, as president and general manager, built them into the American League's premier team. The A's were a family business or "plaything" with all of the stock owned by Finleys — Charlie, his wife, and their children. Involved in all aspects of the club's operation, from boardroom to ball field, Finley even had a hand in designing the Athletics' avant-garde "mix and match" uniforms. In June he paid his players to grow mustaches as part of a promotional event and, although the special occasion was over, most of the A's had retained their long hair and manicured mustaches. For many in the viewing audience, the Athletics represented the antiestablishment forces across the land.

Finley had been labeled "antiestablishment" for some time, at least by the staid fraternity of baseball owners. He had lobbied for "prime time" television coverage of the weekday World Series games and had won. In 1972 the games in Oakland began at 5:30 P.M., allowing fans in the eastern section of the country to watch in prime time. The A's owner was also making noises about having a "designated hitter" to bat for the pitcher and using orange baseballs during night games.

The scene was set for the 1972 matchup between Cincinnati and Oakland. Each franchise was looking for its first championship in many years. The last time the Reds won was in 1940, and the Athletics had not grabbed the brass ring since 1930, when the team was in Philadelphia with Connie Mack as the manager and an elephant — not a mule named "Charlie O" — as its mascot.

Roger Angell wrote about the contrast on the field: "They [the Reds] looked over at the hairy young A's, in their outlandish green and gold and white costumes, with a patronizing curiosity that was perhaps shared by the great majority of baseball fans everywhere."[2]

The *New York Times* referred to the teams as "The Hairs" and "The Squares."[3] Sparky Anderson, the Cincinnati manager, was more direct, claiming his "clean-shaven Reds were a better example to American youth than the shaggy haired A's."[4]

Whether it was style or dress or skill, the National League's pennant winner was the odds-on favorite to win the 1972 World Championship. In *Sports Illustrated* Ron Fimrite examined the Senior Circuit's superiority: "The National League has all the superstars, the batting averages, the stolen bases, the home runs and the crowds. American League stars — such as they are — are merely recycled National Leaguers."[5]

The Reds' manager added, "If I said the American League was as good as the National League ... I'd be lying. Yes, Oakland could come over and play in our league and maybe Boston. But they're the only ones."[6]

And even the A's Reggie Jackson supported that opinion: "The National League ... has more depth, better personnel overall and more good young black players. We just don't have an Earl Williams or a Rennie Stennett in our league."[7]

The '72 series was tightly contested, and it was laced with a sizable portion of social rhetoric. And the second contest produced another memorable October moment.

Riverfront Stadium, Cincinnati, was the site of the opener on October 14. Nolan and Holtzman faced each other in game one. Gene Tenace, who had come out of the bullpen late in the season to become the Athletics' regular catcher, was instrumental in all of the A's runs in their 3–2 victory. He homered with a man on base in the second inning, giving Oakland a 2–0 lead. He connected again with the bases empty in the fifth, becoming the first player in history to hit round-trippers in his first two World Series at bats.

The following day, the Athletics posted another close victory, 2–1, and moved ahead in the series, 2–0. They tallied once in the second inning, and Rudi slammed a homer in the third that proved to be the winning run. Hunter pitched 8⅔ innings before Fingers nailed down the victory, retiring Julian Javier on a pop foul with the tying run on base.

The Reds had base runners in six of the innings, getting the leadoff man on five times. However, they were unable to score a run off Hunter until the final frame. Oakland's ability to prevent the "spark plugs" from igniting "the Big Red Machine" was a major factor in their success. In game two, Hunter and Fingers held Rose, Morgan, and Tolan to a single and a gift base, the result of an error. In the two losses, the trio had combined for two hits in 23 at bats. Bench, who was expected to drive in runs, found himself leading off in six of his eight plate appearances.

Rose believed the playoffs had taken a lot out of the Reds. He said, "We're flat as hell. That's a good word for it. We don't have any momentum. Everybody's sitting there waiting for things to happen, but in baseball you can't do that. If you just sit there and wait, they don't happen."[8]

In game two Oakland had not been content to sit back and wait for things to happen. Players like left-fielder Joe Rudi, for example, made them happen. His spectacular catch saved the A's victory and became another of baseball's special moments.

With the Athletics leading, 2–0, the Reds came to bat in the bottom of the ninth. Perez led off with a single to left. Dennis Menke drove Hunter's next offering toward the left-field wall. Rudi ran back as far as he could go and, feeling with his right hand for the wall, leaped for the ball. His hand cushioned the impact with the fence, and the ball remained securely lodged

October 15, 1972: Joe Rudi saves the day for Oakland with his spectacular catch of Reds batter Denis Menke's left-field fly. (AP/Wide World).

in the webbing of his glove. It was an all-important first out. As the buzz about the catch was subsiding, first baseman Mike Hegan followed with another fine grab of a sharp sizzler by Cesar Geronimo down the line for the second out. Hal McRae then stroked a run-producing single, making the score 2–1. Fingers replaced Hunter and retired Javier for the final out.

After the game, Rudi spoke about his catch, saying, "The ball was hit over my head … and I turned to my left to turn into the ball. At first I didn't think I had a chance. But I caught it just before it hit the wall and I was lucky to get it in the webbing."[9]

The vision of Rudi's fully-extended body silhouetted against the wall is a lasting one. A headline in the *New York Times* the following day gave a hint about the quality of the catch: "Rudi Snares a Ranking with Gionfriddo, Mays."[10]

Manager Dick Williams, of the victorious A's, compared Rudi's grab with several others in World Series games:

> "I put this catch ahead of the one Al Gionfriddo pulled on Joe DiMaggio. I put it ahead of the one Willie Mays made on Vic Wertz."
> "How about the catch of Sandy Amoros?" someone asked.
> "That was excellent, but this was the best," said the blissful Williams. "This one was for me."[11]

Without Rudi's leaping, backhand grab, the game's outcome might have been very different. The consensus was that if Rudi had not been able to make the catch, Menke would have had at least a double. Perez would have been home, and the tying run would have been in scoring position. As it turned out, the Reds never got the second run to deadlock the game.

The Reds headed for Oakland, two games down to the Athletics. As reported in the New York press: "The Hairs have put the clippers to the Squares, and these throwbacks from the Gay Nineties have struck a damaging blow against the clean-cut, American boy image. The hirsute A's have displayed mustaches, beards, shaggy locks, pitching, hitting and fielding. The Reds haven't done much more than look old-fashioned.[12]

Game three began in the twilight and shadows of the Oakland Coliseum. The 5:30 P.M. starting time caused massive rush-hour traffic jams in sections of Oakland, as the mass of baseball fans heading for the ballpark traveled the same roads that were being used by the mass of other citizens heading for their homes. Finley's television dream had become a nightmare for motorists. Also, the late-afternoon shadows presented a challenge for the hitters. The outcome was a 1–0 victory for the Reds behind the pitching of Billingham and Carroll.

Perez scored the only run of the game in the seventh inning, barely beating the throw to the catcher after slipping to the ground on the wet turf as he rounded third base. It was that fall's third straight one-run victory in the series.

A truly rare play occurred in the eighth inning, with the Reds in front, 1–0 — a play which helped them protect their lead. With one out, Cincinnati had runners at second and third, and Fingers had a three-and-two count on Bench. Williams, the A's manager went to the mound for a chat with his ace reliever. Before the next pitch, Tenace pointed to first base to indicate he wanted Fingers to throw a fourth ball, giving Bench an intentional walk. Then Tenace quickly ducked back into his crouch behind the plate, and Fingers blazed a called third strike past the unsuspecting Bench for the second out of the inning. Commenting about the move, the surprised strikeout victim said, "I was sort of half-ready.... Joe Morgan hollered down from third to be alive, so I knew something might be on, but probably I wasn't as ready as I could have been. He made a very good pitch, and caught me looking."[13]

A single run provided the margin of victory in the fourth game, also. Holtzman and Gullett hooked up in a duel that eventually went to the Athletics, 3–2, when they scored twice in the bottom of the ninth. Tenace contributed another homer, putting the A's ahead, 1–0. The Reds came back with two in the eighth and, with a 2–1 lead, had visions of bringing the teams even. In Oakland's final at bat and with one away, Gonzalo Marquez singled over second base. Tenace continued his torrid hitting, smacking a single, and Don Mincher tied the game with a hit to right field. Then, pinch hitter Angel Mangual dribbled a "seeing-eye" single between Perez and Morgan to bring home the winning run. Oakland went ahead three games to one.

After Cincinnati took games five and six, the clubs were tied at three apiece. The fifth contest, in Oakland, was a continuation of the one-run sagas. In the ninth inning, Geronimo broke a 4–4 tie, scoring the winning run on Rose's liner to center for a hit. Cincinnati's top three "spark plugs"— Rose, Morgan, and Tolan — did their jobs in game five. They combined for two walks, five hits, three runs, three stolen bases, and four runs batted in.

When the clubs returned to Riverfront Stadium for game six, the trio continued their work. In the Series' only runaway, the Reds' "top three" led an assault on Blue and three other Oakland pitchers in an 8–1 romp.

Cincinnati had won its first home World Series game in three Octobers spread over 11 years. One more victory would bring them the 1972 World Series crown, and they would become the first team to win it all after having dropped the first two games at home.

In the 16 League Championship and World Series games that season, 10 had been decided by a single run. Game seven was to be the 11th nail-biter in that amazing string. Oakland led the finale all the way, winning by a slim margin, 3–2, and wrapping up the title. "The losing Reds' manager, Sparky Anderson, called this the best-played and most exciting Series in his memory, and one would have to strain to fault him. Six of seven games were decided by a single run, a Series record. Despite the tenseness of one close game after another, both teams fielded with almost nonchalant grace.[14]

During the seven contests, Tenace, the A's one-time backup catcher, was virtually a one-man offensive show, knocking in nine of the Athletics' 16 runs and stroking four homers. Rudi added one more game-saving catch to the magical lore of the Fall Classic. And for the first time, a kelly green, gold, and white Championship flag fluttered high above that haven of new ideas, handlebar mustaches, and Charlie's mule — the Oakland Coliseum. The Bay Area proudly celebrated its first championship for any of its professional sports teams at the major-league level.

1975
World Series
Boston Red Sox and Cincinnati Reds

Third Game — October 14 at Cincinnati

Team												R	H	E
Boston	0	1	0	0	0	1	1	0	2	0		5	10	2
Cincinnati	0	0	0	2	3	0	0	0	0	*1*		6	7	0

Wise, Burton[5], Cleveland[5], Willoughby[7], Moret[10]
Nolan, Darcy[5], Carroll[7], McEnaney[7], Eastwick[9]

Sixth Game — October 21 at Boston

Team												R	H	E
Cincinnati	0	0	0	0	3	0	2	1	0	0	0	0	6	14	0
Boston	3	0	0	0	0	0	0	3	0	0	0	*1*	7	10	1

Nolan, Norman[3], Billingham[3], Carroll[5], Borbon[6],
               Eastwick[8], McEnaney[9], Darcy[10]
Tiant, Moret[8], Drago[9], Wise[12]

The 1975 World Series was one of the most entertaining, exciting, and exhausting in the history of baseball. The "Twelve Days in October" produced a seven-game extravaganza, with five games decided by one run, the winning team coming from behind in six of them, two going into extra innings, and neither team ever ahead in the series by more than a game. Two of baseball's most memorable moments — one a collision at home plate and the other a climactic home run — were part of the legacy of that Fall Classic when two of baseball's oldest franchises, the Boston Red Sox and the Cincinnati Reds, battled for the World Championship.

The Boston Red Sox became the American League pennant winner, after eliminating the three-time World Champion Oakland A's in three straight playoff games. In a break with tradition, the Bosox were sporting red hats with dark blue bills and the familiar Boston "B." They were in pursuit of their first World Championship since 1918. Boston would not get the ring but would add monumentally to the lore of the Red Sox and Fenway Park.

Two rookies, American League MVP Fred Lynn and Jim Rice, contributed mightily to a Sox attack, that also included "wall bangers" Carl Yastrzemski,

Dwight Evans, Carlton "Pudge" Fisk, Bernie Carbo, and Cecil Cooper. Bill Lee and Luis Tiant headed a colorful and crafty pitching staff that also featured Rick Wise, Reggie Cleveland, and Roger Moret.

"The Big Red Machine" rolled into Boston for the opener on October 11. By the end of the regular season they had carved out a chasm of 20 games between themselves and their nearest foe in the National League West. After disposing of the Pittsburgh Pirates in three games, the Reds had raised the Senior Circuit's pennant flag above Riverfront Stadium. Pete Rose, Joe Morgan, Johnny Bench, George Foster, Tony Perez, and Ken Griffey had helped the Reds pound out an incredible 108 regular-season victories. Starting pitchers Gary Nolan, Jack Billingham, Don Gullett, and Fred Norman, together with a deep and talented bullpen, had been vital cogs in the well-oiled machine. The Reds were a compelling favorite to win it all and had shifted into high gear for the final leg of the drive to their first World Championship since 1940.

Boston threw a monkey wrench, named "Loo-ie," into Cincinnati's gears, taking the opener, 6–0. A tight duel between Tiant and Gullett lasted until the bottom of the seventh inning, when the Red Sox scored all of their runs. Tiant's father, who had just arrived from Castro's Cuba, sat in the stands, watching his son toss a five-hitter. With chants of "Loo-ie ... Loo-ie ... Loo-ie" resounding through the friendly confines of the antique and idiosyncratic ballpark known as "Fenway," the veteran of many baseball battles held the Reds at bay with his own special brand of magic. Roger Angell described the special treat in store for those who watched Tiant pitch:

> His repertoire begins with an exaggerated mid-windup pivot, during which he turns his back on the batter and seems to examine the infield directly behind the mound for signs of crabgrass. With men on bases, his stretch consists of a succession of minute downward waggles and pauses of the glove, and a menacing sidewise, slit-eyed, Valentino-like gaze over his shoulder at the baserunner. The full flower of his art, however, comes during the actual delivery, which is executed with a perfect variety show of accompanying gestures and impersonations.[1]

The pregame ceremonies for game two featured a special observance of the 200th anniversary of the United States Navy. Secretary of State Henry Kissinger threw out the first ball. With the focus on the water, it was appropriate that rain visited Fenway that Sunday afternoon, along with wind and chilly temperatures.

Billingham and Lee faced each other in a game marked by spectacular defense. Amazing grabs in the sixth inning by Cooper, Fisk, and Lynn prevented the Reds from breaking a 1–1 tie.

The Bosox went ahead, 2–1, in the bottom of the same inning when Yastrzemski, who had singled and then advanced to second on an infield error, scored on a hit by Rico Petrocelli.

There was a 27-minute rain delay in the seventh inning. When the game resumed, Boston was able to maintain their one-run lead into the top half of the final frame. Lee was still pitching for the Red Sox. The left-handed social critic, who had angered many Boston citizens when he chastised them for their bigoted views on the city's school-busing dilemma, had begun to hear cheers replace the boos that had greeted him when he was introduced before game one. Lee kept the Reds off balance with a "lollipop" curve and occasional blooper ball. Some saw the latter pitch as a reincarnation of Rip Sewell's "eephus ball," except it was delivered from the port side. The "Spaceman" had held the mighty Reds to a single run through eight innings. When he took the mound to face Cincinnati in their final at bat, the Beantowners' hearty applause was a sign that, at least for the moment, all was forgiven.

Bench led off the ninth with a double, prompting manager Darrell Johnson to bring in Dick Drago to close out the game. Perez grounded out, with the tying run moving over to third. Foster flied to left for the second out, but it was not deep enough to allow Bench to score. With two outs and victory virtually in their grasp, the Red Sox fans gasped when Dave Concepcion hit a grounder up the middle. Second baseman Denny Doyle knocked it down but was not able to make the throw to first, and Bench scored the tying run. After Concepcion stole second base, Griffey stroked a shot to left center out of the reach of the fleet Lynn, and the Reds took a 3–2 lead. Boston was unable to score in the bottom of the ninth, and the teams were deadlocked at a game apiece.

The Bosox and the Reds left Fenway Park's inviting "Green Monster" and curiously carved outfield and headed for Cincinnati's modern, symmetrical and artificially turfed Riverfront Stadium. Wise and Nolan went to the hill in game three. Before the final out was registered in the tenth inning, eight other pitchers would follow them to the mound. Each club hit three home runs, the most memorable being Evans's clout that produced two runs and tied the game, 5–5, in the top of the ninth.

It was a game of round-trippers, but a sacrifice bunt created the most commotion. In the bottom of the tenth inning, Cesar Geronimo led off with a single. Ed Armbrister, pinch-hitting for the pitcher, laid down a bunt in front of the plate. Attempting to field the ball, Fisk collided with Armbrister. The catcher said, "I took the ball and this man was underneath me like a linebacker. I certainly must have tagged him. Hell, he ran into me. It was really like smashing into a linebacker."[2] Fisk attempted to throw out Geronimo at second base. The throw bounded into center field, and the base runners ended up at second and third base. After a heated argument about the collision and the call, play resumed. An intentional walk to Rose loaded the bases, and Morgan singled home the winning run.

The argument centered on whether or not Armbrister had hesitated, causing interference with Fisk as he was lunging for the ball. Larry Barnett, the

October 14, 1975: Boston catcher Carlton Fisk collides with Cincinnati's Ed Armbrister (AP/Wide World).

home plate umpire, explained his call: "I ruled that it was simply a collision. It is interference only when the batter intentionally gets in the way of the fielder."[3]

The following description of the play seemed consistent with the general consensus that Armbrister had paused for an instant before breaking for first base: "The ball struck hard AstroTurf in front of the plate and hopped high into the air. Armbrister hesitated, gaping at the ball as though it were a visitor from outer space. The catcher, Carlton Fisk, lunged over Armbrister's shoulder to grab the ball. For a moment their uniforms melded together."[4]

Armbrister acknowledged the hesitation but suggested another reason for the collision: "After I bunted ... I kind of watched it for just a second as it took a high bounce. I think he came from behind me. He reached out and hit me on the leg. He interfered with me."[5]

The Red Sox catcher was the player most visibly upset by Barnett's call — or noncall. As Geronimo was scoring the run to seal the Reds' victory, "Pudge" was firing his mask to the screen behind home plate. Later in the clubhouse, he blasted the umpire saying, "'It's a gawddamn shame to lose a gawddamn game because of that gawddamn call,' the catcher finally said. Then he stood up, scooped up three magazines from his locker and flung them across the room."[6]

Lee, always direct and to the point, claimed he "would have 'chewed Barnett's ear off,' if he had been within biting distance. 'I would have Van Goghed him.'"[7] Yastrzemski continued the blistering attack, questioning the procedure for choosing umpires for the World Series. He charged: "The best teams in baseball are in the Series ... but the best umpires aren't. They take turns no matter how competent they are. Why don't the teams take turns? Next year, how about San Diego and the Angels playing, no matter where they finish."[8]

Years later, when asked about the play, Barnett said, "The rule was on my side, but I won't try to convince people of that.... They threatened to shoot my 2-year-old daughter, and I had more security around me than Henry Kissinger, and he was Secretary-of-State."[9]

Tiant went the distance in the fourth game and led Boston to victory, 5–4. "El Tiante" was not as sharp as he had been in game one. He went deep in the count a number of times and ended up delivering 163 pitches. Cincinnati went up early, scoring twice in the bottom of the first. The Sox responded, scoring five times in the fourth inning. After the Reds came back with two in their at bat, the score stood at 5–4.

Pitch number 161 from Tiant was critical to the game's outcome. In the ninth Cincinnati had runners on first and second base. Griffey drove a shot to the deepest part of center field, 400 feet from home plate. After a long dash to the farthest reaches of the ball yard, Lynn gathered in Griffey's blast for the second out. Two pitches later Morgan popped to Yastrzemski, ending the game.

Gullett's pitching and Perez's two home runs and four RBIs provided the power for "the Big Red Machine's" 6–2 victory in the fifth contest and a 3–2 Series lead.

Following a day off for travel, the teams lingered in Beantown during three days of rain. Sportswriters scurried about searching for interesting tidbits to fill their columns during the unexpected delay. The sixth game was played on the evening of October 21 and into the morning of the following day. The writers' void overflowed. The long and memorable confrontation provided endless print for those on the beat as well as for others who, down through the years, have been fascinated with that amazing contest.

Game six of the 1975 Classic has been called "the greatest game in World Series history" and "the greatest game in the greatest World Series." It was an exciting back-and-forth struggle in a spectacular back-and-forth set of games. After mentioning some of the great contests of the past, the November 3, 1975, issue of *Sports Illustrated* described the marvelous event: "Terrific games, all of them. But for the 35,205 wedged into misshapen Fenway on the pleasantly cool October evening, and the millions who watched on television, the sixth game of the 1975 Series will be the standard by which all the future thrillers must be measured."[10]

Lynn put the Sox on the hand-operated Fenway scoreboard in the bottom of the first inning. With two on base, he hit a Nolan delivery into the right-center-field bleachers for a three-run Boston lead. Cincinnati, which seemed to have adjusted to Tiant's tantalizing tactics, tied the score, 3–3, with Griffey and Bench driving in runs. The Reds went ahead, 5–3, in the seventh, when Foster blasted one of Tiant's pitches off the center-field wall to score Griffey and Morgan. In the eighth inning, Geronimo's home run down the right-field line knocked Tiant out of the game, gave Cincinnati a 6–3 cushion, and set the stage for a memorable Red Sox moment.

In the bottom of the eighth, Lynn started a rally with a single off the leg of pitcher Pedro Borbon. After Petrocelli drew a walk, Rawly Eastwick replaced Borbon. Eastwick, who had pitched well in his four previous appearances, retired Evans and Rick Burleson for the first two outs of the inning and seemed poised to retire the side. For the second time in the series, Carbo came to the plate as a pinch hitter against his former teammates. In game three he had hit a home run. With four outs standing between the Reds and the World Championship, Eastwick and Carbo battled to a 3-2 count. After struggling to stay alive with a full-count, foul dribbler, Carbo's short compact swing powered the next pitch, a fastball, to the deepest part of Fenway Park into the center-field bleachers. "As the ball began its long flight into the record books, a vague roar, almost subterranean in quality, began to make itself heard. Then it gathered momentum and erupted into a full 35,205-throated bellow in an intensely partisan salute to the utterly absurd scenario played out in front of them: The Red Sox were still alive!"[11]

As Carbo circled the bases, he yelled to Rose, "'Don't you wish you were that strong?' And he [Rose] yelled back, 'This is the way baseball is supposed to be!'"[12]

The game was deadlocked, 6–6, at the end of eight. The crowd cheered again, in anticipation, when the Red Sox loaded the bases with no one out in the home half of the ninth inning. Doyle had started the inning by drawing a free pass. Yaz lined a single to right, and Fisk was given an intentional walk. Lynn followed with a short fly ball down the left-field line, near where the stands jut out, narrowing foul territory. It would be generous to say it traveled 200 feet. Foster made the catch, and Doyle tagged up at third, making a bold dash for home. The Reds' outfielder, not blessed with a strong arm, fired a short-range "bullet" to Bench, nailing the sliding Doyle for the second out of the inning. Petrocelli bounced out to end the Sox threat and squelch the fans' excitement.

The score remained tied through the tenth. In the eleventh, the Reds' Griffey was on first base when Morgan shot a long line drive to the right-field corner. It was targeted for home-run territory, but Evans, hurtling toward the wall, made a leaping catch and stole the ball from the stands. Then he unloaded one of baseball's most powerful "rifles" and gunned-out Griffey before he could get back to the bag. As Evans later recounted, "It all happened so fast and I was running so hard that I couldn't really remember what happened on the catch. Somehow I got my glove on the ball to catch it, and threw to first base to double off the runner and end the inning. I'm sure that Morgan's drive would have made the seats if I hadn't caught it and, at that point, it could've been the end for us."[13]

Fisk came to bat to lead off the bottom of the twelfth. After addressing home plate with all of his methodical and preparatory rituals, he entered the batter's box. At precisely 12:33 A.M. EST, he attacked Pat Darcy's second pitch, a slider down and in, and drove it high into the night and down the left-field line.

A television camera, positioned in the left-field scoreboard, caught a powerful picture of Fisk bouncing down the first base line, using body English to keep the ball in fair territory. "But truth be known, the NBC cameraman stationed in the Green Monster captured the moment only because a giant rat at his feet had scared him motionless. Instead of following the ball as he was instructed, the cameraman's focus remained stuck on Fisk at the plate."[14]

The announcer excitedly proclaimed, "There it goes ... a long drive ... if it stays fair ... home run!"[15] The ball kissed the yellow mesh attached to the foul pole and dropped majestically to the grass below. As Fisk circled the bases, brushing aside several fans along the way on his magnificent gallop, John Kiley, the Fenway Park organist, triumphantly pounded out the "Hallelujah Chorus." Soon, church bells rang out from the Episcopal Church in Charlestown, N.H., the tiny New England town where Carlton's parents resided. The world seemed aglow. History had been made during the long four-hour-and-one-minute extravaganza, with the last moments bringing forth a lasting vision.

Long before A. Bartlett Giamatti became president of Yale University, he had received another special calling. Even before he ascended to the presidency of the National League and then to the Commissioner's desk, he had served as a lifelong, long-suffering, die-hard Red Sox fan. He recalled the thrill of that unforgettable moment in 1975: "Everyone in America remembers where he was when Fisk hit his home run. My wife, Toni, and I were home in bed on Central Avenue, in New Haven, with the set on — it was after midnight, of course — and our three kids were supposed to be asleep, but, of course, they were outside, prowling around. Then they heard us yelling, and they came rushing in pretending they didn't know what was happening. We all ended up jumping up and down on the bed together."[16]

Don Conkey of the *Springfield* (MA) *Union-News* described the perspective of one of the losing players: "Baseball lore cherishes the moment that Cincinnati's Rose ran off the field after Carlton Fisk's game-winning homer in Game Six of the 1975 World Series, excitedly yelling over and over to manager Sparky Anderson about what a great game it had been. When Sparky pointed out to Rose that the Reds had lost the game, Rose yelled back that it didn't matter — that it was the best baseball game he'd ever played in, regardless of the score."[17]

October 21, 1975: Carlton Fisk is airborne when he sees his twelfth-inning homer hit the left-field foul pole to win game six of the World Series over Cincinnati (AP/Wide World).

Ray Fitzgerald of the *Boston Globe* began his column of October 22 — entitled "The best game ever!" — with these words, "Call it off. Call the seventh game off. Let the World Series stand this way, three games for the Cincinnati Reds and three for the Boston Red Sox."[18]

As much as some may have wished that Fitzgerald's request would be granted, game seven was played later the same day that the monumental sixth contest had come to its fantastic finish. Left-handers Gullett and Lee were matched for the final confrontation of the 1975 season, and it also went down to the wire.

As they had done the previous day, the Red Sox broke on top, 3–0, helped mainly by four Gullett walks. Those would be Boston's final runs of the season, and they were not enough to outdistance the Reds. After scoring twice in the sixth and once in the seventh, Cincinnati came to bat in the top of the ninth with the score even, 3–3. Boston's rookie left-hander Jim Burton, who had seen limited action in 1975, was in the game in relief. Griffey walked to lead off the inning, and two fielder's choices moved him around to third. With two outs, Rose walked on a 3–2 pitch. Then Burton threw the ball low and away to Morgan, and Joe reached with one hand and hit a chip shot off the end of the bat, lobbing it over the infield. It dropped in front of Lynn in short–center field, and the winning run crossed home plate.

There were no more miracles for the Boston Red Sox. They went quietly in their last at bat. The third out was recorded when Yastrzemski flied out to center.

The final play had been made, and the World Series was over. It had consumed 12 days from start to finish. Five of the games had gone to the winner by a single run, and on two of those occasions it took extra innings to decide the outcome. In all but one contest the victorious team came from behind to pick up the win. Cincinnati was the World Champion, but Boston proved a valiant foe.

As a fitting conclusion to that wonderful October, Red Smith of the *New York Times* wrote:

> Better than fruitless comparisons is the memory of a lively tournament of seven games, all tautly played and stoutly contested, two carried into overtime, all won with distinction and lost with credit. The best was the sixth, which consumed four hours and one minute and proved a point which needs to be proved as often as possible. Year after year the complaint is that baseball is grown weary, dull, stale, flat and unprofitable ....Thousands in Boston and millions elsewhere watched for four hours and one minute Tuesday night and Wednesday morning. Does one of them feel that a good baseball game can be too long?[19]

1977
World Series
Los Angeles Dodgers and New York Yankees

Sixth Game — October 18 at New York

Los Angeles	2	0	1	0	0	0	0	0	1		4	9	0
New York	0	2	0	*3*	*2*	0	0	*1*	x		8	8	1

Hooton, Sosa[4], Rau[5], Hough[7]
Torrez

During their storied careers, many of the greats of the game acquired nicknames descriptive of their character, style, or persona. Fans came to recognize a certain player as "The Splendid Splinter," "The Say-Hey Kid," "The Yankee Clipper," or "The Man." A small group received just as much recognition and adulation at the mention of a familiar form of their baptismal names. A few have become one-word celebrities. One of those was "Reggie." Before the end of his Hall of Fame career, the legend of "Mr. October" would be added to the mystique of Reginald Martinez Jackson. But for the 1977 World Series, when the Yankees and the Dodgers renewed their long and treasured rivalry, "Reggie" would do.

In their division, the Los Angeles Dodgers finished ahead of the decade's "star in the West," the Cincinnati Reds. They went on from there to capture the National League pennant in a four-game set with the Philadelphia Phillies. Freshman skipper Tom Lasorda penciled in a daily lineup that included four players who had slammed 30 or more home runs — Ron Cey, Steve Garvey, Reggie Smith, and Dusty Baker. Tommy John, Don Sutton, Burt Hooton, Rick Rhoden, Doug Rau, and reliever Charlie Hough handled the bulk of the mound duty for the pennant-winning Dodgers.

Manager Billy Martin led the New York Yankees into the World Series for the second year in a row. In 1976, after taking the American League East by a comfortable 10½ games and then beating Kansas City in the American League Championship Series, they had done the unthinkable. They were drubbed in the Fall Classic by Cincinnati in four straight contests.

The result so angered the Yankees' principal owner George Steinbrenner that he vowed not to allow the same indignity to befall his team ever again. Steinbrenner, the chairman of the board of the American Shipbuilding Company, had owned the Yanks since 1973. He had the funds available to go into the deep waters of the off-season's free agent pool. Out of it he pulled star left-hander Don Gullett, who had been the winning pitcher in the 1976 series opener for the Reds.

Steinbrenner also tossed a five-year lure worth $2.6 million into the Chesapeake Bay. After some expert angling, he reeled in Reggie Jackson of the Baltimore Orioles, landing him on the shore of the Hudson River in the Bronx.

Jackson's first full year in the major leagues had been 1968, as a member of the Oakland Athletics. In his initial season, his patented "all-or-nothing swing" produced both 29 home runs and a league-leading 171 strikeouts. The following year, after slamming 49 round-trippers, he went to A's owner Charles Finley and asked for a sizable raise. Finley countered with an offer of much less. After a lengthy holdout, a dejected Jackson signed and came back to the fold. Both his batting average and home-run output took significant dips that season.

Oakland's glory years were 1972, 1973, and 1974, when they won three World Championships. Reggie played an integral part in those accomplishments. His high point was 1973, when he led the circuit in most of the offensive categories and pocketed the league's Most Valuable Player award.

In 1975, Reggie's final season in Oakland, the A's won the American League West but were beaten in the ALCS by the Boston Red Sox. Shortly before the start of the next season, Jackson was traded to the Orioles where he spent a single campaign. In 1977 Steinbrenner and the Yankees brought him to the hallowed "House that Ruth Built."

If Steinbrenner believed that controversy was the handmaiden of motivation, then the Yankees were set for a highly charged season. On November 29, 1976, Reggie signed a multiyear contract to wear baseball's most prestigious pinstripes. From that point forward the battle lines were drawn. Martin, who never ran from a battle on or off the field, made it clear that Jackson's services were not needed on his talented pennant-winning team.

The 1977 campaign produced a number of direct confrontations between manager and player. Their most public squabble took place on June 18 in a jammed Fenway Park, Boston, before a national television audience. Martin removed Reggie from the game after, in his estimation, Jackson made only a token effort to catch a ball hit by Jim Rice to right field. That ignited a highly visible and verbal dugout scrimmage. Only the presence of teammates with cooler heads prevented it from turning into a physical battle.

Reggie, who had been playing in deep–right center for the power-hitting Rice, had a distance to run to reach the short fly ball and rejected Martin's charge. He challenged the manager's action, saying, "The man took a position today to show me up on National T.V.... Everyone could see that."[1] Jackson went on to criticize the entire Yankee situation: "It makes me cry the way they treat me on this team. The Yankee pinstripes are Ruth and Gehrig and DiMaggio and Mantle. I'm just a black man to them who doesn't know how to be subservient. I'm a big black man with an IQ of 160 making $700,000 a year and they treat me like dirt. They've never had anyone like me on their team before."[2]

Captain and catcher Thurman Munson was angry at both the Yankees' owner and Reggie. By signing Jackson, the club had broken its promise to him that he would be their second-highest-paid player (behind Jim "Catfish" Hunter). Other Bronx Bombers had their own axes to grind with Steinbrenner, and Reggie represented an omnipresent reminder of their grievances. In the minds of many, Jackson was "George's boy," and Reggie did not help matters. In a magazine article he boasted, "I'm the straw that stirs the drink. Munson thinks he can be the straw that stirs the drink, but he can only stir in bad."[3]

The stage was set for high drama. It would be the "George and Billy and Reggie Show," and it would be an "off Broadway" spectacle from the start of spring training until the final out of the World Series — and beyond.

On the field, the Yankees joined Baltimore and Boston in a fierce battle for the pennant. The Bronx Bombers' ticket to the Series was punched by a 2½-game victory in the American League East and a tight 3–2 ALCS win over the Kansas City Royals.

Reggie finished the embattled season batting .286, hitting 32 home runs, and driving in 110 runs. His lowest and angriest moment came prior to the fifth and final game of the ALCS. Jackson was 1-for-14 in the first four games, and Martin started Paul Blair in his place against Royal left-hander Paul Splittorff. For Reggie, the decision represented more than a manager's strategy. As he claimed later:

> I couldn't believe that after my heroics in September — I won't say I carried the team because so many others played well, but that September was a tug-of-war, I was the anchor man at the back of the line — that it could all end in a nightmare.
> But as we got ready to face lefty Paul Splittorff in the fifth game, I knew I was all dressed up to be the scapegoat. All season long Billy had been telling people that the Yankees had made it to the World Series in '76 without me. Now there was a chance that the Yankees weren't going to make it to the Series with me.[4]

With the support and advice of his teammate and friend Fran Healy, Jackson refrained from approaching Martin in another direct confrontation. He waited with volatile emotions burning beneath the surface until the manager called him to pinch-hit for Cliff Johnson in the eighth inning. He singled to drive in the Yankees' second run, making the score 3–2. Three more Bronx Bombers crossed the plate in the ninth, providing the margin of victory. New York had fought their way into the 1977 Fall Classic.

There was a burning question in Jackson's mind as the opener approached. Would he be a starter in the first game against the Dodgers? When the lineup card was posted, Reggie's name was there along with Munson, Chris Chambliss, Graig Nettles, Willie Randolph, and the other "regular" pinstripers who had been instrumental in the Yankees' pennant-winning fight. Gullett started the opener for the second year in a row. In 1976 it had been against the Yankees; in 1977 it was for them.

The Dodgers scored twice in the top of the first on RBI hits by Bill Russell and Cey. New York bounced back with one in the bottom half of the inning on Munson's single, Jackson's looper into center, and Chambliss's hit to right. The Yankees scored a run in the bottom of the sixth and another in the eighth. Los Angeles tied the game, 3–3, in the top of the ninth, taking it into extra innings. The Yankees nailed down the opener in the bottom of the twelfth when Blair, a late-inning defensive replacement for Jackson, singled home the fourth run.

The vivid contrast between the two teams was clear in remarks made prior to the start of the second contest:

> Lasorda appears beatific before the game. He arrives on the field in the company of a priest, and he advises newsmen of his love for his fellow man, particularly his fellow Dodgers. "I believe in togetherness," he says. "I believe a team is like a family. I can eat with my players. I have drinks with them in my office. I know the names of their wives and children. They make my life enjoyable."
>
> Advised of these remarks, Martin smiles, though not beatifically. "That's wonderful," he says. The Yankees, too, are a family. A family like the Macbeths, the Borgias and the Bordens of Fall River, Mass.[5]

"Love" conquered "war" in game two in Yankee Stadium. Los Angeles, behind a five-hitter by Hooton, topped New York, 6–1. The visitors got round-trippers from Cey and Smith early in the game. After three innings the Dodgers had built a quick 5–0 lead off a sore-armed Hunter. Following the game Jackson was furious with Martin for starting Hunter and for having subjected his longtime friend and former Oakland teammate to public embarrassment. In the clubhouse he charged, "The man hasn't pitched since September 10.... It's like me sitting on the bench for a month and then expecting to get two hits and drive in a run. If you're going to pitch him in the World Series, then use him before then."[6]

Grumbling among the Yankees continued as the teams moved to Dodger Stadium for game three. Martin shot back at Jackson for his comments about Hunter, and Munson expressed his desire to escape it all and wear a Cleveland Indian uniform in 1978. Amid the hassle, New York went out and edged the Dodgers, 5–3, on a route-going performance by Mike Torrez. Reggie, who had gone one-for-nine in the first two games, hit a hard single to left field and scored twice. Baker contributed a three-run homer for all of Los Angeles' runs.

Before the third game, the season's two major combatants held a "summit conference." By the end of game four, strange words were being spoken by Billy and Reggie — words of togetherness, unity, and respect — as if they had become blood brothers. And during the contest, a "feel-good" Jackson began to move to the front of the pack. He gave fans throughout the baseball world a glimpse of the powerful metamorphosis that occurred during a number of Octobers. Before a record crowd of 55,995, Reggie drilled a double and a homer, leading the Yankees and lefty Ron Guidry to a 4–2 victory and a 3–1 series advantage.

Following the win, Jackson remarked:

> "You probably should give Billy Martin the Nobel Peace Prize for managing the damn team."
> "I accept," Martin said when informed of Jackson's nomination. "With deep humility, I accept. Thank you very much."
> And what would you nominate Reggie for, Billy?
> "The Good Guy Award," the manager said and he smiled.[7]

Television cameras caught Jackson and Martin embracing and whispering "sweet nothings" in each other's ear. The picture shocked the baseball world, which had watched their season-long confrontations.

The newly discovered camaraderie was not enough to halt the Dodgers in game five. Sparked by Steve Yeager's four RBIs, Los Angeles streaked to a 10–0 lead on their way to a 10–4 victory. Jackson singled in the seventh and homered in the eighth for his fourth hit in his last eight at bats. New York held a 3–2 series lead as the teams traveled across country to the Bronx for the sixth game.

The grand finale was played on October 18. That evening Reginald Martinez Jackson stepped to the plate for three at bats in majestic Yankee Stadium, swung the bat three times and took his place in history alongside the "Sultan of Swat."

Hooton and Torrez faced each other in the Stadium matchup. The Dodgers broke on top in their first at bat when Garvey's two-out triple scored Smith and Cey for a 2–0 lead. The Yankees countered with the tying runs in the second. Jackson walked on four pitches, and Chambliss shot the ball deep into the right-center-field bleachers.

By the time Reggie came to bat for the second time, the Dodgers had regained the lead on a third-inning home run by Smith. With the Yankees trailing, 3–2, the Yankee outfielder drove Hooton's first pitch into the right-field grandstand, scoring Munson ahead of him and putting New York in front to stay.

One inning later Jackson came to the plate with Mickey Rivers on first base and Elias Sosa on the mound for the Dodgers. He, too, delivered only one pitch to Reggie, which landed deeper in the right-field stands than the earlier shot. The score was New York 7–Los Angeles 3.

"Number 44," swinging from the heels, was in a special groove. He had been that way all evening. He recalled:

> Batting practice can confuse the hell out of you.
> But BP on October 18 was something special. I cannot ever remember having one like it. The players around the batting cage were amazed, and so were the writers. The crowd, especially out in right field, was going crazy; people show up earlier for Series games, and the ones who did on this night got themselves a show. I hit maybe forty balls during my time in the cage. I must have hit twenty into the seats. Upper deck. Bullpen. Into the black in center. Didn't matter. The baseball looked like a volleyball to me.[8]

Reggie came to the plate for the final time in the bottom of the eighth. Hough, a knuckleballer, had replaced Sosa. Jackson remembered: "When I was playing in winter ball one year, about 1970, my manager was Frank Robinson. He told me a lot about how to hit the knuckleball. So when I went up there against Hough, I thought if he threw me anything good, I could hit another homer. But when I walked to the plate and heard all that cheering, I knew I had nothing to lose. Even if I had struck out against Hough, they would have cheered me back to the dugout."[9]

Reggie had the crowd in the palm of his hand as he waited in the batter's box. Fans were on their feet, rhythmically chanting "Reggie! Reggie! Reggie!" "On the first pitch if he got it anywhere near the plate, I knew I'd have a good pass at it. The crowd was insane with noise as I dug in. They were expecting a home run. They wanted a home run."[10]

Hough made his one pitch to Jackson. It was a dancing, darting knuckleball, and Reggie did not miss it. He deposited it in the seats in dead–center field, 450 feet from home plate. Home run number three was in the record books and in the memory banks of the baseball fans in Yankee Stadium and those far beyond the confines of New York City.

Los Angeles scored once in the ninth. The final tally was 8–4, and New York became the World Champions for the first time in 15 long years. After the Dodgers' final out, Reggie turned into a bruising halfback, dashing from his right-field position into the dugout to avoid the onrushing crowd. He carried the World Series record of five home runs with him. Four of them had come on successive swings in games five and six. His three round-trippers in the final contest matched Babe Ruth's achievements in 1926 and 1928.

Red Smith wrote in the *New York Times*: "It had to happen this way. It had been predestined since Nov. 29, 1976, when Reginald Martinez Jackson sat down on a gilded chair in New York's Americana Hotel and wrote his name on a Yankee contract.... That day the plot was written for last night — the bizarre scenario Reggie Jackson played out by hitting three home runs, clubbing the Los Angeles Dodgers into submission and carrying his supporting players with him to the baseball championship of North America."[11]

Lasorda, the losing manager, praised Jackson: "It's the greatest performance I've ever seen in a World Series.... We tried to throw the ball in a certain area on him, but if you don't get it where you want it, we all know he's
tough."[12]

Yeager, the Dodger catcher who had called the pitches, recounted, "I
remember Jackson walked the first time at bat, but I never caught another
pitch we threw to him. The next three times up he hit the first pitch each time
for a home run. Talk about frustrating! There's not much you can do when a
batter is in the groove like that. Nobody was going to get Jackson out that
day."[13]

Los Angeles' first baseman Steve Garvey paid what was perhaps the finest
tribute. After watching the third home run disappear into the stands, he admitted, "When I was sure nobody was looking, I applauded in my glove."[14]

When the excitement of the Yankees' victory began to subside, it became
evident that many of the problems that had plagued the team throughout the
season were still with them. Rifts between the owner, the manager, and the
players were too deep to be covered over by victories or even a World Championship.

It also was clear that a new and powerful personality had emerged in New
York — a personality that was to grace the baseball scene for years to come.
Two descriptions of the man known as "Reggie" presented a glimpse into his
complex nature. The first was written by Thomas Boswell in *How Life Imitates the World Series*: "Jackson's basic difficulty, one that may take him years
to solve, is that, like politicians and poets on a grander scale, Jackson does not
live a life in the conventional, everyday sense. He manufactures a legend, a
personal history, with himself and his exploits at the center. Jackson's sin is
that he has always been uniquely bad at hiding this conscious myth-making
process."[15]

The Reverend Jesse Jackson offered another perspective on Reggie:
"Because of his intelligence and his gifts, Reggie's domain is bigger than baseball. All the bad pitches to him do not come on the diamond. He has a sense
of history, which so many athletes don't have. I think that's why he gets up
for the big games. He has a sense of moment. Greatness against the odds is
the thing. Anyone can be famous. Just by jumping out of one of these build-
ings you can be famous. To be great is a dimension of the authentic."[16]

1978
American League
Eastern Division Playoff
Boston Red Sox and New York Yankees

American League-East Playoff— October 2 at Boston

										R	H	E
New York	0	0	0	0	0	0	4	1	0	5	8	0
Boston	0	1	0	0	0	1	0	2	0	4	11	0

Guidry, Gossage[8]
Torrez, Stanley[7]

The road to the 1978 American League pennant was marked by two great comebacks, a midsummer switch in managers, Lady Luck's change of allegiance, and a memorable moment.

The defending World Champion New York Yankees spent the first half of the campaign swirling in the turmoil that had engulfed the team throughout the previous season. George Steinbrenner, Billy Martin, and Reggie Jackson continued to be the stars on the "off–Broadway" stage, delivering their lines of direct challenge, insinuation, and innuendo. Their ongoing clashes, both on and off the field, offered Yankees fans their major excitement. They were rivaled only by the new candy in town, the "Reggie Bar." On opening day, 50,000 had been given away at the Stadium.

On the field the team was far from being a serious challenge to the Boston Red Sox. Injuries to key members of the club were bothersome into the fourth month of the campaign. Through mid–July only hard-throwing lefty Ron Guidry's outstanding 13–1 record had kept the Yankees' faint hopes alive.

The pivotal point in the season for the Bronx Bombers was the latter part of July. Jackson had been seething since June 26, when he was demoted from full-time right fielder to part-time designated hitter. On July 17 he was promoted from the sixth position in the batting order to his preferred "clean-up" spot. One could not miss a bit of irony in Martin's choice of that particular day to move Jackson up in the order. The Yankees were scheduled to face Kansas City left-hander Paul Splittorff, who had supposedly spurred the manager's decision to bench Reggie in game five of the American League Championship Series the preceding October.

Martin justified his move of July 17, saying, "He's starting to swing the bat decently lately.... And the way we're going now, maybe hitting fourth will make him happier. And if it helps him and makes him happy, maybe he'll hit better and we'll win some games and make me happy."[1] In the bottom of the tenth inning, Jackson came to bat with the score tied, 5–5. No one was out and Thurman Munson was on first base. Martin flashed Reggie the bunt sign. Kansas City pitcher Al Hrabosky's fastball sailed by the batter's head. With the infield drawn in, the manager wiped off the bunt signal and told Jackson to hit away. On the second pitch, Reggie attempted to sacrifice. Dick Howser, the third-base coach, ran toward home plate to confer with the batter about the missed sign. Jackson informed Howser that he was going to bunt anyway. Ignoring the manager's signal, he attempted to lay the ball down two more times. His second try produced a foul pop to the catcher, Darrell Porter, for the first out of the inning.

After the game, Martin, still livid at his indignant player, flung a clock radio and a beer bottle against the clubhouse wall. Reggie expressed his anger about being the designated hitter, charging, "How can they say I'm a threat to swing the bat? I'm not an everyday player. I'm a part-time player."[2]

The incident earned Jackson a hefty five-day suspension and a $9000 fine. New York won four games during his absence and the fifth upon his return when Martin refused to put him in the lineup.

On July 23 Martin was still at odds with Jackson. He had also heard that, earlier in the season, Steinbrenner had considered trading managers — Martin for the White Sox's Bob Lemon. While waiting at Chicago's O'Hare Airport for a flight to Kansas City, Billy lashed out at his two adversaries, Jackson and Steinbrenner, telling reporters, "The two deserve each other.... One's a born liar, the other's convicted."[3]

The next day in Kansas City, the Yankees' embattled skipper resigned before Steinbrenner could fire him. Lemon, who earlier in the campaign had been dismissed by Chicago, was hired by the Yankees' owner to lead the struggling Bronx Bombers. The aftershock was felt on July 29 at the Old-Timers Game in Yankee Stadium, when Steinbrenner announced that he had rehired Martin to manage his club in 1980!

But at least for the remainder of the 1978 season, Lemon would be at the Yankees' helm. He brought calm to a hostile battlefield. As Graig Nettles, New York third baseman, said, "It wasn't Billy's fault, but as long as he was there, the turmoil would have kept going.... Lem was the perfect guy for that team at that time. He just kept things loose and easy, no commotion, and let us play. That's all we needed."[4]

On July 19 the Bronx Bombers reposed in fourth place, 14 games behind Boston. The events shortly before and following that date were instrumental to the start of one of the greatest comebacks in American League history.

As the Yankees began to chip away at the Red Sox lead, health was also returning to the New York squad. A struggling and sore-armed Jim "Catfish" Hunter mended, posting a 6–0 record in August with a 1.64 ERA. If Lady Luck was in anyway involved in preventing injuries, she must have turned her gaze away from Boston. During the latter part of the season, a number of the Red Sox, including Carlton Fisk, Rick Burleson, Fred Lynn, and Butch Hobson, came down with nagging physical problems.

Together with the "ups," the Yankees also had a few bad moments. In early August the Bosox came to Yankee Stadium, leading New York by 6½ lengths. Boston swept the Yanks in two straight to drop them back again into fourth place, 8½ games off the pace. Guidry was beaten the next night by Baltimore, and many thought the bubble had burst. That was only his second loss of the season, and the major leagues' leading pitcher recounted, "We knew we lost a big chance when we lost to Boston ... and I don't think anybody really envisioned at that time what would happen. But we were the defending champs, and the general feeling was, if we were going to lose, let's lose with dignity, let's make it close."[5]

Over the remainder of the season, the Yankees never lost more than two in a row in their 41–14 rush to the pennant. During the last weeks of July, the Red Sox began to watch their lead over the fourth-place Yankees dissipate. Both Milwaukee and Baltimore fell off the pace, and New York climbed into the runner-up position for the first time. Boston's darkest hours came during the period between August 30 and September 16, a stretch when they won only three games and lost 14. "'I've never seen a good team do absolutely everything so poorly,' says Manager Don Zimmer. Boston hit .192; Tiant was the only starting pitcher to win a game; the fielders made 33 errors."[6]

Head-to-head meetings with the hard-charging Yankees were the crucial battles. On September 7, the Bronx Bombers came to Fenway Park to open a four-game series. New York stood four games back of Zimmer's stumbling Sox. Bill Lee, the Red Sox left-hander, sized up the situation: "No team ever looked more intense than they did. Getting on the field with them was akin to stepping into a wading pool with Jaws. Every time we made a move, they would bite off another limb. It was terrifying to watch. We had expected at least to split with them in our own ballpark. That's what everyone said and wrote, 'All we need is a split and we're in good shape.'"[7]

What took place the next four days could be called "The [Second] Boston Massacre." The Yankees torched the Sox in a four-game annihilation. That left the Red Sox dead-tied for first place and Fenway fans in mourning. It wasn't just the losses that were so difficult for Boston to swallow; it was the way New York had done it, by the scores of 15–3, 13–2, 7–0 and 7–4. The Yankees rattled 67 hits around "friendly Fenway," whereas the hometown Sox managed only 21.

A week later Boston visited New York. "The darkest moment came on

Sept. 16 with a ninth-inning, 3–2 defeat in Yankee Stadium. It was the Sox's sixth straight loss to New York and left them 3½ games behind. Privately, the players conceded the race was over."[8]

The next day Boston ace Dennis Eckersley, with bullpen help from Bob Stanley, stopped the Yankees and the streak by the count of 7–3. While the New Yorkers were rushing to a pennant on the wings of their amazing and historic comeback, the Red Sox had just begun to mount a phenomenal recovery of their own. They went to Detroit and Toronto during the next-to-last week of the campaign and gained ground on the league-leading Yankees.

On Sunday, eight days before the end of the regular season, New York held a one-game lead over Boston with seven remaining to be played. After that day's contest in Cleveland, the Yankees would finish at home with Toronto and Cleveland, the division's two weakest teams. Following their Sunday encounter in Toronto, the Red Sox would close with the Tigers and the Blue Jays in Fenway Park.

Neither team could afford to lose and neither team did — until the last afternoon of the regular season. The rejuvenated Red Sox won all seven games, knowing that to lose even one would probably seal their doom. They closed the season picking up victories in 12 of their final 14 games, and they were still one monumental game behind. After Luis Tiant shut out Toronto, 5–0, in the Bosox's 162nd game, there was nothing to do but hope that Cleveland would close their season with a win over New York. Hunter did not have his "August sharpness," giving up five runs in 1⅔ innings. Rick Waits pitched the Indians to a 9–2 victory, becoming something of a celebrity in Boston. The Red Sox had gained a tie for the Eastern Division flag.

The American League East would require a one-game playoff in order to crown its champion. As reported in *Sports Illustrated*: "So baseball's Athens and Troy would be brought together for a 163rd game. 'After all that has happened to both teams,' Carl Yastrzemski said, 'this is probably the only way it should be settled. But I feel sorry that either team must lose. The two best teams in baseball, the greatest rivalry in sports. There should be no loser. I know after the way this team came back, I'll always think of it as one thing — the winner.'"[9]

For the Boston Red Sox 1978 brought back memories of 1948. Cleveland had lost and Boston had won on the final day of the regular season, 30 years earlier. That had created a tie for the American League pennant between those two teams and brought about the first-ever Junior Circuit playoff. Cleveland won that game three decades earlier, but Boston was hoping for a different outcome in 1978.

Fenway Park was the site of the "one-game season." October 2 was a glorious early autumn day in New England. That afternoon, one more memory would be added to the history of the Red Sox's special ball yard and to all of baseball as well.

Each starting pitcher brought a story of his own. Guidry wanted to guarantee a happy conclusion to his incredible American League season, entering the game with a 24–3 record. Boston's Mike Torrez was the same pitcher who the record books listed as the winner of two games for the Yankees in the 1977 World Series. He welcomed the opportunity to try again in 1978 with his new team. Torrez had been one of the few to escape "the Bronx Zoo," coming to Boston via free agency. Perhaps an omen was on his side. The only three pitchers to have beaten Guidry that season were also named Mike — Caldwell, Flanagan, and Willis.

Yastrzemski homered in the second inning, putting the Red Sox on the hand-operated Fenway Park scoreboard. Jim Rice's run-scoring hit added to the lead in the sixth.

Going into the top of the seventh, Torrez was protecting a 2–0 advantage, having surrendered only two hits. Chris Chambliss and Roy White singled to start things off for the Bronx Bombers. They watched as Torrez got the next two Yankees out. Bucky Dent, the ninth hitter in the New York lineup, came to bat, bringing a .243 average and four home runs to the plate with him.

Dent took the first pitch for a ball. He fouled Torrez's second delivery off his ankle. While Bucky was hobbling around the batting area on his throbbing ankle, Mickey Rivers grabbed Dent's bat. He had the bat boy replace it with a new "Roy White" model. It was later learned that Rivers had been trying to convince Dent to make the switch but to no avail. With Bucky in agony, Mickey worked his chicanery!

"The heavy air lifted a bit when Dent brought the count to 1-1 and brought Red Sox worries nearly to rest. But sometimes when you least expect it…"[10] When Bucky swung at Torrez's next pitch, the Red Sox announcer gave the fatal account "Deep to left, Yastrzemski will not get it…. It's a home run!"[11] Dent had lifted a three-run fly ball into the netting just over the top of Fenway's "Green Monster." As reported in the *Boston Evening Globe*, Dent's "blast" was "a 306' Home Run over a fence 305' away."[12]

The Yankees took the lead, 3–2. Yastrzemski later recalled the tragic moment and lamented, "When he first hit the ball I thought it was an out. I just kept going back — and then when it slid over the wall it just almost nicked the back part of the wall. I couldn't believe it. I didn't think it was going to be a home run. We talked about loving Fenway Park so much. It's probably the one time I hated Fenway Park, on the Bucky Dent home run."[13]

Commenting on his homer, Dent said, "I've been dreaming of this…. You know you dream about things like this when you're a kid. Well, my dream came true."[14]

In later years Dent kept the dream alive at the "Bucky Dent Baseball School" in Delray Beach, Florida. The instruction and competition took place in a replica of Fenway Park with the numbers on the scoreboard appearing exactly as they were at the moment he drove Torrez's pitch over the Green Monster.

For a number of the Yankees there could not have been anything sweeter than the home run off Torrez. His abandonment of New York had not been overlooked. Following the game, Nettles spoke about how happy he was to have won and especially to have beaten Torrez. He said, "He's been bad mouthing us all year. We didn't appreciate that. If it wasn't for us, he wouldn't have been in a position to sign a $2.7 million contract. Maybe this will teach him to keep his mouth shut."[15]

Bucky's home run landed a bit to the right of where Fisk's dramatic homer had struck the foul pole in game six of the 1975 World Series. Fisk's "shot" had brought ecstasy to Fenway; Dent's was a blast of doom.

Stanley replaced Torrez. Before he could get the third out, Rivers walked and Munson doubled-in the fourth run. An inning later, Jackson homered for what would become the decisive run, putting the Yankees ahead by the margin of 5–2.

Fenway spirits received a brief boost in the bottom of the eighth when the Red Sox scored twice off Goose Gossage on RBI singles by Yastrzemski and Fred Lynn.

With Boston trailing, 5–4, they came to bat in the last of the ninth, hoping for one more comeback. With one out, Burleson walked, and Jerry Remy followed with a shot to right field. As Yankee outfielder Lou Piniella moved toward the ball, it suddenly disappeared in the bright sunlight, and he extended his arms in panic. He later explained, "Remy's ball, I didn't see it at all. I didn't know where it was going to land. Over my head. In front of me. I didn't know if it was going to hit me on the head. I was just fortunate that I somehow lined myself up right. So when the ball bounced in front of me I had a play."[16]

He was able to play the ball on the first bounce and fired it back to the infield. Burleson, who was rounding second base, decided not to chance going to third and headed back to the bag. That proved to be a critical break for the Yankees. Rice followed with a long fly to Piniella, which was deep enough to advance Burleson to third. Certainly, had Burleson already been on third when Rice hit the ball, he would have scored the tying run.

One out remained. Yastrzemski, probably the most poignant symbol of the struggles of the Red Sox through the years, came to bat. He took a hefty cut at a Gossage pitch, and made contact.

> The ball had floated into the air, the laziest sort of a pop up and a certain out, whether the third baseman was Graig Nettles or the kid next door.
> And as Nettles grabbed the ball, amid the stunned silence of Fenway Park, you thought, this isn't the way it should end. Not like this. Not with Yaz making the final out.[17]

The game was over. Yaz wept in the training room. He had driven in two runs with a single and a homer, but he had ended the season with a futile pop fly to third base. Perhaps Nettles's glove had gobbled up the 39-year-old's final chance to play for a World Champion.

A headline in the *Boston Globe* put the painful loss in perspective, at least from the point of view of Beantown's battle with futility. It read: "Destiny 5, Red Sox 4."[18]

Bucky Dent's seventh-inning home run off Mike Torrez would be the lasting memory that the baseball world would carry away from a very special game in that very special season. The New York Yankees, under the leadership of manager Bob Lemon, were the champions of the American League East. They headed off to meet the western winners, the Kansas City Royals. The victor would go on to the 1978 World Series.

1984
National League
Championship Series
Chicago Cubs and San Diego Padres

Fifth Game — October 7 at San Diego

Chicago	2	1	0	0	0	0	0	0	0		3	5	1
San Diego	0	0	0	0	0	2	*4*	0	x		6	8	0

Sutcliffe, Trout[7], Brusstar[8]
Show, Hawkins[2], Dravecky[4], Lefferts[6], Gossage[8]

When baseball was in its infancy, Henry Chadwick, the game's pioneer sportswriter, invented one of the necessities of his trade — the box score. For this and other contributions to the Great American Pastime, Chadwick became one of the earliest members of the Hall of Fame in Cooperstown, being inducted in 1938. As he covered baseball's first professional team, the Cincinnati Red Stockings, he used his creation to keep track of who did what along the way. Chadwick's box scores included a category called "Fatal Errors," those miscues that led directly to a team's loss. Had the scorekeepers at the 1984 National League Championship Series used that designation, Leon Durham of the Chicago Cubs would have been given an "FE" for a misplay that cost his club both the ball game and the league pennant.

When the gates of Wrigley Field, Chicago, were opened for business on October 2, 1984, some of baseball's greatest fans came to see the first postseason game played there in nearly four decades. The Cubs had earned the right to play beyond the regular season for the first time since 1945, when they had lost the World Series to Detroit, four games to three. Chicago was in a best-of-five-game set for the National League pennant against the winners in the West, the San Diego Padres.

The Cubs' home on Chicago's north side — major-league baseball's oldest ballpark — was a unique and historic place. Opened in 1914 as Weeghman Park, a 14,000-seat stadium, it was renamed "Cubs Park" in 1920 and, finally, Wrigley Field in 1926. A hand-operated scoreboard was installed in 1937. A year later

Bill Veeck planted ivy at the base of the brick wall in the outfield. The absence of light standards was another distinguishing mark of the aging and cherished park. Red and green tones of the brick backstop and the ivy-covered outfield wall suggested summer-long Christmas spirit, inviting celebration and joyful times. Roger Angell, in *Season Ticket*, gave a glimpse into Wrigley Field's special character: "The scoops of bunting set around the gray-blue facing of the steep upper deck were also astir, and, farther out, the tall center-field flagpole above the gray-green scoreboard and the rising pyramid of bleachers flew a double row of pennants (team flags, in the order of finish, top to bottom, of the National League divisions), which kept up a gala, regattalike flutter all through the shining afternoon."[1]

Angell went on to describe the faithful "Windy City" folk who were enjoying a brief respite of joy and hope in the midst of what had been a lifetime of broken dreams and dashed possibilities:

> It is the Cub fans who will have to sort out this season — most of all, the unshirted, violently partisan multitudes in the Wrigley Field bleachers, who sustain the closest fan-to-player attachment anywhere in baseball — and I will not patronize them by claiming a share of their happiness during the summer or pretending to understand their pain and shock at its end. Baseball, as I have sometimes suggested, is above all a matter of belonging, and belonging to the Cubs takes a lifetime. But to Chicago the Cubs are something more than just a team.[2]

Chicago had finished in fifth place in 1983. After beginning their spring training schedule by absorbing 11 straight losses, it looked like it would be another typical Cub season. In years past the bubbling enthusiasm of "Mr. Cub," Ernie Banks, had turned a short winning streak into "pennant fever." But reality always seemed to destroy the rosy vision of the Chicago legend who had retired after the 1971 season.

During the ceremonies before the first game of the NLCS, Banks — an honorary Cub captain in 1984 — threw out the first ball. Rick Sutcliffe, a mid-season Cub acquisition, took over from there and set down the Padres without a run through seven frames. Warren Brusstar came on in relief and dealt the Padres two more goose eggs. Cub leadoff hitter Bob Dernier produced the only run the Bruins needed that joyous afternoon, driving Eric Show's second pitch into the left-field screen. Two batters later, Gary Matthews lifted one into left field and beyond the ivy-covered wall.

In the third inning Sutcliffe added his own home run, and it was just the beginning of the Cubs' raucous romp over the Padres. The final tally of that first and memorable game was Chicago 13–San Diego 0.

Game two also went to the "Cubbies." It was a more normal contest, with the final score 4–2. Steve Trout, whose father "Dizzy" had pitched the Detroit Tigers to the win over Chicago in the fourth game of the 1945 World Series, picked up the victory with relief help from Lee Smith. For the second day in a row the Windy City's heroes took a first-inning lead. The go-ahead run was the product of routine grounders and Dernier's aggressive baserunning, rather than a home-run smash. By the end of the third, the Cubs had added two more tallies and held a 3–0 lead, which was enough of an offensive output to put game two in their win column.

Two sterling defensive plays by first baseman Leon Durham were important in Chicago's victory. In the fourth inning, he knocked down a hard smash by Steve Garvey behind first base. The ball caromed off his arm into the air. He grabbed it and flipped it to Trout who was covering the bag, just in time to nip the hustling Garvey. San Diego scored one run in the inning, but Durham's play helped limit it to that.

In the sixth Alan Wiggins was on first base when Tony Gwynn hit a hard shot that took a high bounce toward Durham. The first-sacker leaped high for the ball, caught it in his outstretched glove and beat the runner to the base.

The game report in the *New York Times* mentioned a couple of the key individual contributors. It also noted what devout Cubs fans would later view as painful irony. Also, there was a serious warning by the Chicago manager, Jim Frey:

> It wasn't as rollicking as the 13–0 caper that the Cubs produced in the opening game of the series. But they got five-hit pitching from Steve Trout, no-nonsense relief pitching from Lee Smith in the ninth inning and two sparkling plays at first base from Leon Durham. No team in the league has ever lost the first two games of the playoff and survived.
>
> ———————
>
> "Now everybody's asking, in a nice way, if we can blow three in a row," said Jim Frey, the manager of the Cubs. "Well, I won't feel confident till we get the 27th out in the final game."[3]

When the turnstiles clicked in Jack Murphy Stadium, San Diego, on October 4, 1984, Padre fans were coming to see the first postseason major league game ever played there. The team began its first season in 1969, the same year the Montreal Expos joined the National League's Eastern Division. During the 1980 and 1981 seasons, San Diego finished dead-last in the Western half of the Senior Circuit. The next two years they began moving up in the standings, ending in fourth place each season.

The Padres had been built with experienced veterans and quality young players. Garvey came from the Dodgers as a free agent, and Graig Nettles arrived through a trade with the Yankees. In the outfield Kevin McReynolds and Gwynn were youngsters who had shown flashes of brilliance.

After an 18–18 start in 1984, San Diego went on a tear. They won 53 of their next 83 games, opening up a sizable lead and coasting to their first division crown. They finished 12 games ahead of Atlanta and Houston.

Standing on the brink of elimination from the NLCS, the Padres were buoyed by the comfort of being home and playing in front of 58,346 exultant fans. Two insurance agents, a schoolteacher, and an explosives test expert were on the playing field, serving as umpires for game three. The regular "men in blue" were on strike, seeking more money for postseason games and increased job security.

For the third straight game, the Cubs opened the scoring. Keith Moreland's double and Ron Cey's single off the Padres' Ed Whitson in the second inning put Chicago in front, 1–0. The rest of the day's runs went to San Diego, as they coasted to their first victory, 7–1.

Game four belonged to Garvey. San Diego jumped off to a 2–0 lead in the third, when Gwynn, the major league's leading hitter at .351, delivered a sacrifice fly to score Gary Templeton and Garvey doubled to bring Wiggins home. Chicago rebounded, going ahead, 3–2, in the top of the fourth on a two-run homer by Jody Davis and a shot into the right-field seats by the next hitter, Durham. Garvey singled to tie the game, 3–3, in the fifth and put San Diego ahead with another hit in the seventh.

The game was deadlocked, 5–5, when the Padres' first-sacker came to the plate in the bottom of the ninth. With one out and Gwynn on first base, Garvey was looking for his fourth hit. Smith, the Cubs' fireballing reliever, was on the mound. The first pitch was a ball. The second was to the liking of the day's hero, and it ended in the stands as a game-winning two-run homer. The final score was San Diego 7–Chicago 5, and the series was deadlocked, 2–2. The National League pennant race suddenly became another of those special "one-game seasons."

Show, who had been mauled by the Cubs in the opener, went to the hill for San Diego. In the first inning, Chicago continued their brutal attack on the right-hander. With two outs, both Matthews and Durham slammed 3–1 pitches over the right-center-field fence for two quick runs. Davis led off the second and blasted a homer to left field, giving the Cubs a 3–0 advantage. Before the inning ended, Andy Hawkins received a hurry-up call from the bullpen and relieved Show.

Sutcliffe, the Cubs' ace, was given the ball by manager Jim Frey. He had carried Chicago's hopes on his broad shoulders since being acquired in a trade with Cleveland on June 13. It had been three months since the tall redhead had suffered a defeat. He continued his mastery over the Padres through five innings, allowing them only two infield singles.

In the sixth San Diego's Wiggins dragged a bunt past the mound for an infield hit. Gwynn lined a single to right, and Wiggins stopped at second. Garvey drew a walk to load the bases. Nettles banged Sutcliffe's second pitch 400 feet to deep center where the speedy Dernier pulled it in. Wiggins tagged-up and scored the Padres' first run. Terry Kennedy followed with a hard liner to left on which Matthews made a diving, tumbling catch. Gwynn trotted home on the sacrifice fly, bringing San Diego to within a run of Chicago.

Hawkins, Dave Dravecky, and Craig Lefferts brought effective relief for the Padres and held the Cubs scoreless. With Chicago still leading, 3–2, San Diego came to bat in the bottom of the seventh. After the traditional "seventh-inning stretch," the home fans watched their team move a giant step closer to their first National League pennant.

Sutcliffe dug the first shovel of dirt out of his "grave," walking Carmelo Martinez to start the inning. Templeton sacrificed Martinez to second.

The next few moments are best forgotten by Cubs fans. In the painful blinking of an eye, an event occurred that was critical to the game's outcome and became another of those special "what if" situations that are part of the lore of playoff and World Series history.

Tim Flannery came to bat as a pinch hitter for San Diego. He rolled a grounder toward Durham at first base. The ball slipped painfully beneath Durham's outstretched glove and rolled into right field, as the tying run crossed the plate on the potential "second out" error. Consecutive hits by Wiggins, Gwynn, and Garvey knocked Sutcliffe out of the game and gave the Padres a 6–3 lead. That would be the final score, as "Goose" Gossage slammed the door in Chicago's face in the eighth and ninth innings.

San Diego, after opening with two losses, had made history by winning three straight playoff games on the way to their first National League Championship. They would welcome the Detroit Tigers to Jack Murphy Stadium for the start of the 1984 World Series.

The utter dismay of Chicago fans was expressed in 12 letters emblazoned across the top of the front page of the Sports Section of the *Chicago Tribune* the day following the crushing defeat: "Paradise Lost."[4] The lead story added:

> Today, the Cubs' pennant hangs at half-staff. The franchise's fervent hopes of capturing its first National League flag in 39 years died Sunday when the San Diego Padres rallied for four runs in the seventh inning to defeat the Cubs 6–3 in Game 5 of the National League Championship Series.[5]

The Cubs' discouraged general manager, Dallas Green, said, "I've never been a good loser. I really feel bad for our guys and all the Chicago fans.... We had them by the throat but we just didn't go for the jugular. It all came down to one ballgame and we just didn't get the job done. We played good until the last three games of the season."[6]

Durham, whose error had opened the floodgates, felt the brunt of the disappointing finish. He painfully recalled, "You know it's going to come up somewhere, but it stayed flat.... It had a little behind it, but it was nothing like a hot shot. I'll remember it, for sure. It hurts a lot. We had a chance to go to the World Series, but now it's out the window."[7]

Sutcliffe claimed major responsibility for the loss, having walked Martinez to start the seventh inning downfall. He minimized the error by his first baseman. A number of critics thought Frey had gone too long with Sutcliffe, and they placed a sizable portion of the blame on the manager's decision not to remove his starter.

But the vision of the "flat" grounder going through the legs of Durham, as if they were the gates of Hell, seemed to be the "cause" that lingered longest in the minds of the fans of baseball, especially those who claim Wrigley Field as their own special ballpark. A caustic Bernie Lincicome, writing in his column in the *Chicago Tribune*, asked:

> Today's word, boys and girls, is choke. Can you say choke? Can you spell it? Will you ever forget it?
>
> Can you say ground ball? Could you catch one if you were eight outs from the World Series? Could you catch two?[8]

Trying to play the error down just a "wee bit," Jerome Holtzman of the *Tribune* wrote, "DURHAM'S ERROR was crucial. But it wasn't a blunder that matched the fly ball Hack Wilson lost in the sun in 1929 or Mickey Owen's dropped third strike in 1941. Those occurred in the World Series. Durham's boot came in the fifth game of the National League playoffs."[9]

One wonders if that was adequate consolation for all the long-suffering Cub fans whose hopes, like the enthusiasm of Ernie Banks, had risen almost annually only to discover that the World Series was a distant land they never quite reached. In 1984 they had stood just beyond the entrance.

The three straight losses, which had snatched defeat from the jaws of victory, were only the most recent reminder of an almost annual trauma described in the ballad, "A Dying Cub Fan's Last Request." The song's painful story, which was reborn in the events of the 1984 NLCS, asks what a Chicago fan is to do "when you raise up a young boy's hopes and then just crush them like so many paper beer cups, year after year after year after year ... til those hopes are just so much popcorn beneath the 'El' tracks to eat."[10]

The lyrics had been written by composer and folksinger Steve Goodman. A Chicago native, Goodman had died on September 20, 1984, at age 36, losing a 15-year battle with leukemia. He had been asked to sing the national anthem at the opener of the NLCS in Wrigley Field if the Cubs made the playoff. On the day he died, his Cubs were eight games ahead of the second-place Mets, their division-clinching magic number was three, and all Chicago was hopeful.

1986

American League Championship Series

Boston Red Sox and California Angels

Fifth Game — October 12 at California

```
Boston      0  2  0    0  0  0    0  0  4    0  1    7  12  0
California  0  0  1    0  0  2    2  0  1    0  0    6  13  0
```

Hurst, Stanley[7], Sambito[9], Crawford[9], Schiraldi[11]
Witt, Lucas[9], Moore[9], Finley[11]

Neither of the teams in the best-of-five-games playoff for the 1986 American League Championship had known much recent success in the postseason. The Boston Red Sox had won their last World Series in 1918, defeating the Chicago Cubs. A standout pitcher named George Herman Ruth posted two of Boston's four victories. They lost three times after that, most recently in the exciting and memorable series against Cincinnati in 1975.

The California Angels played their first major-league game in 1961. Their first postseason appearance was in 1979, when they were defeated in the American League Championship Series by the Baltimore Orioles, 3–1. That was not nearly as painful as their playoff collapse in the five-game set in 1982 against the Milwaukee Brewers. After winning the first two contests, the Angels dropped the next three to become the first team in history to take that path to defeat in a league championship series.

Fans of both teams were anticipating three weeks of excitement. Much of the attention was focused on the starting pitchers for the initial contest. Young fireballing right-hander Roger Clemens had posted a 24–4 record and was about to pocket the Cy Young and the Most Valuable Player awards for the American League. He would go to the mound for the hometown Bosox.

Mike Witt, a curveballing, 6'7" right-hander with a 90+ mph fastball, would start for the Angels. He had won 18 games and had finished second in the league in earned run average, right behind Clemens. According to one writer, "At his best, Witt is probably the only pitcher in the league capable of beating Clemens."[1]

Two other pitchers — on the other side of "young and promising" — were attracting special attention. Don Sutton of the Angels, at age 41, was completing his twenty-first major league season and had added 15 victories to his career total. On the opposing bench sat Tom Seaver, also 41, and nearing the end of his outstanding career. Boston had acquired Seaver from the Chicago White Sox in June, but because of an injury, he would not be an active participant. His presence and experience, however, would provide encouragement for his Boston teammates. Each of the masterful right-handers had earned his "ticket" to that October matchup.

"Mr. October" was back in another postseason spectacular, wearing an Angel uniform. Although he was being platooned as a designated hitter and had hit a subpar .241 with 18 home runs, Reggie Jackson often made the World Series his "Magic Kingdom." He came into his eleventh pennant playoff in the throes of a 2-for-30 batting slump and suffering with a sore hand — the result of an attack on a watercooler and a dugout wall in Arlington Stadium, Texas. Although reason told the baseball fan not to expect much from the 40-year-old Jackson, memory whispered exciting possibilities.

Manager Gene Mauch of the Angels was in his twenty-fifth major league season. Only three managers in history had more longevity than the California skipper. Not once in all those years had he taken his team to a World Series. In 1964 Mauch's Philadelphia Phillies had led the National League pennant race by 6½ games with 10 remaining to be played. In an astounding collapse, they lost it all to the St. Louis Cardinals. He was also at the helm in 1982, when California won the first two games in the ALCS but then were beaten three straight times and lost the series to the Brewers. Sentimentally, many hoped that '86 would be Mauch's year for glory.

The American League Championship Series began in Fenway Park, Boston, on October 7. Clemens, who had been hit on the elbow by a line drive six days earlier, was not as sharp as usual. In the second inning, after striking out the first two batters, Clemens walked Bob Boone and Gary Pettis, the Angels' number eight and nine batters. Three hits followed, and California had a 4–0 lead. They added their fifth run an inning later.

Witt held the Red Sox hitless until two were out in the sixth. He walked Spike Owen, and then the league's leading sticker, Wade Boggs, sent a high hopper halfway down the third base line for a scratch hit. Marty Barrett singled to drive in Owens with Boston's only run of the game. The Angels and Witt captured the opener, 8–1.

The tables were turned the following day. Pop-ups lost in the sun and botched ground balls were the distinguishing marks of the game. The sun's gift enabled the Red Sox to break a 2–2 tie in the fifth, when Bobby Grich lost Dwight Evans's short fly with two outs. Three Angel errors gave Boston three more runs in the seventh inning. Left-hander Bruce Hurst worked in and out of trouble, surrendering 11 hits and going the distance in the 9–2 victory. Commenting on his team's sloppy play, Sutton said, "The last time I saw a game like this ... our coach wouldn't take us to the Tastee-Freeze for a milkshake afterward."[2]

The teams moved to Anaheim Stadium for game three. In the bottom of the fourth inning, with Boston leading, 1–0, both Wally Joyner and Brian Downing singled. "Then — in rapid order — there was a full swing squibber, a foul ball that decided to be fair, a tag that may or may not have been made in time, an Angel run that lasted about 15 seconds, a manager tossed out for swearing at the wrong umpire and a ruling that had everyone baffled long after the fact."[3] Doug DeCinces hit a dribbler in foul territory along the first base line. The ball rolled fair at the last moment and struck the bag. Bill Buckner grabbed it and threw it home to Rich Gedman, but the onrushing Joyner "stepped over" the catcher's tag. Home-plate umpire Terry Cooney, who had gotten himself out of position, called the runner "safe." The Red Sox argued vehemently. After a conference with the third-base umpire Rich Garcia, Cooney reversed his decision and thumbed Joyner "out." That led to a classic confrontation with the Angels on the attack and an irate Mauch being ejected. As the *New York Times* reported the following day, "Until something better comes along — something really weird — it will be known as 'The Play' of the 1986 American League Championship Series."[4]

California scored in the bottom of the sixth when Jackson singled in a run to tie the game, 1–1. One inning later, the Angels took a 4–1 lead. The first run came across when Dennis "Oil Can" Boyd hung a slider, and Dick Schofield slammed it for a homer. Then Boyd, who Mauch had called "Dipstick"[5] because of his stalking and glove-pounding antics around the mound, served up a two-run shot to Pettis, giving California a three-run cushion. John Candelaria held Boston in check the rest of the way, and the home team went on to a 5–3 victory.

Clemens returned in game four, pitching with three days' rest for the first time that season. Some criticized manager John McNamara for changing the normal rotation. Sutton was making his first appearance for the Angels. Boston broke a scoreless tie in the sixth, when Buckner doubled home the go-ahead run. They increased their lead to 3–0 in the eighth inning as California tried to match their defensive horrors of game two. In that frame they committed two errors, threw a wild pitch, had a passed ball, and misplayed two other grounders.

During 1986 victory was imminent when the Red Sox went into the ninth inning holding a three-run lead with Clemens on the mound. DeCinces shook the stadium, leading off with a home-run blast. One out singles by Schofield and Boone chased Clemens from the game, bringing in Calvin Schiraldi. Pettis sent a line drive toward Jim Rice in left field. As he was breaking in on the ball, it sailed over his head, and another Angel crossed the plate, making the score 3–2. After an intentional walk to load the bases, Grich struck out. Schiraldi faced Downing and quickly threw two fastballs by the batter. With a 2–1 count, the right-hander landed a slider on Downing's thigh to force home the tying run. "'It was the stupidest pitch of my life,' Schiraldi said later, 'I tried to throw the perfect pitch and choked it.'"[6]

The game moved to extra innings. In the bottom of the eleventh, a Grich single scored Jerry Narron with the run that brought the win. The 4–3 victory handed the Angels a 3–1 series lead. The stage was set for game five, one of the most exciting games in the history of postseason play.

On October 12 California was a single win away from moving on to the franchise's first appearance in a World Series. Mauch, in his silver-anniversary season, would finally get the chance to grab the brass ring. Witt, the Angels' best pitcher, was facing the Red Sox. Hurst was entrusted with the task of bursting California's bubble.

Gedman's two-run homer off Witt in the second frame gave the Bosox an early jump. California rebounded with a single tally in the third, cutting Boston's lead to 2–1.

With two outs in the sixth, the first of a number of unbelievable events occurred, events that would stamp that memorable game as "Amazing," "Outstanding," "Phenomenal" — choose any one or all three.

DeCinces lifted a routine fly toward right–center field. The ball dropped between Dave Henderson and Evans for a sun-aided, windblown, confusion-marked double. But the worst was yet to come. Grich followed with a long, high drive deep to left–center field. Henderson out-raced the shot, leaped against the wall and made a magnificent catch — for a moment. The center fielder, who was only in the contest because of a second-inning injury to starter Tony Armas, described the catastrophe, saying, "I knew I'd have to go to the wall and leap to catch it. The ball hit the heel of my glove as I was going up but I had it in the pocket until my wrist hit the top of the wall and the ball fell over the fence for a two-run homer."[7] Grich had a two-run "break," the Angels had a 3–2 lead, and Henderson had been transformed into the "goat."

California tacked two more runs on the board in the seventh and entered the top of the final frame with a 5–2 lead. The Angels were three outs away from grabbing the American League pennant, and their ace was in control. It sounded amazingly similar to the situation the Red Sox and Clemens had been in one day earlier. The similarities to the earlier game were about to multiply.

With one out and one on, Don Baylor mimicked DeCinces and did him one better, slamming a two-run clout and bringing the Red Sox closer. But Witt settled down, disposing of Evans for the second out. Mauch, the master of the "percentages," brought in southpaw Gary Lucas to face the lefty, Gedman. The Red Sox catcher had homered, doubled, and singled off Witt in the game. As it turned out, Mauch would be roundly criticized for removing his ace with one out to go and the pennant a breath away. Some would resurrect the charges that he had mishandled his pitchers in 1964, leading to the Phillies' great collapse. But the manager had his reasons for making the move.

Lucas plunked Gedman on the hand with his first and only delivery — a reminder of what Schiraldi had done to Downing one game earlier. Mauch had seen enough of Lucas and went to the Angels' dominant right-handed closer Donnie Moore to face Dave Henderson.

Moore started the right-handed hitting Henderson off with a 95-mph fastball, which the Bosox slugger took for a called strike. He swung helplessly and missed the next blazing delivery. The next two pitches were out of the strike zone. With the count 2-2, "Hendu" fouled off a pitch. Moore came within a whisker of wrapping up the ALCS when Henderson barely tipped the next offering for a foul dribbler. "Hendu" reached for the fatal pitch, a low outside forkball, and powered it into the lower left-field seats for the inning's second two-run homer, giving the Bosox a shocking lead. Suddenly, Boston led, 6–5, with the Angels coming to bat in the bottom half of the ninth.

Bob Stanley had the job of protecting the Red Sox lead. Boone singled to center, leading off for California. Pettis sacrificed pinch runner Ruppert Jones to second base. Joe Sambito relieved Stanley and quickly surrendered a single to Rob Wilfong. Jones's acrobatic slide around Gedman beat a rifle-throw from Evans, tying the game, 6–6. McNamara went to his bullpen once more and brought in Steve Crawford, who was making his first series appearance. Schofield greeted Crawford with a solid base hit to right field. Then, Downing was intentionally walked to load the bases.

DeCinces came to bat, hoping to finish the Bosox and bring the pennant to the Angels. Later, when asked how he felt at that point, Crawford confessed, "If there was a toilet on the mound at the time, I would have used it."[8] "Shag" got DeCinces to pop the first pitch to shallow right, recording the second out of the inning. Grich followed with a soft liner back at Crawford, which he grabbed, ending the threat.

Moore and Crawford did not surrender any runs in the tenth. The Bosox had men on first and third with one away, but the Angel reliever got Rice to ground into an inning-ending twin-killing.

The score remained deadlocked until the day's "goat-turned-hero" came to bat again. By then it was the top of the eleventh, the inning in which the previous day's thriller had been decided. Henderson came up with the bases loaded and delivered a game-winning sacrifice fly, putting the Sox on top, 7–6. That was the score at the game's end, as Schiraldi retired the Angels in order in their last chance at bat.

"Hendu," who had been rescued from Seattle with Owen in an August trade, talked about his dramatic ninth-inning blast:

> "It was a big hit. It came at the right time. I don't get too many chances to do that." But Henderson knew what he had done. He has hit enough homers to know the difference between a double and something over the fence.
> "Right when I swung [I knew]," he said. "I hit the ball solid out of the park. When I hit it like that, I knew it was gone."[9]

McNamara, Boston's jubilant manager, exclaimed, "That baseball game ... was the best baseball game, the most exciting baseball game, the most competitive baseball game I've ever seen."[10]

It was also a special experience for those who played in it. "When Baylor was hit to start the 11th, he trotted to first and stood beside Grich, his close friend since they signed with the Orioles in 1967. 'What do you think?' Grich asked Baylor. 'Greatest game I've ever played in,' Baylor replied. Grich slapped Baylor's hand, 'Me, too, partner.'"[11]

When game five reached its unexpected conclusion, attendants rushed to hastily remove the chilled champagne from the Angels' locker room. Preparations for the awards ceremony were cleared away. The American League pennant trophy was packed up. It would be awarded to one of the teams in another place, at another time.

When California Angels fans entered Anaheim Stadium on the afternoon of October 12, most had envisioned their team winning its first pennant on the home turf and anticipated a joyous celebration at game's end. That dream was dead. As they headed home, they could probably sense the impending nightmare that was to follow.

After a day for travel, the teams took the field in Boston. The Red Sox brought their potent bats home to Fenway Park for game six. By the end of the third inning they were spanking the Angels, 7–2. Boyd, with relief help from Stanley, held the visitors at bay. Five of the Red Sox starters collected two or more hits, with Owen leading the way with four. The Bosox rolled to a 10–4 win, and the clubs were tied at three games apiece.

The dream of an American League pennant, which had seemed so close for the California Angels before Henderson's dramatic ninth-inning homer, was slipping away. Momentum had surged to the charged-up Boston Red Sox. Candelaria was the Angels' last hope. Clemens was right where every Boston fan wanted him to be — on the mound for the all-important seventh game. Even though he was fighting the flu, Roger was strong enough to pitch into the eighth inning. He limited the Angels to four hits and one run. For the second day in a row, Boston broke from the gate quickly and held a 7–0 lead after four frames. Home runs by Rice and Evans, along with crucial lapses in California's defense, led to an easy Red Sox victory, 8–1.

The California Angels had suffered another excruciating near-miss, especially for the older players who would not have another opportunity. Grich had already announced his retirement.

The 1986 ALCS had not been one of Reggie's best, as the Red Sox staff kept "Mr. October" in check. He ended with a .192 average and a strikeout in his final appearance in game seven.

Boston had the American League pennant in hand. Henderson and his teammates were happily looking forward to meeting the New York Mets in the 1986 World Series, which was set to begin in Shea Stadium, Flushing, N.Y., on the evening of October 18.

The pain was especially obvious for the defeated manager. Mauch had brought another team to the brink of the World Series, only to watch them fall short of the goal:

> Ghosts? Mauch would not address his past — not 1964 or 1982 or this latest collapse — but he could not hide the anguish. An 8–1 defeat to the Boston Red Sox tonight left Mauch without a pennant after 25 seasons of managing in the big leagues.
>
> "There's not a hell of a lot to say," he finally said, almost inaudibly. "I hurt like hell for these players. I hurt like hell for Gene Autry. Those players laid their hearts out there and got stepped on. Eight months of hard work.... We feel like we got the job done. It just got away."[12]

For Mauch, the lost opportunity was a monumental disappointment; for Donnie Moore, it was something much more tragic. He couldn't erase the one disastrous pitch he had served to Henderson. The pain from one catastrophic moment in sport had become all consuming, and it would not go away. In July 1989 he shot and seriously wounded his wife before turning the gun on himself. Shortly after the pitcher's death, the Associated Press reported, "Those close to him said Moore was obsessed by his failure to record the final out in 1986's American League playoffs.... What set Moore apart [from others who had given up similarly critical hits] was that his torment never dimmed."[13]

1986
World Series
Boston Red Sox and New York Mets

Sixth Game — October 25 at New York

Boston	1	1	0	0	0	0	1	0	0	2	5	13	3
New York	0	0	0	0	2	0	0	1	0	3	6	8	2

Clemens, Schiraldi[8], Stanley[10]
Ojeda, McDowell[7], Orosco[8], Aguilera[9]

The Boston Red Sox and the New York Mets battled through memorable League Championship Series and earned berths in the 1986 World Series.

Boston, coming off the exciting comeback victory over the California Angels, was seeking its first title since the World War I era. The vision of Dave Henderson's climactic home run in game five, when the Red Sox were one pitch away from elimination, had been etched in the minds of baseball fans. Whether the Beantowners' newfound hope would neutralize "the Curse of the Bambino" was yet to be answered.

The New York Mets won 108 games in the National League East and took the division crown by a whopping 21½ games over the Philadelphia Phillies. Like the Red Sox, the Mets were also involved in a spectacular set of games for their league's crown against the Houston Astros, winners of the West.

With the National League Championship Series tied at two games apiece, 39-year-old Nolan Ryan of the Astros and 21-year-old Dwight Gooden of the Mets hooked up in a masterpiece in Shea Stadium. Ryan allowed New York two hits through the nine innings he pitched, and Gooden scattered nine hits in his ten innings of work. The game was finally decided in the bottom of the twelfth, when the Mets scored and claimed a 2–1 victory.

The finale of the NLCS, which took place in Houston, also went into extra innings. In the top of the sixteenth, New York scored three times to take a 7–4 lead. The Astros bounced back with two of their own but fell one run short. The Mets prevailed and captured the National League flag.

For the first time since 1916, two teams from the "Eastern Establishment" baseball cities — Boston and New York — were facing each other in October.

The Red Sox had beaten the Brooklyn Dodgers for the grand prize in that series 70 years before.

There was a somber reminder mixed with all of the hoopla surrounding the National and American League pennant winners. Had the ball bounced just a bit differently, the fans at the 1986 "Fall Classic" would have been casting their eyes on the modern-day wonders of the Astrodome and Disneyland rather than on time-honored sites such as the Empire State Building, Bunker Hill, and "the Fenway."

Bruce Hurst of Boston and Ron Darling of New York were matched in the opener in Shea Stadium, Flushing, on Sunday, October 18. On a chilly night, with the temperature dropping into the 40s, the pitchers put a sting in the bats and fashioned shutouts through six innings. In the bottom of the sixth, with runners at first and second for the Mets and no one out, Hurst struck out Darryl Strawberry on three straight curveballs and induced Ray Knight to bounce into a double play, providing a great escape for the Red Sox left-hander.

The game's first and only run scored in the top of the seventh. The "rally" began with a walk to Jim Rice. A wild pitch by Darling moved him to second, and a grounder by Rich Gedman, which handcuffed second baseman Tim Teufel, allowed Rice to score. Boston won the first contest, 1–0, with a tainted tally.

Game two was advertised as the "Pitching Match-up of the Year." Gooden of the Mets, the 1985 National League Cy Young winner, and Roger Clemens of the Red Sox, about to be named the 1986 recipient of that award in the American League, were the major leagues' most heralded right-handed superstars. The anticipated duel never materialized because the Red Sox refused to follow the script, banging out 18 hits and scoring nine runs against Gooden and four other New York pitchers. The Bosox grabbed a three-run lead in the third on run-scoring hits by Wade Boggs, Marty Barrett, and Bill Buckner.

New York rebounded with two in their half of the inning, but they would not catch their opponents from the Back Bay. Home runs by Henderson in the fourth and Dwight Evans in the fifth widened the lead. Boston went on to a 9–3 victory for their second straight win. Clemens tired and lasted only 4⅓ innings, not long enough to be the pitcher of record.

The games moved to Boston's Fenway Park, and the Bosox fans were ecstatic. Their team had two victories before ever setting foot in "friendly Fenway." However, the next two games would be more amicable to the Mets than they would be to the "Olde Town Team."

New York's Lenny Dykstra led off the third game with a home run, the Mets' first extra-base hit of the series. A defensive lapse by the Red Sox — when they lost two runners in run-downs on the same play — along with run-scoring hits by Gary Carter and Danny Heep, helped the New Yorkers to a quick 4–0 first-inning lead. Behind Bobby Ojeda, who had been a Boston starter a year earlier, the Mets went on to a convincing 7–1 victory.

Game four featured a matchup of Boston's crafty Al Nipper and New York's Darling. In the top of the fourth the Mets put the first three runs on the board, highlighted by Carter's two-run blast over "The Green Monster" in left field. Dykstra added a two-run blast in the seventh, and Carter stroked his second round-tripper of the evening an inning later. The Mets pounded out a 6–2 victory and tied the World Series at two apiece.

So far that October, there were some observable patterns. First, the home team lost each game; and second, the team that scored first never surrendered the lead in its march to victory.

Game five repeated only one aspect of the pattern. Boston finally won at home, with Hurst besting a struggling Gooden and Sid Fernandez, 4–2. The Mets' starter left the game with no one out in the fifth, trailing, 4–0. With one down in the second, Henderson, who had tripled to right–center field, scored on Spike Owen's sacrifice fly.

An inning later, Evans lined a single to center, driving in Buckner from second base. Roger Angell, in *Season Ticket*, described "Billy Buck's" scoring jaunt: "No one wanted to laugh at his journey home after Evans bounced the ball up the middle, but you couldn't help yourself. He looked like Walter Brennan coming home — all elbows and splayed-out, achy feet, with his mouth gaping open with the effort, and his head thrown back in pain and hope and ridiculous deceleration. When he got there, beating the throw after all, he flumped belly-first onto the plate and lay there for a second, panting in triumph, and, piece by piece, got up a hero."[1]

The Boston first baseman, who had suffered an Achilles tendon injury in the seventh game against the California Angels, was playing in pain and wearing black high top shoes to support his injured ankle. Injuries to his knees and ankles caused Buckner to hobble every time he had to move — offensively and defensively. Before and after each game, the injuries, which seemed to be gradually spreading over his entire body, were treated with ice bags. The grit and determination of the Red Sox first sacker, who had driven in 102 runs during the regular season, was extolled by Ira Berkow in the *New York Times*: "Bill Buckner of the Red Sox runs the bases as if one foot is on a curb and the other on the street. He runs from side to side, lopsided, part hobble, part stumble, part desperation.... Watching Buckner run is painful, but not nearly as painful as running is for the 36-year-old Buckner."[2]

After the 4–2 victory, the object of the fans' affection was their Red Sox, who had drawn to within one win of the elusive World Championship. The object of the fans' playful derision was Strawberry, the tall, lean right fielder of the New York Mets, who had been piling up strikeouts and failing to do any productive hitting during the series. Chants of "Dar-ryll ... Dar-ryll" greeted him at the plate and in the field. Strawberry, a sweet-swinging left-hander, hit .259 during the regular season, slugging 27 homers and driving in 93 runs. In the NLCS, two of his five hits had been for the circuit. In some circles his graceful stroke had been compared to the classic swing of Fenway's one and only Ted Williams, "the Splendid Splinter." Perhaps, the Boston faithful were challenging the veracity of that comparison at a level that went deeper than playful humor.

Game six was played in Shea Stadium on the night of October 25. There were 55,078 fans who had come to the Stadium to watch and millions more who were in front of their television sets. It could be the night that the Red Sox broke "The Curse." It would be a night to remember.

Clemens and Ojeda faced each other. Whereas most of the hype had focused on the game two matchup, the starters in the sixth game could very well have been their teams' most valuable pitchers that year.

Early in the game, Clemens was overpowering. In the first two innings, 27 of his pitches were clocked at 95 mph and above. Four Mets were "the Rocket's" strikeout victims.

Also on target was a yellow-clad parachutist, carrying a sign reading "Let's go Mets," who dropped to earth near the pitcher's mound in the top of the first, while a stunned Buckner waited in the batter's box. After the intruder was rushed from the field by embarrassed security guards, the Red Sox landed on the scoreboard with the game's first run. They added another in the second.

New York knotted the contest with two tallies in the home-half of the fifth. Boston came back, retaking the lead, 3–2, in the top of the seventh, when Knight made a high throw to first base on a grounder, allowing a run to score.

The Red Sox returned the favor, committing a critical boot in the bottom of the eighth. With Lee Mazzilli on first base, Calvin Schiraldi — who had just replaced Clemens — threw Dykstra's sacrifice bunt into the dirt at second base on an attempted force out. After Wally Backman successfully advanced the runners, the Red Sox walked Keith Hernandez to load the bases. Carter swung at a 3–0 pitch and lined it deep enough to left to allow Mazzilli to tag up and score the New Yorkers' third and tying run.

The game remained deadlocked until the momentous tenth inning. Henderson, the hero of game five of the ALCS, struck a blow for a new honor. He led off for the Bosox and drove the second pitch from relief pitcher Rick Aguilera down the left-field line for another potentially "historic" round-tripper. With two outs, Boggs doubled, and Barrett singled him home for what the Red Sox hoped would be the icing on a very special celebration cake.

Schiraldi had two runs to work with as the Mets came to bat, trailing, 5–3. Backman flied to left field for out number one, and Hernandez followed with a fly out deep to center. After his out, Hernandez took a slow, painful walk back to the Mets' dugout. "He picked up his glove and his cap and took another long walk to the clubhouse. Hernandez walked through the door. He turned left into the office of manager Dave Johnson, put his cap and glove on the manager's desk, sat in a folding director's chair and looked at a television set."[3]

Boston was one out away from ending its 68-year postseason drought.

Red Sox players were perched on the dugout steps, poised to charge onto the field to mob their heroes and usher in a new era in Boston sports history. For a brief instant, the message board in Shea Stadium flashed: "Congratulations, Red Sox." Sportswriters had chosen Hurst as the Series' MVP.

A woman seated in the box behind home plate, who had been making circular motions with her hands throughout the game in an effort to hex the Red Sox pitchers, attempted her black magic one more time.

Carter, the potential final out, stayed the Mets' execution with a single to left. Kevin Mitchell, batting for Aguilera — who was in Strawberry's spot in the lineup as the result of a "double-switch" in the ninth inning — banged a single to center. Knight, with two strikes on him, connected for the Mets' third consecutive hit, scoring Carter, and sending Mitchell to third. Suddenly, it was a 5–4 ball game!

Bob Stanley, called from the bullpen to replace a shell-shocked Schiraldi, ran to the mound, took his allotted number of warm-up pitches and then stared in at the next hitter, Mookie Wilson. Wilson battled the sinker-baller to a 2-2 count and then fouled off the next two pitches. Stanley came inside to the left-handed hitter — a bit too far inside — and it ticked off Gedman's glove, rolling to the screen behind home plate. Mitchell dashed in from third base. Miraculously, the game was tied, 5–5!

The Red Sox were still one out away from, at least, limping into extra innings. Knight stood at second base. Wilson fouled off another pair of Stanley's offerings.

The rest is "page one" in the annals of baseball history. Wilson recounted, "I don't recall whether Stanley's next pitch was a fastball or a slider, but I didn't hit it solid. I beat it into the ground, a three bouncer that — like I said — was hit about 22 miles-an-hour right at the first baseman, Bill Buckner."[4]

> "I hate to say I missed a ground ball," Buckner said later. "I was playing deeper than usual, and he's a pretty good runner getting down the line. I did concentrate on the ball. I saw it well. It bounced and bounced, and then it didn't bounce. It just skipped.
>
> "I can't remember the last time I missed a ball like that, but I'll remember that one. It just shows you that anything can happen."[5]

Knight scored as the ball rolled into right field. The Mets' amazing comeback had produced a 6–5 victory. In a fleeting moment, the Red Sox's pot of championship gold had turned to dross.

It was another powerful example of nineteenth-century sportswriter Henry Chadwick's designation: "Fatal Error."

The ball that had rolled through Buckner's legs lay unattended on the right-field grass. Umpire Ed Montague picked it up and took it with him to the umpires' locker room. Later that evening, he presented it to Arthur Richman, the Mets traveling secretary and special assistant to the general manager. In 1992 the ball went on the auction block at Leland's Auction House in New York. Actor Charlie Sheen paid a whopping $93,500 for the piece of historic memorabilia, which bore the inscription:

> To
> Arthur
> The Ball Won
> it For Us
> Mookie Wilson
> 10/25/86[6]

The "out" that Schiraldi and Stanley couldn't get was described this way: "The slings and arrows of outrageous fortune pierced the Red Sox again moments later when, just a pitch away from ending the inning, the worst that could happen, did. For Mets fans it was the best of times. For Red Sox fans, especially eyewitnesses, it was an unbearable moment."[7]

Two years later, Rene Lachemann, who had been Boston's third base coach that fateful night, returned to Fenway Park as a coach for the Oakland Athletics. He was in town with the A's to begin the 1988 ALCS. One of the teams playing that day would go on to another Fall Classic. In the midst of that new opportunity, he remembered the past:

> I'm out on the step of the dugout and waiting for Stanley to close it out. I'm ready to start the celebration. I'm gonna rush out and lift Hindu on my shoulder and carry him out of Shea Stadium.
> Then there's a ball ... and another ball. I drop to the second step. A wild pitch. Oh, now I'm down on the third step. Then Wilson hits that little grounder and Buck can't make the play. Ugh...
> I can't help it. That sixth game won't go away. Oh, what might have been.[8]

Besides Buckner, others were measured for a goat's costume. Stanley's wild pitch allowed the Mets to tie the game. "'The pitch just took off the other way,' he said, 'I had been going inside on him and I wanted to go outside just one time.'"[9] Many questioned whether it was a wild pitch caused by Stanley's inaccuracy or a passed ball caused by Gedman's slow adjustment to the pitch. The pitcher, who altogether threw 6⅔ innings of relief with one save and an 0.00 ERA, lamented, "Seventy eight was bad, but this is the worst."[10]

Some critics aimed their shots at manager John McNamara. Why was Buckner still in the game at the time? Why hadn't McNamara pinch-hit Don Baylor for the hobbled first baseman in the eighth? Or, why hadn't he replaced Buckner with Dave Stapleton as a defensive measure in the last of the tenth? Others offered another line of questioning. Why hadn't Baylor been the first baseman at the start of the game against the left-handed Ojeda? The rationale given was that the manager had faith in Buckner. McNamara said, "I never thought about taking him out tonight. He has very good hands."[11] He went on to describe his usual way of substituting and added, "We have not changed the pattern of what got us here."[12]

Lou Gorman, the Red Sox general manager at the time, remembers the loss with great pain. Many of the players he had signed as G.M. for the Mets were on the field that night. He commented, "Even to read about this many years later, still brings back such painful memories.... There will always be a question as to why Bill Buckner was still at first base defensively in the 9th inning for he played injured throughout the entire season. Yet in retrospect we would not have reached the World Series without him."[13]

There were two sides to the story of the sixth game. Boston lived it this way: "The Red Sox and their fans might have thought they had seen everything since Babe Ruth helped pitch them to a World Series title in 1918 and was sold off a season later, but Bucky Dent's homer in the 1978 playoff, and Country Slaughter's mad dash home with the winning run of the 1946 World Series may now be equalled by this morning's terror."[14]

Sportswriter Leigh Montville shared a few of his thoughts in the *Boston Globe*: "One pitch away from a World Championship. One pitch away from an end to 68 years of frustration. One pitch. Not close enough."[15]

And the people of New York described it in this manner: "Not since Bobby Thomson hit his pennant-winning home run for the New York Giants off Ralph Branca in the ninth inning of their decisive 1951 playoff game with the Brooklyn Dodgers had a New York team won such an important game in such an improbable, if not impossible, manner. Two out, nobody on, two runs behind. But somehow the Mets won."[16]

After a day of raindrops — or maybe they were tears streaming down from the north — play resumed in Shea Stadium before 55,032 fans. Each of the starting pitchers, Darling and Hurst, had two strong outings in earlier games. Originally, McNamara had nominated Dennis "Oil Can" Boyd for the start, but after the postponement he changed his mind and went with the series' only two-game winner. The disappointed and emotional Boyd was told that he would receive the first call from the bullpen. The call never came.

In the second inning, the Red Sox recaptured the momentum that had been stifled early in the morning of October 26, when Evans launched a home run that cleared the pavilion in left field. The next batter, Gedman, stroked another long drive. The ball landed in and, then, out of right-fielder Strawberry's glove, falling over the fence into home-run territory. Later in the same inning, Boggs's single scored Henderson from second base, and the Bosox took a 3–0 lead. It appeared that, remarkably, the good spirits were back with Boston.

Hurst, who came into the game having given the Mets only two runs in

17 innings, held New York scoreless through five frames. The Red Sox's 3–0 advantage disappeared in the sixth, and with it went a large measure of hope. For some who were familiar with Boston's past, it rekindled unpleasant memories of a lost three-run lead in the seventh game of the 1975 World Series. Pinch hitter Mazzilli and Wilson hit consecutive singles, and Teufel walked to load the bases. Hernandez came to the plate in the crucial situation for the Mets. Angell called it the "acute moment in Game Seven": "Anyone who does know baseball understood that this was the arrangement — this particular batter and this precise set of circumstances — that the Mets wanted most and the Red Sox least at the end of their long adventures. It was the moment that only baseball — with its slow, serial, one-thing-and-then-another siftings and sortings — can produce from time to time, and its outcome is often critical even when reexamined weeks later. I think the Red Sox would have won this game if they had got Hernandez out."[17]

But the Red Sox weren't able to handle Hernandez. On an 0-1 pitch, Keith rapped a long single to left–center field, driving in Mazzilli and Wilson and bringing the Mets to within a run, 3–2. Before the sixth inning was over, the Mets pushed across a third run to tie the contest. New York added three more scores in the seventh, the first of which came when Knight homered to left field off Schiraldi.

Boston rebounded with two in the top of the eighth to whittle the score to 6–5. Evans's double chased home a limping Buckner, followed by Rice. But before the Bosox could get any closer, the Mets' Strawberry homered and Jesse Orosco bounced a single through the middle to score Knight. The Mets' lead had ballooned to 8–5, and the Bosox were down to one final at bat.

Boston had been a pitch away from winning it all in game six and now were three outs away from one more failure. Orosco, the fourth Met pitcher, faced the number-nine hitter Ed Romero, who fouled out to the first baseman. Two outs remained. Boggs bounced a grounder to second base for the next-to-last out.

Met fans stood and waited expectantly for one more Boston batter to be retired. Mounted police were poised in the bullpen, ready to protect the players and the playing field from the onrushing masses bent on celebrating their World Championship.

> Boston's Marty Barrett, who had tied a Series record in the second inning when he got his 13th hit, was standing at the plate in swirling mists, a ghost of Series past for all those Red Sox fans who have dutifully borne more than their share of suffering. And then someone tossed a red smoke bomb onto the grass in left centerfield. What cruel symbolism. There went a season of hope, an incredible escape from defeat in the playoffs and a World Series of such promise (two straight wins at the start) and maybe the last chance for New England fans to believe that it's possible for their team not to bomb in the big ones. There it all went, up in a puff of red smoke.[18]

After the smoke faded, the Red Sox's final hope met the same fate. Barrett swung and missed a 2-2 pitch, and the Mets had won the championship. It was New York's 116th win of the season. They were one of the few teams in history to have lost the first two games at home and then recovered to grab the brass ring.

As jubilant Mets fans and players began to celebrate the victory, the television audience's gaze was drawn to the Red Sox dugout, where Wade Boggs, the major leagues' leading hitter, sat alone, with tears streaming down his face.

Schiraldi, one pitch away from winning game six and a World Championship, was the loser for the second straight game. He wondered: "'When will I get over it? In about 20 years,' Schiraldi said at the time."[19]

Postseason 1986 offered a roller coaster ride of joy and sorrow, of hope and disappointment for many fans of the Great American Pastime. In the end, while New Yorkers celebrated and Bostonians cried, everyone held on to the precious — and sometimes painful — memories born in that outstanding set of League Championship and World Series games. There had been the Angels' dreams and Henderson's home run, the final two titanic battles between the Astros and the Mets, the memorable moment in the sixth game of the World Series, and all of the other special remembrances in between.

The Mets were the World Champions for the second time in their history, and they were ecstatic. The postseason had carried the Red Sox from "The Thrill of Victory" in Anaheim to "The Agony of Defeat" in Flushing. And "The Curse" still hung over them.

Angell, in *Season Ticket*, wondered if fans were asking "if all this really did come to pass at the end of the 1986 season and if it was all right for us to get so excited about it, so hopeful and then so heartbroken or struck with pleasure. To which let it be said again: Yes, it did. Yes, it was. Yes, absolutely. What matters now, perhaps, is for each of us to make an effort to hold on to these games, for almost certainly we won't see their like again soon — or care quite as much if we do."[20]

1988
World Series
Los Angeles Dodgers and Oakland Athletics

First Game — October 15 at Los Angeles

Oakland	0	4	0	0	0	0	0	0	0	4	7	0
Los Angeles	2	0	0	0	0	1	0	0	2	5	7	0

Stewart, Eckersley[9]
Belcher, Leary[3], Holton[6], Pena[8]

During the latter part of the 1980s, a number of motion pictures telling stories set against a backdrop of the Great American Pastime came to neighborhood theaters. *Bull Durham, Eight Men Out, Major League,* and *Field of Dreams* presented baseball themes. Some were based in history; others were founded in fantasy.

Bernard Malamud's 1952 novel, *The Natural,* had made it to the silver screen a few summers earlier, in 1984. It was the story of Roy Hobbs, an 18-year-old-phenom who, on the eve of his major-league tryout, was shot and seriously wounded by a mystery woman. After 15 years of aimless meanderings, he attempts a baseball comeback, hoping to fulfill the dream that had been shattered by a silver bullet.

Following a tryout with the New York Knights, Hobbs is given a spot on their roster. The season progresses, and his feats become legendary. As fate would have it, the hero is hospitalized at the very end of the regular season. The Knights lose their final three games to the lowly Reds and finish in a flat-footed tie with Pittsburgh. Weak and not fully healed, Hobbs leaves the hospital, joining the Knights for the one-game playoff against the Pirates. The winner's prize would be a berth in the World Series.

Hobbs, in excruciating pain, strikes out in his first two plate appearances — the second time on three feeble swipes at the ball. The Knights trail, 2–0, in the bottom of the ninth. Roy comes to bat with two outs, two on base, and the season on the line. The left-handed slugger faces a young left-handed relief pitcher with "a blinding fastball and an exploding curve."[1] Blood is oozing from Roy's unhealed wound, staining the front of his Knights uniform.

Hobbs slams a two-and-two pitch into the stands in right field, but it is just foul. On the drive, he splinters his bat. The bat boy picks out a "special" piece of timber for him to use. And then the miracle happens. With a twist of his pain-wracked body, he drives the next pitch high into the light standard in deep right field for the game-winning, pennant-clinching home run. The collision of ball and incandescent bulb sets off a fireworks display of exploding light and sound. Roy Hobbs lives his dream, and the Knights win the crown. The story was pure fantasy. However in the minds of some, it would later be born in real life.

Away from the silver screen, the teams in the real-life 1988 World Series brought their own brand of entertainment to baseball fans. Foremost was the unbelievable blast in game one, which lit up the evening sky, began the joyful celebration for the Dodger faithful, and set the series on an unexpected path.

While the star of the game was being mauled by his ecstatic teammates on the field, the bullpen coach was placing a sign over the hero's locker. It read: "Roy Hobbs."

The combatants in the eighty-fifth edition of the World Series were the Athletics of Oakland and the Dodgers of Los Angeles — not far from Hollywood.

Oakland, winner of 104 games, was the front-runner in the American League's Western Division throughout the regular season. They displayed their awesome power and pitching in a four-game sweep of a talented Boston Red Sox squad in the American League Championship Series.

In the National League Championship Series, Los Angeles had a much more difficult time disposing of the New York Mets, whom many considered the strongest team in the Senior Circuit. In the exciting set of seven games, the Dodgers prevailed four games to three.

The A's and the Dodgers were each led by two major headliners. Each of the four players had continued his regular-season heroics during the League Championship Series. Oakland had Jose Canseco and Dennis Eckersley. Los Angeles countered with Orel Hershiser and Kirk Gibson.

Canseco, the 6' 3", 230-pound Cuban-born strongman of the Athletics' attack, connected for 42 home runs during the regular season. He also displayed another side of his amazing physical ability, stealing 40 bases to become the first player in major league history to reach the coveted "40–40" mark.

Some wondered about Jose's amazing strength. On a CBS television show a week before the start of the ALCS, *Washington Post* columnist Tom Boswell suggested that Canseco was "an example of a major leaguer who has used steroids to build up muscles, add strength and pounds."[2] The A's outfielder denied the charge and threatened a lawsuit.

During the ALCS, fans in Fenway's right-field bleachers began their playful banter with Canseco. Chants of "ste-roids ... ste-roids" greeted his every move. For some, it was a reminder of "Dar-ryl ... Dar-ryl," which had welcomed Darryl Strawberry to that area during the 1986 World Series.

Canseco commented after the game about the chants and the charges against him, saying, "I thought it was kind of fun. The fans were chanting rumors. Honestly, I had a lot of fun with them. They really didn't mean any harm. I've heard so many rumors and criticisms about me it doesn't make any sense. So, I just try to make the most of the moment and that's what I did today."[3]

Eckersley had a spectacular summer coming out of the bullpen for the Athletics. He collected 45 saves — a mark reached previously by only three pitchers. Earlier in his career, Eckersley had been a member of the Red Sox and had left them as a "washed-up" starter. He then spent time in the National League. He made his way back to the American League and found a rejuvenated career in the Bay Area as a closer. During the ALCS, he appeared in all four of Oakland's victories, picking up a save in each game. His performance earned him the Most Valuable Player Award.

The Dodgers' Hershiser, a 23-game winner, set one of baseball's most amazing records in the sport in his final appearance of the regular season. He broke Don Drysdale's mark for consecutive shutout innings, extending his own string to 59 straight. In the first game of the NLCS he added eight more goose eggs to his total. The streak ended in the ninth inning.

Gibson, the Dodgers' supercharged outfielder, was the fourth headliner. Prior to the 1988 campaign he had spent his entire major league career with the Detroit Tigers. In January of that year, he became one of the players declared a free agent in a collusion case against major-league owners. A month later he signed a $4.5 million, three-year contract with Los Angeles.

The Dodgers had finished the previous two seasons with identical 73–89 records. Upon his arrival at spring training, Gibson sensed a lackadaisical attitude pervading the camp. He did not appreciate the team's casual acceptance of their losing records during the past couple of seasons.

There were also the practical jokes. When Jesse Orosco put black eye shadow inside of Gibson's hat, Kirk failed to see the humor in it. An enraged Gibson confronted manager Tommy Lasorda, and then he stormed out of the clubhouse. "When he came back the next morning he called a team meeting, reportedly labeled his new teammates 'clowns' and suggested in the strongest terms they keep their hands off his equipment and their jokes to themselves when he was preparing for a game. Any game."[4]

The Dodgers' intensity changed with the addition of the "hard-driving man." They learned to win with more regularity, and losing became harder to accept. Even though his personal statistics for the season were not eye-popping (.290 average, 25 home runs, and 76 RBIs), he was being mentioned as a leading candidate for the National League's Most Valuable Player Award. During the NLCS, however, Gibson reinjured the hamstring in his left leg and had also jammed his right knee.

Those four — Canseco, Eckersley, Hershiser, and Gibson — were the headliners. When the rest of the casts were assembled, it appeared as if the Oakland Athletics had too much power and more than enough pitching to handle their intrastate foes from the National League. Some were predicting a quick and merciful series, similar to that which the A's had just completed with the Red Sox.

Game one took place on October 15 in Los Angeles. Tim Belcher was manager Lasorda's choice to try and stifle Oakland's power. Tony La Russa sent gritty, 20-game winner Dave Stewart to the mound for the Athletics.

Gibson was held out of the lineup because of his injured legs and hadn't even been introduced in the official ceremonies prior to the game. He was replaced in left field by Mickey Hatcher, who also had been a free-agent acquisition. Hatcher gave the Dodgers a big lift in the bottom of the first inning, belting a two-run homer off Stewart and putting Los Angeles in front, 2–0.

As one would expect in a well-written drama, Canseco came to bat in the top of the second with the bases loaded. He wanted to make Belcher pay for having hit him with a pitch, taking the bat out of his hands in his first at bat. He turned one of Belcher's pitches into a low, whistling line drive. The ball ended its quick journey when it slammed into an NBC television camera beyond the fence in deep left–center field. Four runs were in, and Oakland had regained the lead, 4–2, in a very convincing manner. Canseco had homered in four of his last five games, and each of the blasts had either tied the contest or put the Athletics ahead.

The Dodgers scored a singleton in the last of the sixth inning and came to bat in the bottom of the ninth trailing, 4–3. Seven shutout innings from Tim Leary, Brian Holton, and Alejandro Pena had kept L.A. in the game.

As he had done so often during the season, La Russa dialed the bullpen for Eckersley and asked him to protect another Oakland lead. Mike Scioscia popped up to the shortstop for the first out. Eckersley struck out Jeff Hamilton for out number two. Lasorda sent up Mike Davis to pinch-hit for Alfredo Griffin, while another pinch hitter, Dave Anderson, waited in the on-deck circle.

The flight of Canseco's second inning grand slam had been ended by a television camera. An upcoming journey into the realm of the unbelievable was started by one. Gibson had received a shot of cortisone and xylocaine in his injured right knee prior to the game and had spent most of the contest in the clubhouse. Late in the game, an NBC television camera panned the Dodgers' dugout. The announcer Vin Scully commented that Gibson wasn't anywhere to be seen. Kirk was in the trainer's room and heard Skully say:

> "The man who is the spearhead of the Dodger offense throughout the year, who saved them in the League Championship Series, will not see any action tonight, for sure. [Gibson] is not even in the dugout."
>   With that, Gibson had slid off the trainer's table. "____ it," he shouted, grabbing an ice bag for his injured right knee. "I'll be there."[5]

Gibson recalled what happened next:

> "I jammed an ice bag on my knee and pulled on my uniform top," said Gibson, who asked Hines [the hitting coach] to get him a batting tee.

Hines found one and told Poole [the Dodger batboy] to put the balls on the tee for Gibson. "We didn't want him bending over and hurting himself," Hines said later. After he'd hit about half a bucket of balls, Gibson said, "I told Mitch to go down and tell Tommy [Lasorda] that if someone got on, I wanted to try to hit." Lasorda came up the runway, and Gibson told him he was ready. "As soon as he heard that I wanted to hit, he took off. I never got a chance to say 'I think'...."[6]

On the playing field, Davis was trying to disrupt Eckersley's rhythm, stepping out of the batter's box after each pitch and making him wait. With a 3-1 count, the .196 hitter succeeded in working the Oakland reliever for a base-on-balls. It was an uncharacteristic gift from a pitcher who had given up only nine unintentional passes during the entire regular season.

Davis headed toward first base, and Anderson left the on-deck circle, returning to the dugout. Later, Lasorda spoke about having used Anderson as a decoy: "I figured Eckersley would pitch more carefully to Davis with the right-hander on deck. If he'd seen Gibson, he would have pitched Davis differently."[7]

A total of 55,983 fans watched in amazement as Kirk Gibson hobbled to the plate, in obvious discomfort. For the first time in the 1988 Fall Classic, two of the headliners were facing each other, one-on-one. The clear advantage appeared to rest with the Oakland ace.

Attempting to keep the ball away from the left-handed swinging Gibson and not allow him to generate any power from his gimpy legs, Eckersley fed Gibson fastballs on the outside part of the plate. Kirk fouled off the first two pitches weakly to the left. The count stood at 0-2. He took a tortured swing at the third delivery, and the ball rolled slowly down the first base line, going foul just before Mark McGwire could reach it. By that time Jack Buck in the CBS radio booth was telling the listeners how painful it was to watch Gibson's futile swings.

The next pitch was a ball, followed by another foul down the left-field line. Eckersley threw a fastball high and outside, evening the count at 2-2. Ball three came inside. On the pitch, Davis took off for second base, but Ron Hassey, the A's catcher, did not attempt to throw him out.

The Los Angeles scouting staff had researched the A's pitching patterns. One bit of information had to do with Eckersley's approach to specific situations. While he was waiting for the next pitch to be thrown, Gibson remembered Dodger scout Mel Didier's words, "Pahdnuh, sure as I'm standing here, if you're a left-handed batter with a 3-and-2 count, Eckersley is gonna throw you a back-door slider every single time."[8]

On the 3–2 count, Eckersley tried to "backdoor" Gibson with a slider. "Then, with a quick turn of his hips and a snap of his wrists, Gibson, using virtually one hand, sent Eckersley's pitch over the right-field wall to complete an exhilarating 5–4 comeback victory by the Dodgers before a crowd of 55,983 that simply would not stop cheering, even after the players had left the field."[9]

Three times, Buck announced excitedly and quizzically, "'I don't believe what I just saw!' He went on to ask, 'How could he do it?,' and 'Is what I saw the truth?' And then he declared to his broadcast partner Bill White, with a stunned radio audience listening in, 'It was simply one of the most dramatic moments in sports, Bill.'"[10]

Gibson's trip around the bases formed a powerful image: "He knew what he'd done the instant the ball exploded off his bat. He raised his arm and held it aloft until he reached first base coach Manny Mota. Then he limped around the bases as if he were straggling home from the Russian front, dragging his right leg and stepping gingerly on his left. His home run hobble was probably the slowest passage around the bases of all time, and it stood in stark contrast to Hatcher's first-inning scamper around the diamond, then noted as the fastest in World Series history."[11]

The Los Angeles Dodgers had taken a 1–0 Series lead and looked with anticipation for Hershiser to get them their second win.

By game time the next day, Roy Hobbs had been recast in "Dodger Blue." The television lead-in for game two featured a replay of the final scene from the "The Natural," with fade-ins of Kirk Gibson in the title role. Because of painful legs, the real, live Gibson was not in the lineup. The memory of his first-game heroics was foremost in the minds of the fans in Dodger Stadium and for those tuned in on their television sets and radios. Whether it would live as another of those eternally vivid postseason moments was, perhaps, dependent on the future course of the 1988 World Series.

Game two was a family affair. The traditional first pitches were thrown out by the "Little League Parents of the Year," Orel III and Millie Hershiser, the proud parents of Orel IV. Son took over from dad and mom, and fashioned a 6–0 whitewash job, becoming the first pitcher to hurl shutouts in the LCS and the World Series in the same year. In his last 92⅔ innings, Hershiser had registered a phenomenal 0.29 ERA. He limited Oakland to three singles, all by Dave Parker. The Dodgers' Mike Marshall, with a three-run homer and a triple, sparked the winners' offense. Orel contributed two doubles and a single, becoming the first pitcher to get three hits in a Fall Classic game since Art Nehf did it in 1924.

The clubs traveled north to Oakland where the final three games were played. The A's were in the midst of a 16-inning scoring drought. During the season they had slammed 156 home runs, second highest in the majors. So far in the series they trailed the number-twenty-two finisher three round-trippers to two. In the most important set of numbers, the Athletics trailed the Dodgers, two games to nothing.

Bob Welch was the A's pitcher for game three. Lefty John Tudor, who the Dodgers had acquired from St. Louis during the season, started for L.A. but faced only four batters. He had to leave the game with a sore elbow on his

October 15, 1988: Kirk Gibson celebrates as he circles the bases in his two-run homer, which led his team to a 5–4 victory over Oakland (AP/Wide World).

throwing arm, joining Gibson on the "doubtful" list for future appearances. The Dodgers' cleanup hitter, Marshall, was also removed from the game in the fourth when his back stiffened.

Oakland took a 1–0 lead in the third, when Hassey singled home Glenn Hubbard. Two innings later, the Dodgers' Franklin Stubbs doubled to score Hamilton, tying the game, 1–1. It remained that way until the bottom of the ninth. With one out, McGwire delivered a quick finish to the third game, slamming a dramatic home run off Jay Howell and bringing the A's their first win.

The opening-game pitchers, Stewart and Belcher, went to the mound for game four. Injuries were decimating Los Angeles. Bob Costas, NBC television's announcer, proclaimed the Dodgers' makeshift lineup, "possibly the worst ever to be put on the field in a World Series game."[12] In the fourth, their problems intensified when catcher Scioscia twisted his right knee sliding into second base on an unsuccessful stolen base attempt. Unfortunately for the Athletics, while L.A.'s starting lineup was being riddled by injuries, Oakland's defense was becoming painfully porous. Two errors, the A's first in the series, gave Los Angeles key runs to help them to a 4–3 win and a 3–1 Fall Classic lead.

In the fifth and final contest, Hershiser gave up two runs! With their "super subs," Hatcher and Davis, each powering two-run homers, and backup catcher Rick Dempsey driving in the fifth run with a sixth-inning double, the Los Angeles Dodgers triumphed, 5–2. They were, to the astonishment of many, the 1988 World Champions.

There were a number of reasons for the stunning outcome. Hershiser had continued his masterful pitching, picking up two victories and the Most Valuable Player Award.

Also, there was the "Blue back-up crew." As reported in a West Coast newspaper:

> From somewhere in the left-field seats came the shrill cry of a desperate man. The cry was directed at Oakland A's pitcher Storm Davis, who was in the process of walking Mike "196" Davis.
> "C'mon!" the man wailed. "This guy's nobody!"
> Exactly
> If you ask who, besides the pitchers, won this World Series for the Dodgers, the answer would be "Nobody."[13]

"Nobodies" were in "Dodger Blue," with the names "Hatcher," "Davis" and "Dempsey" sewn on the backs of their uniforms.

Dave Anderson of the *New York Times* had written about the anticipated matchup of headliners Canseco and Gibson. He mentioned that Gibson was moving on tender legs, whereas Canseco, "moves muscularly with a nonchalant swagger that's more boyish than boastful. In this World Series it's as if Kirk Gibson of the Dodgers and Jose Canseco of the Athletics have drawn lines in the dirt with their bats. Lines that only they dare cross in a rare rock concert of dueling slugging outfielders who are likely to win the two most valuable player awards for the season."[14]

The expected confrontation never materialized. Each of the players had one hit; for Canseco it was traumatic — for Gibson it was ecstatic. Jose went 1 for 19. His only hit was the grand-slam home run in the opening game, and he finished with an anemic .053 batting average. Canseco and the other "Bash Brother," McGwire, were a combined 2 for 36.

A century earlier, in 1888, Ernest Lawrence Thayer's "Casey at the Bat" first appeared in print in the *San Francisco Examiner*, across the bay from Oakland. The mighty batsman, from whom the crowd expected so much, struck out and brought utter disappointment.

The strikeout that might well have been expected in the 1988 World Series never came. Instead, it was Kirk Gibson's only hit in his only appearance in an injury-marred October. His stunning ninth-inning home run off Eckersley in the first game became one of baseball's most memorable happenings.

Over the long winter months, Eckersley would not forget that moment. When he was asked the following spring about his pitch to Gibson, he recalled, "I'd like to say, 'Don't take people lightly, but I didn't take him lightly,' the 34-year-old right-hander said. 'What I learned was that you're not supposed to give a cripple a breaking ball.'"[15]

Through a window in time, future generations will look back and remember. The victory propelled the Los Angeles Dodgers, heavy underdogs, to a one-game lead over the powerful Oakland Athletics. They had taken the A's best shot — Canseco's mammoth grand slam — and had withstood the blast.

Oakland never recovered from losing the opener, after coming so close to victory. Los Angeles, although battered by injuries, built their confidence from game to game and grabbed the brass ring.

Comparisons were made between Gibson's thrilling blast and Bill Mazeroski's home run in game seven of the 1960 World Series. Kirk's homer was also mentioned in the same breath as Bobby Thomson's "Shot Heard Round the World" off the Dodgers' Ralph Branca in the final game of the 1951 National League playoff. Both Mazeroski's and Thomson's momentous homers ended historic struggles, delivering the championship on one occasion and the pennant on the other.

In 1988 Kirk Gibson's game-winner brought victory in the opening game of the World Series, and it set the tone for what would follow. Perhaps for that reason, it would be more appropriate to compare its impact to Willie Mays's breathtaking catch in the opener of the 1954 Fall Classic. In a similar fashion, the title in 1988 was not won by an amazing event on the final day. Rather, it was a championship that was put in motion and then achieved from the front end.

1989

World Series

Oakland Athletics and San Francisco Giants

The most memorable postseason series since 1940 may not be 1961 and "Maz," or 1975 and "Pudge," or 1986 and "Billy Buck." It may be the Fall Classic of 1989 — a four-game sweep! Among the championship games that have been marked by unforgettable moments, it may forever be a natural disaster in the San Francisco–Oakland Bay Area that will take top billing. At 5:04 P.M. PDT on Tuesday, October 17, the earth shook and rattled, and the series stood still. It was an eerie event that transposed the World Series — the centerpiece of so many memorable moments — into a "modest little sports event."[1]

Two games had been played prior to the "Earthquake of '89," the most damaging quake in the San Francisco area since the disastrous shaker of 1906. Before it struck, the Oakland Athletics and the San Francisco Giants had battled twice in the Oakland Alameda County Coliseum. The A's had handled the Giants by the scores of 5–0 and 5–1. Twenty-game winner Dave Stewart stifled San Francisco on five hits in the opener. Right-hander Mike Moore, with relief help from Rick Honeycutt and Dennis Eckersley, shut down the Giants' attack in game two.

Rickey Henderson, who had owned the American League Championship Series against the Toronto Blue Jays, continued his postseason romp, banging out five safeties in eight at bats. Mark McGwire was hitting .500, going four-for-eight.

The 0–2 Giants had been ineffective in all aspects of their game and were hoping that the trip across the bay to Candlestick Park would be rejuvenating. Without a quick recovery, it promised to be a very short and uneventful World Series for the National League pennant winners.

Game three was scheduled to begin in the late afternoon of Tuesday, October 17. That October day had brought "Indian-summer" weather to a stadium often ridiculed for its windchill factor in July. Many of the 62,000 fans in the sold-out "Stick" were moving to their seats, and a huge television audience had just joined the festivities. ABC-TV sportscasters Al Michaels, Jim Palmer, and Tim McCarver were in the booth on the stadium's second level, and fellow announcer Joe Morgan was down on the field preparing to interview Willie Mays, who would be throwing out the ceremonial first pitch. The A's and the Giants were gathering in the dugouts, awaiting the introduction of the players. And at 5:04 P.M. PDT, a massive earthquake rolled up and down the San Andreas Fault from its epicenter near Santa Cruz. San Francisco was in its path, 75 miles to the north. The park shook, the center section of the Bay Bridge collapsed, I-880 in Oakland fell in upon itself, and fires broke out in a number of places.

Michaels had only been able to utter the words, "We're having an earth..." before the television screen went fuzzy. In a few short seconds, people were killed, injured, and made homeless. And a watching nation witnessed a disaster unfold before its eyes.

For a period of time, the fans and the national television audience wondered how long the delay would last before the countdown to the opening pitch resumed. Some fans in Candlestick Park cheered the quake, not knowing the devastation that had occurred throughout the area. It took a while before they realized that the third game was not going to be played that evening, or for some days to come, or maybe ever. The public address system had gone silent, and the lights in the stadium were out. Police used megaphones to announce the game's postponement.

The breadth of the disaster caused by the earthquake, which registered 7.1 on the Richter scale, was revealed very slowly to those in Candlestick. Transistor radios and a few miniature TVs brought the grim news to fans in the park. Because of the power outages, the vast majority of people in the immediate vicinity of the quake did not hear the reports or see the pictures of the devastation that had happened around them.

By the next morning it had become clear that it would be some time before the series could be resumed. Baseball commissioner Francis "Fay" Vincent, Jr., stood behind a podium in the St. Francis Hotel and announced the postponement of Wednesday night's game. In his statement he put the World Series, the Fall Classic, the climaxing ritual of the Great American Pastime — whatever you want to call the two-week extravaganza — in its proper perspective. He said, "Obviously there's been a substantial tragedy in this community.... Baseball is not the highest priority to be dealt with. We want to be very sensitive as you would expect us to be to the state of life in this community. The great tragedy coincides with our modest little sports event."[2]

Some were suggesting that the Series should be cancelled. Massive human effort and time would be required before the damaged lives and fallen structures in San Francisco and Oakland would regain any sense of normalcy.

Mike Littwin, writing for the *Baltimore Sun*, represented the sentiment of those who thought that the games should be called off: "Games do not have to go on. Sometimes, life — and, especially, death — intrudes, and the games, no matter how far-reaching their scope, no matter how glorious their tradition, can trivialize a tragedy."[3]

The horror of October 17 and its aftermath served as a jolting reminder that the Great American Pastime was just that — a pastime. Sensibility and necessity demanded that the "fun and games" cease while many residents of the Bay Area faced the gruesome task of reconstructing their lives. The bodies of the dead and injured had to be recovered, taken care of, and grieved over.

The devastation in San Francisco, Oakland, and other California communities brought deep despair during a year that had delivered other suffering to the National Pastime. The season-long Pete Rose saga formally ended with his banishment from the game by Commissioner A. Bartlett Giamatti on August 24. On the field, Rose had banged out more hits than any other player in the history of the game. Throughout his illustrious career as a player and manager, his special brand of hustle had brought excitement and entertainment to the fans of the sport. Off the field, he had lost touch with the values inherent in the game, and he had gambled away his right to represent it.

On September 1, a brief, televised special report announced that Giamatti had died unexpectedly at the age of 51. The worlds of academia and sport were stunned. Giamatti had been more than an administrator of a university and of a sport. His lifelong love of baseball had made him an interpreter and an ambassador of its greatness to others. One of Giamatti's hopes for his administration was that he would become known as the "fans' commissioner." When this renaissance scholar wrote about baseball, he helped many to understand how this kid's game served as a symbol of life itself. And then, life suddenly was taken from him, and he was taken from the game. Ironically, the two cities in the World Series were linked by the Bay Area Rapid Transit system, or "BART." The 1989 Fall Classic had been dedicated to the memory of Bart Giamatti.

There had been another personal tragedy that summer. In July former California Angel pitcher Donnie Moore had shot and wounded his wife. He then turned the gun on himself and took his own life. Three years earlier, with the Angels one out away from winning the American League pennant, he had served up the memorable home run to Dave Henderson of the Boston Red Sox. The round-tripper kept the Bosox's hopes alive, and they went on to capture the flag. Moore never recovered from that historic defeat, and suicide was his escape.

During the summer of '89, another human drama came from the world of baseball to the public's attention. San Francisco pitcher Dave Dravecky had shown a special strength for others to emulate. After undergoing surgery the previous October to remove a cancerous tumor from a muscle near his left shoulder, he appeared to have battled back from the disease. He had rebuilt his body and returned to the mound for the Giants. On August 10, the left-hander pitched a dramatic 4–3 victory over the Cincinnati Reds. Five days after baseball fans had joyously witnessed his personal triumph, they watched in horror as he writhed in agony after breaking his left humerus delivering a pitch against the Montreal Expos. Later, Dravecky fractured the same bone in another spot in a freak on-the-field accident during the Giants' celebration after winning the National League pennant. What had been cause for optimism had become bleak once again.

And baseball's future was ominous as well, with the possibility of a strike looming large for the start of the 1990 campaign. The World Series was supposed to be a bright spot in an otherwise distressing and painful season.

Commissioner Vincent worked closely with the mayors of the two cities to determine when and if the games could be appropriately resumed. Initially, Tuesday, October 24 was considered. The need for additional time to continue rescue efforts on I-880 and in other areas, along with anticipated rain, made it unwise to aim to restart the series that day. In the belief that a resumption of the series would help the healing process in the Bay Area, the Fall Classic was scheduled to begin again on Friday, October 27 in Candlestick Park.

Game one in Oakland had begun with a moment of silence for A. Bartlett Giamatti. For the second time that October, a moment of silence was observed. It marked the official start of the 1989 World Series: Part Two. The ceremonial first pitches were thrown by 12 representatives drawn from the many thousands of area citizens who had helped in the rescue efforts. The fans let out a loud roar of relief and excitement, and game three got underway.

It quickly became clear that not much had changed on the ball field. Oakland continued its unswerving path to the World Championship. San Francisco did not get its game together. The third meeting went to the A's, 13–7. Only a late Giant rally brought any semblance of challenge to the Athletics. The handwriting was on the wall after the A's number three and five hitters came to the plate in the top of the first inning. Jose Canseco singled to left, breaking a personal 0–23 slump. He went on to add a home run and another single to his day's output. With Carney Lansford on third and Canseco on second, Dave Henderson, who had been unable to hit a ball out of the infield in the two earlier contests, doubled off the top of the right-field fence to drive in the first two runs. He also banged out two round-trippers later in the game. Stewart, later chosen the Most Valuable Player, picked up his second win in seven innings of work.

The Fall Classic came to an unceremonious conclusion the following day. Moore returned to the mound for his second start and was quickly bequeathed an 8–0 lead. Rickey Henderson chipped in with three hits to lead the A's to a 9–6 victory. Oakland had taken all four games in one of the most lopsided series in history. Because of the catastrophe in the Bay Area, the Athletics' victory celebration was a somber one. No champagne corks were popped in the locker room.

History books will show that the Oakland Athletics captured the 1989 World Championship. Only two pitchers started for each of the teams, setting a record and creating an oddity. It may be the only interesting statistic about that set of games.

As the years pass, few people will recall the on-field events of those four contests spread over a grueling 15 days. There was little of the exciting competition that usually enraptures us during that time of year.

Nevertheless, many will think back and recall what took place in the midst of the Fall Classic and what made it stop. Few baseball fans will ever forget what happened to our country's "modest little sports event" at 5:04 P.M. on October 17, 1989.

1991

World Series

Atlanta Braves and Minnesota Twins

Seventh Game — October 27 at Minnesota

Atlanta	0	0	0	0	0	0	0	*0*	0	0		0	7	0
Minnesota	0	0	0	0	0	0	0	0	0	1		1	10	0

Smoltz, Stanton[8], Pena[9]
Morris

The 1991 World Series, the eighty-eighth edition of the Fall Classic, matched two teams that had finished in the cellars of their respective divisions the previous year. After its exciting conclusion, many players, fans, and writers placed this seven-game set at the top of the list of the greatest World Series. The Minnesota Twins had climbed from the basement to the pinnacle of the American League in one season, and the Atlanta Braves had done the same in the National League. These two "last-to-firsts" battled through five one-run games, with four being decided on the final pitch of the contest. Three of the encounters required extra innings, setting a record.

The seventh and deciding game was a ten-inning masterpiece in which 36-year-old Jack Morris bested the Braves, 1–0. On the way to their victory, two of the Twins' middle infielders worked a masterful decoy on Atlanta base runner Lonnie Smith, and October's game had another moment to remember and debate. And another "goat" roamed its green pastures.

In 1990 Minnesota had a 74–88 record and finished in the cellar of the AL West, 29 games behind the pennant-winning Oakland Athletics. The following January they signed Morris, a free agent, to a three-year contract that, including incentives, would pay him $11.6 million. Morris had been born and raised in St. Paul and was coming home. He was leaving the Detroit Tigers, the only major-league club he had been with during an illustrious 13-year career. The strong right-hander had led the majors in wins during the decade of the '80s but had struggled to a 21–32 record and a 4.65 ERA during his final two seasons with the Tigers. Some suggested that the Twins were gambling with a "has been."

Eleven games into the '91 season, Minnesota found themselves back in the basement, having won only twice. On June 1, carrying a 23–25 record, and in fifth place, the Twins began a sprint that would eventually lead to the crown. The Twins played outstanding baseball during June and were 22–6 for the month, including a club-record 15 consecutive victories. By mid–August, Minnesota was 2½ in front of the Chicago White Sox. They continued to build their lead and finished eight games ahead of the second-place White Sox.

Kirby Puckett (.319), Brian Harper (.311), and Shane Mack (.311) were the Twins' leading hitters. Chili Davis, another off-season free agent acquisition (from the California Angels), powered 29 round-trippers, and Kent Hrbek contributed 20.

Scott Erickson was a 20-game winner (20–8), and Morris finished the season with an 18–12 record. Kevin Tapani chipped in with a 16–9 mark. Minnesota manager Tom Kelly tapped the trio to do the bulk of the Twins' postseason pitching. Rick Aguilera was ready in relief, having picked up 42 saves during the regular season.

The Twins met Toronto in the American League Championship Series. The path to the pennant had only one rough spot, as Minnesota topped the Blue Jays, 4–1, including three victories in the Toronto's Skydome. The Twins were set to meet the Atlanta Braves in the 1991 Fall Classic.

The Braves had arrived in Atlanta from Milwaukee in 1966. A third consecutive basement-finish in the National League Eastern Division in 1990 provided little optimism for any change in the Braves' near future.

Their path to the NL West title was bumpier than the road taken by the Twins. In early June Atlanta was 25–19 and were only ½ game behind the league-leading Los Angeles Dodgers. However, at the All-Star break the Braves were a game under .500 and 9½ out of first place. Even after a strong start, especially for this particular franchise, it was probably expected that their upward movement had ceased and that they would continue a downward slide through the division to their home in the basement.

A glance at the standings on August 17 showed that, surprisingly, they were back nipping at the heels of the Dodgers and only a game behind. In mid–September, they had taken over the top rung and were 1½ games ahead. One of those victories had been the Senior Circuit's first three-man no-hitter, by the triumvirate of Kent Mercker, Mark Wohlers, and Alejandro Pena.

Atlanta and Los Angeles waged a nip-and-tuck, down-to-the-wire battle — a battle that wasn't decided in Atlanta's favor until the final weekend of the season.

In Atlanta the Southeastern Savoyards Light Opera Company performed "H. M. S. Pinafore" and celebrated the Braves' pennant-clinching win. At the beginning of the concert, the conductor, in white tie and tails, turned to the orchestra and raised not a baton … but a tomahawk.

The Braves had tomahawked their way to victory. "America's team" had done it.

On the final day of the season, Terry Pendleton, a free-agent acquisition during the winter, clinched the National League batting title with a .319 average, barely out-pointing Hal Morris of Cincinnati in one of the tightest batting races in history. Ron Gant hit 32 home runs for Atlanta, drove in 105 runs, and had his second consecutive 30 HR–30 SB season.

Tom Glavine's 20–11 record, 2.53 ERA and 246⅔ innings pitched led the Braves' staff. Steve Avery (18–8), Charlie Leibrandt (15–13), and John Smoltz (14–13) were the other major contributors. Avery and Smoltz were undefeated after August 1.

Just as the regular season had gone down to the wire for the Braves, the National League Championship Series was no different. Atlanta finally outdistanced the Pittsburgh Pirates in a battle of seven games. The Braves pitchers tossed three shutouts at the Pirates, including two 1–0 gems.

Feathered headdresses, tom-tom drumming, tomahawk chopping, and war chanting had become the signature of the Braves. The whooping and chanting had also drawn the ire of Native Americans. The controversy would not go unnoticed at the opening game of the Fall Classic in Minneapolis. About 200 demonstrators marched outside the Metrodome, protesting the desecration of symbols of Native American culture by the Atlanta organization and their fans. There was a caption inside Atlanta's postseason media guide that proclaimed: "With weapons issued, Braves fans tomahawked the club to one of its biggest victories of the season over the Dodgers."[1] The reference was to the club's giveaway of thousands of Styrofoam tomahawks during a series against Los Angeles in September.

Clyde Bellecourt, director of the American Indian Movement, was concerned about a larger issue that had been raised previously on a number of college and university campuses. Bellecourt said, "We're calling for the Atlanta Braves to change their name.... It is wrong for sports teams to be using the symbolism and regalia that we use for ceremonial purposes. Why don't they just call them the Atlanta Negroes? Or the Atlanta Klansmen? Do you think that American Jews or blacks would stand for that kind of treatment?"[2]

Others were angered by the behavior of actress Jane Fonda, noted social activist and fiancée of Braves owner Ted Turner. Fonda had been seen doing the "tomahawk chop," which some felt was inconsistent with her earlier activities in support of Native American causes.

The issue would not be settled, and the tension would continue. Other incidents would occur during the progress of the Fall Classic, and the Braves organization would be left with demands to consider and decisions to make before the start of the 1992 season.

The opener took place indoors in the Hubert H. Humphrey Metrodome in Minneapolis on Saturday, October 19. For the fourth year in a row, the teams represented the "Wests" of the National and American leagues.

The Twins picked up a 5–2 victory. Greg Gagne's three-run homer in the fifth broke the game open and gave the Twins a 4–0 lead. Kent Hrbek, who had not hit well in his previous World Series appearances in 1987, contributed a double and a home run to the cause. Rookie second baseman Chuck Knoblauch banged out three hits, giving him a total of ten for the post-season. He also made a sprawling grab of a ground ball in the eighth inning to start an important double play. Morris picked up the win, pitching seven innings and giving up both of the Braves' runs. Leibrandt took the loss. "Homer hankies," the special weapon of the Twins' fans, were waving in all their glory.

The following day, Davis, the Twins' designated hitter, banged a two-run homer off Glavine, continuing the home team's charge. The ball landed 20 rows deep in the left-center-field stands, 380 feet from home plate. The Braves rebounded, scoring singletons in the second and fifth frames, each coming on sacrifice flies.

A memorable and controversial play occurred in the third inning. Gant singled to left field with two outs and a runner on first. He took a wide turn around the bag, drawing a relay throw to first baseman Hrbek. Gant scampered back to the base, coming in standing up. Hrbek caught the ball, and the beefy first sacker wrapped his glove around Gant's leg, lifting him off the base. Umpire Drew Coble, thinking that Gant's momentum had carried him off the bag, called the Atlanta runner out. Gant raged that he had been forcibly removed from the base, and the television replay appeared to support his argument. The Twins first baseman, who had spoken about trying his hand at professional wrestling upon retirement from baseball, had won his first match. His savvy move had been too quick for even the eyes of an umpire.

In game one it had been Minnesota's number nine hitter, Gagne, who delivered the decisive blow — a three-run homer. The heroics in the second game were provided by the Twins' eighth man in the lineup, Scott Leius. With the score tied, 2–2, the rookie infielder drove Glavine's first delivery in the home half of the eighth inning into the seats, providing the margin of victory.

After a travel day, the series resumed in Atlanta–Fulton County Stadium. Again, the cultural battle was revived. Picketers marched outside the ballpark, protesting the tomahawk chop and the other affronts to Native Americans.

Since the tomahawk first arrived at the ballpark sometime in early May — possibly in the hands of some Florida State Seminoles who were in the stands — it had become the rage. Paul Braddy, a 38-year-old Atlanta entrepreneur, had quit his job as sales manager for a urethane company to manufacture tomahawks full-time for Braves fans.

The movements of the chop were something that fans needed help with and the directions were provided:

1. With a straight back, hold upper arms at a 45 degree angle to body and lower arm vertically.
2. Now, prepare to chop with force and determination.
3. Chop continues with upper arm moving to 90 degree angle to body.
4. Head nods.[3]

Inside Atlanta–Fulton County Stadium, 50,878 fans were there to see the first World Series game ever played in their hometown. Their city was 0–83 in combined years of having professional teams fighting unsuccessfully for a world title. What the Braves, Falcons, Hawks, and Flames had failed to do in previous years, this baseball team was hoping to achieve.

Avery, the young Atlanta left-hander, was the Brave charged with keeping Minnesota from picking up their third consecutive win. Erickson went to the mound for the Twins, who were playing outside on real grass for the first time in over two weeks.

Avery, perhaps a bit jittery with the weight of the city of Atlanta resting on his shoulders, struggled in the early going. Dan Gladden tripled to open the game, the ball falling between David Justice and Gant and rolling to the wall. Better communication between the two outfielders might have turned the three-bagger into an out. A Knoblauch sacrifice fly scored Gladden, and Minnesota was first on the scoreboard for the third straight game. The run also broke Avery's 16⅓ consecutive scoreless-inning streak in postseason play.

However, the next run off the Atlanta lefty didn't come until the seventh inning, when Puckett deposited a pitch into the left-field seats. By that time, home runs by Justice and Smith had helped the Braves build a 4–2 lead.

Davis, the Twins' powerful designated hitter, was relegated to pinch-hitting duties for the three contests in Atlanta, since National League rules did not allow the designated hitter. He was called to pinch-hit in the eighth inning, with Harper on first. He greeted the reliever, Pena, and slammed a two-run homer to left, tying the score, 4–4.

Steve Bedrosian, Carl Willis, and Mark Guthrie held the Braves scoreless from the sixth through the eleventh innings. With the managers making maximum use of their rosters, the game went into the twelfth inning. In the top of that frame with one out and a runner on first base, Mark Lemke, the Braves second sacker, bobbled a routine double-play ball. Mercker saved Lemke from the goat horns, striking out Hrbek with runners at the corners. Kelly sent up his only available pinch hitter, pitcher Aguilera. Jim Clancy retired him on a line drive to center.

Lemke, the near "goat," turned "hero" a few minutes later when he drove home a sliding Justice, who had singled and stolen second base to move into scoring position.

Game three went to the Braves, 5–4. It was the longest night game in World Series history — four hours and four minutes with an ending time of

12:42 A.M. Forty-two players made the boxscore, and only two position players failed to see action.

The fourth contest was also a one-run thriller, with the Braves prevailing, 3–2. For the fourth straight game, the Twins struck first, getting on the board in the top of the second inning. A Mike Pagliarulo single off Smoltz scored Harper, who had doubled. Pendleton countered with a homer in the third off Morris to knot the game, 1–1.

In the fifth the Braves had two base runners tagged out at home. Smith was gunned down in a bone-crushing collision with Harper. Later in the inning Pendleton was cut down at the plate, trying to score from third on a wild pitch in the dirt.

Pagliarulo and Smith traded home runs in the seventh and the score remained tied, 2–2.

In the bottom of the ninth, the previous night's hero, Lemke, tripled to center. After an intentional walk to Jeff Blauser, Jerry Willard (one of only two position players to miss action the previous night) came to bat as a pinch hitter. His sacrifice fly to right scored Lemke with the winning run of game four.

In the fifth matchup, the suspense ended much earlier than it had in any of the games to date. Atlanta scored four times in the fourth and added six in the seventh on their way to a 14–5 romp — the most runs ever scored by a National League team in World Series history.

The Braves pounded their drums, tomahawk-chopped, and bagged 17 hits off five Minnesota hurlers. Justice, Smith, and Brian Hunter cracked home runs. For Smith, it was his third in as many games. Lemke added a pair of triples to continue his magical October and tie a World Series record for three-base hits.

Atlanta had captured the three games in Fulton County Stadium to take a 3–2 lead. Games six and seven would be played back indoors under the Metrodome's cream-colored Teflon ceiling. The tomahawk would take a back seat to the homer hankie.

In the immortal words of Yogi Berra, Minnesota was hoping for "déjà vu all over again." In 1987 they had beaten the St. Louis Cardinals twice in the Metrodome and then had proceeded to drop all three games in Busch Stadium. Returning home, they regained their winning ways and finished off the Cardinals, picking up their first championship.

Erickson, who had been chased by the Braves in the fifth inning of game three, started game six for the Twins. Avery, who had pitched into the eighth in the same contest, took the mound for Atlanta.

Minnesota broke on top, as had been the pattern in the series with but a single exception. They restored the optimism of the home folks, scoring twice in their first at bat. In the top of the fifth, the Braves rebounded to tie the game, 2–2, only to fall behind again when the Twins added a tally ½ inning later.

Atlanta came back to knot it, 3–3, in the visitor's half of the seventh. For the second time, the teams were headed for an extra-inning affair.

The name of the game that night was "Puckett." The Twins 5' 8" fireplug center fielder got Minnesota to the eleventh inning and ended it there. Along the way, he had singled, tripled, driven in a run on a sacrifice fly, and scored a run himself. He had also made a leaping catch against the center-field Plexiglas panel, above Tony Oliva's retired red "#6," robbing Gant of extra bases and the Braves of an almost certain run.

As a fitting conclusion to "his night," Puckett, the Twins powder keg, faced Leibrandt, leading off the bottom half of the eleventh. He lit up the evening sky, outside the dome, with a blast beyond the fence, delivering a 4–3 victory to the hometowners. The clubs were deadlocked, 3–3.

The players and fans had another "one-game season" to decide the championship of the world. Something memorable happened even before the teams took the field. A scintillating rendition of the National Anthem thrilled the fans in the stands, as well as the radio and television audiences. Jacqueline Jaquez, a seven-year-old youngster of Mexican descent from New Hope, Minnesota, stirred all who heard her. It was another high point in the exciting and well-played set of games. That which followed added to the greatness.

Morris, starting his third game and with one of the Twins wins, was charged with picking up the most crucial victory of the season. Smoltz, who had been nearly unbeatable during the second half of the season, took the hill in the Metrodome for the Braves. As a youngster growing up in Detroit, he had idolized his mound opponent when Morris hurled for the Tigers.

Innings came and went, with each hurler tossing zeroes at the opposition. Minnesota had base runners in scoring position with two out in the second and third frames, but Smoltz retired the Twins before any damage could be done. The Braves had men at first and third with one away in the fifth, but Morris also escaped, getting Pendleton on a pop fly to shallow left and striking out Gant.

With the game scoreless, the eighth inning proved to be a tale of missed opportunities for both teams. Atlanta, batting in the top half of the inning, sent Smith to the plate against Morris. He singled to right field, and Pendleton followed with a line drive hit to left–center field. It became the charge that ignited another postseason memorable moment.

Actually it had begun an instant earlier, when Smith took off on the pitch. With the crack of the bat and the course of the ball unknown, Lonnie raced toward second base. The Twins middle infielders, Knoblauch at second and Gagne at shortstop, played decoy with an imaginary ball. Knoblauch fielded "it" and made an imaginary feed to Gagne at the bag. The shortstop caught "it" and made the "toss" to first to complete the "double play." What was play-acting for the double-play combo was all too real for the base runner; at least real enough to cause him to hesitate as he approached the second-base bag.

By the time Smith picked up sight of the ball near the left-center-field wall, Gladden was about to retrieve it and fire it back to the infield. Smith slowed as he rounded second and could only advance as far as third base. Pendleton arrived at second with a double but no RBI.

Brave runners stood at second and third with no one out. The first run of the game — and perhaps 1991's most important deciding run — was ninety feet away in the person of a most embarrassed Lonnie Smith. With the infield drawn in, Gant hit a weak grounder to first, and the base runners were unable to advance. The Twins' manager called for an intentional walk to the left-hand-hitting Justice, loading the bases. Sid Bream, another left-hander, dug in against Morris.

Instead of driving in the go-ahead run, Bream started one of baseball's rarities, a 3-2-3 double play. This one was not a fake — it was painfully real for the Braves. Bream hit a sharp grounder to Hrbek, who threw home to Harper, forcing Smith. The Twins catcher pegged the ball back to first base, nipping Bream for the final out of the inning. For the eighth consecutive inning, Atlanta had not scored.

The play involving Smith, Pendleton, Knoblauch, and Gagne set off a series of reactions and responses as the principles and others attempted to explain what had occurred in that brief and critical moment. Some reported the effectiveness of the decoy; others focused on Smith's failure to pick up the ball as it came off Pendleton's bat.

Smith, in an article entitled, "OK, so I Blew Series, OK?," attributed his reaction to the latter: "On the ball Terry [Pendleton] hit, if I'd taken the time and looked, that could have been the difference.... Evidently, what nobody realizes, I was going with the pitch on a delayed steal.... I got about halfway and I heard the sound of the bat. I made the mistake of not looking in when I started running. I just assumed that the ball would be hit on the ground.... You know if I saw the ball off the bat, there's a good chance I could have scored. But I didn't see it. I didn't take that look in. That's my mistake.[4]

Knoblauch gave most of the credit to the decoy, which he and Gagne executed. He remarked, "Lonnie Smith stood so long we could have had a conversation."[5]

Bobby Cox, the Atlanta manager, came to Smith's defense: "I think he must have lost it.... There was no reason to go for the deke [decoy], so he must have lost it."[6]

With the dimming of the Braves fans' hopes came the likelihood that the decoy, which had been directly responsible for Smith not scoring, would become a Knoblauch-Gagne-Smith Fall Classic memorable moment. The ultimate influence of the play would not be known until the final out was made and one of the teams was crowned "World Champion."

Some consolation for Atlanta and more frustration for Minnesota followed in the bottom of the eighth. The Twins loaded the bases with one out, and the home team had the go-ahead run only ninety feet away. Hrbek hit a soft liner to Lemke at second base. He stepped on the bag, completing an unassisted double play and keeping Minnesota off the scoreboard.

The Twins had runners at first and second with no one out in the bottom of the ninth and failed to dent the plate again. This time reliever Pena induced Mack to hit into a double play, and he ended the inning by striking out pinch hitter Paul Sorrento. Another game had moved into extra innings.

In the last half of the tenth inning, Gladden hit a broken-bat fly ball to left–center field and hustled to second with a leadoff double. Knoblauch sacrificed Gladden to third. Pena intentionally walked Puckett and Hrbek, loading the bases. Pinch hitter Gene Larkin, with four plate appearances in the World Series and ten in postseason play, was sent to bat for the Twins.

Atlanta brought their outfield in, stationing them about 200 feet from home plate. Their only hope was that a short fly ball would enable them to hold Gladden at third. The infield was positioned so that they could cut the run off at the plate. A repeat of a 3-2-3 twin-killing would be welcomed.

Larkin slapped Pena's pitch to left center, over the head of Hunter, and Gladden easily scored the first and only run of the game. All he had to do was trot in from third and let the celebration begin. He hesitated on his way to the plate. Later, he commented, "I just wanted to enjoy it for a second.... I knew it was finally over, and that we had won."[7]

The 1991 World Series featured outstanding individual efforts. The MVP award, sponsored by Chevrolet, went to Morris, the author of a seven-hit shutout over ten innings — the Fall Classic's longest seventh-game pitching performance.

Smith, the first player in history to appear in four World Series with four different teams (Philadelphia in '80, St. Louis in '82, Kansas City in '85, and Atlanta in '91), contributed three home runs. He also had to claim his part in the event that may be remembered the longest — a costly hesitation around the second-base bag at a crucial juncture of the final game.

An exultant Pagliarulo commented after game seven, "This was the greatest game.... How could the TV guys describe it? They had a chance to win — but they didn't. We had a chance to win — but we didn't. Then we did. I kept thinking of the 1975 Series tonight. This is why baseball is the greatest game there is."[8]

Mike Barnicle, columnist for the *Boston Globe*, reflecting on some of the greatest sporting events of the past, and especially the monumental clash in 1975, echoed similar sentiments: "This World Series, though, was different. It was played out on another level, some high and memorable plane that will be recalled for decades."[9]

The "last-to-first World Series" was one of the greatest of all time. It will long be remembered for the hesitation, for the extra innings, for the intrigue, and for the suspense. Baseball had another feather to put in its cap and another goat to roam its fields.

1992
National League Championship Series
Atlanta Braves and Pittsburgh Pirates

Seventh Game — October 14 at Atlanta

Pittsburgh	1	0	0	0	0	1	0	0	0	2	7	1
Atlanta	0	0	0	0	0	0	0	0	*3*	3	7	0

Drabek, Belinda[9]
Smoltz, Stanton[7], Smith[7], Avery[7], Reardon[9]

Atlanta–Fulton County Stadium was the site for the first game of the 1992 National League Championship Series. The combatants, the Atlanta Braves of the league's Western division and the Pittsburgh Pirates from the East, were repeat champions, and each was hoping to be the Senior Circuit's representative in the World Series. It was the Pirates' third consecutive trip to the League Championship Series, having been unsuccessful in the first two.

Pittsburgh had beaten the odds in making it to the '92 NLCS. After dropping the decisive seventh game to the Braves in 1991, they had also lost a couple of their key performers. Slugging outfielder Bobby Bonilla had gone to the New York Mets via free agency, and 20-game winner John Smiley had been traded to the Minnesota Twins.

Even with those departures, Pittsburgh chalked up 96 victories. Much of the credit went to their manager, Jim Leyland, who had gotten the most out of a team that many had written off. Leyland took the nucleus that remained, and with his personality and expertise, molded the Pirates into another successful competitor.

Andy Van Slyke, one of the Bucs' leaders, commented, "The amazing thing about the team is that the Pirates of 1990 and '91 were more talented but this team was better. We knew how we had to play to accomplish what we did. We sensed all year that this was a team on a mission."[1]

Perhaps this "mission" would be their last for a while. They faced the prospect of losing two more outstanding players — Barry Bonds and Doug Drabek — to free agency before the opening of the 1993 season.

The Atlanta Braves had carried the pride of their league into the previous fall's World Series against the Minnesota Twins. Minnesota had claimed the crown by picking up a scintillating 1–0, ten-inning victory in the seventh and deciding game.

The Braves captured the NL West with a 98–64 record, finishing eight games in front of the Cincinnati Reds. Atlanta's top three pitchers had been experiencing difficulties. John Smoltz (15–12), who had been tapped to open the series, had picked up only a single victory in his last 11 starts. In that time he had chalked up six defeats while compiling a 3.66 ERA. Tom Glavine (20–8) had won 20 games for the second season in a row, but the previous year's Cy Young winner was a paltry 1–5 in his last seven trips to the mound, with a 4.21 ERA. He was also on the mend from a cracked rib suffered late in the campaign. In lefty Steve Avery's (11–11) last 11 starts, he had a disappointing 2–4 mark, surrendering 4.29 earned runs per game.

Charlie Leibrandt (15–7) and Pete Smith, who had gone 7–0 since his recall from the minor leagues, had both made significant contributions to the Braves' season. Bobby Cox would go with Smoltz, Glavine, and Avery, assigning Leibrandt and Smith to the bullpen.

The 1992 NLCS went seven games before the champion was crowned. For the first time in 140 postseason series, a team went from trailing in the game to the winner and champion on the last pitch of the final contest.

While free agency wreaked havoc on Pirates and promised to continue doing so, it was bringing smiles to the faces of the Braves and their fans. The day before the opener, it was reported that Bonds had been house hunting in the Atlanta area, giving rise to speculation that this free-agent-to-be and the NL MVP-to-be might be in a Braves uniform at the dawn of the 1993 season. Bonds had come off a banner year, hitting .311, slamming 34 home runs and driving in 103 runs. He also had stolen 39 bases, making him a rare "30–30" performer.

While Atlanta fans were focusing on Bonds, the Pirate superstar needed to focus on the work at hand and turn around the problems he had experienced once the regular season's statistics were put in the record book. In postseason play, he had posted a .156 average and had difficulty producing runs for his club, especially with runners in scoring position.

The first game of the NLCS took place in Atlanta on October 6. The Styrofoam tomahawks, which had appeared a year earlier, were back in the hands of the Braves' supporters. Smoltz and Drabek were the opposing hurlers. The Atlanta right-hander held the Bucs to four hits over eight innings of pitching on the way to a 5–1 Atlanta win.

The headline in the *New York Times* the next day announced: "Braves and Smoltz Smoke the Pirates."[2] The "smoke" consisted of a two-run inning and three singletons, with two of the runs scoring on plays in the infield. Jose Lind's home run in the eighth was the only score off Smoltz and the extent of the Pittsburgh barrage. Bonds could not shake his postseason woes, striking out on three pitches in his first at bat and failing to deliver a hit in his other plate appearances.

Any excitement in the game was lost on Van Slyke. After the defeat, he commented, "I counted five different messages on the (Goodyear) blimp.... That should give you an idea of the intensity on the field."[3]

If "smoke" was the operative word in the Braves' first victory, then "incinerate" would describe Atlanta's second win. Behind Avery, the Braves destroyed the Pirates, 13–5. Danny Jackson, who had come to Pittsburgh from the Chicago Cubs in July and had gone 4–4 with his new team, was the victim of Atlanta's first explosion in the second inning. Avery delivered a 395-foot sacrifice fly to score one of the runs in the inning. Jackson was long gone by the time Ron Gant smoked a grand-slam homer in the fifth frame to lengthen the Braves' lead to 8–0.

The Pirates battled back, scoring four times in the top of the seventh, ending Avery's playoff scoreless-streak at 22⅓ innings. The Braves added five tallies of their own in the bottom of the same inning, putting the game out of reach.

Foam rubber hooks greeted Atlanta when the clubs met in Pittsburgh's Three Rivers Stadium. The hook took up where the tomahawk had left off. In the third game it worked its magic, as the Pirates, behind a three-for-three effort by Gary Redus, a homer by Don Slaught, and Van Slyke's timely hitting, overtook the Braves.

Van Slyke doubled off Glavine to lead off the sixth and later scored the Pirates second run, putting Pittsburgh on top, 2–1. An inning later, after Atlanta had tied the contest, 2–2, Van Slyke delivered a sacrifice fly, scoring the run that would bring the 3–2 victory. The losing pitcher was Glavine, the Braves' ace left-hander, who had gone 4–0 against the Pirates during the regular season.

Knuckleballer Tim Wakefield went the distance for the Bucs, surrendering only five hits. The 26-year-old right-hander had been drafted by Pittsburgh out of the Florida Institute of Technology, the first player ever chosen from that institution. He was picked as a first baseman, but when his early minor-league experience indicated that he was overmatched at that position, an experiment with the "flutter ball" began. With a scant three years of experience as a pitcher, Wakefield had been called to the majors late in the season. He had dazzled the opposing batters and the Pirate fans en route to an 8–1 record.

Pittsburgh could not keep the momentum going, dropping game four to the Braves, 6–4. Otis Nixon, who had missed the entire 1991 NLCS because of a drug violation and was undergoing treatment in a residential rehabilitation program, was the leading contributor in Atlanta's third victory. He went four-for-five, scored two runs, and stole a base. After the game Nixon said, "I don't think anyone wants to be out there as much as I do. My joy is greater than any fan's, any player's, any manager's."[4]

Smoltz gained his second playoff victory and contributed two timely singles to the offense. Mike Stanton and Jeff Reardon relieved Smoltz late in the game, and together the three pitchers rang up 14 strikeouts.

Two of the whiffs came against Bonds, who was still struggling at the bat and carrying an .091 average. Following the game, he huddled with Leyland, and they talked into the early morning hours, seeking an answer to his postseason futility.

That night another player was up late. Deion Sanders, the two-sport phenom, was flying to Miami to play football for the Atlanta Falcons on the afternoon of game five. He would return after the contest and appear on the Braves bench that night. He had been a nonimpact player in the NLCS to that point, having struck out three times in his five plate appearances. Privately, there was concern within the Braves' organization, as they had a commitment from Sanders that he would be with the team full time.

Tim McCarver, CBS sportscaster and former major-league catcher, expressed his ire more publicly. On the air during game five, McCarver chastised Sanders, saying that he was "flat out wrong"[5] for having flown to Miami and having played in the football game.

On the twentieth anniversary of Pirate legend Roberto Clemente's final game in the major leagues, Bonds broke out of his slump. In what would be his last game in a Pirate home uniform, the outfielder went 2 for 5, drove in a run, scored two more, and stole a base. He broke his 0-for-28 postseason hitless streak with runners on base. He also flashed his defensive skills, robbing Gant of a probable triple with an outstanding catch.

While Bonds was providing the hitting and defense, 35-year-old right-hander Bob Walk was doing the pitching. He was put in the rotation to replace Jackson, who had made a quick departure in game two. Walk delivered a three-hit complete game, and Pittsburgh won, 7–1. Avery, the opposing moundsman, took a quick exit that night. He was gone after ⅓ of an inning, having surrendered four runs. The Braves toted a 3–2 NLCS lead back to their home ballpark.

Before game six, Phil Niekro, who had pitched twenty seasons for the Braves in Milwaukee and Atlanta before his retirement, threw batting-practice knuckleballs to the Atlanta hitters in preparation for facing Wakefield's "dancer" again. However, it was the Pirates' bats that came alive that evening. Pittsburgh coasted to a 13–4 win, tying the NLCS, 3–3. Wakefield continued his mastery of the dazzled Braves, fashioning his second route-going performance.

Bonds led off an historic second inning for the Pirates with a home run over the right-center-field fence. Jay Bell added another round-tripper in the same frame. They were but two of the eight runs Pittsburgh scored off Glavine in the inning. The outburst was the largest ever against a pitcher in a single inning in postseason play. Glavine was blasted from the game before he could retire a batter in the second.

On the home side Dave Justice found the stands twice in the final three innings, but his clouts were far from enough to overcome the damage the visitors had done.

For the second season in a row, the Braves and the Pirates would face each other in a seventh-game showdown. Smoltz and Drabek went to the mound, each hoping to capture the National League pennant. The winner would meet the Toronto Blue Jays, who had won the American League title earlier in the day.

The Pirates did not waste any time building a lead. Alex Cole walked to open the game. Van Slyke, who would experience all the highs and lows the game can offer, doubled Cole to third base. Orlando Merced hit a sacrifice fly, scoring the first run. After the top half of the first, Pittsburgh led, 1–0. Their 13-run outburst the previous day coupled with their quick start in game seven buoyed the Pirates' hopes.

In the second inning, home plate umpire John McSherry called time and excused himself from his duties. Dizzy and in a cold sweat, he was rushed by ambulance to a nearby hospital. His condition did not prove to be a heart attack as was first feared. During the delay to allow Randy Marsh to make the necessary adjustments in preparation for going from first base to behind the plate, Van Slyke and four of his teammates sat on the outfield grass, playing an imaginary game of cards. It was another example of postseason make-believe. Perhaps it brought a recall to Braves fans of the make believe double play in the '91 World Series involving Lonnie Smith, Chuck Knoblaugh, and Greg Gagne.

Bell opened the sixth inning with a double, and Van Slyke singled him home, giving the Pirates a 2–0 lead. In the bottom of the sixth, the Braves loaded the bases with no one out. Drabek continued his masterful work and, with the help of a double play, retired Atlanta without a run crossing the plate. At the end of the inning, he sprinted from the mound to the dugout in celebration of his door-slamming effort.

The score was 2–0 when Atlanta came to bat in the bottom of the ninth inning, hoping for a miracle. What they got in the next 22 pitches was something fans had never witnessed before.

Terry Pendleton doubled to the right-field corner to leadoff the Braves' final at bat. Justice followed with a grounder toward the normally sure-handed Lind at second base, who booted the relatively easy opportunity. Sid Bream followed with a walk on four pitches, and Atlanta had the winning run aboard.

Drabek, after cruising through eight frames, was now hoping to avoid his third loss in the NLCS. He left the game with the sacks full and no one out. Stan Belinda got the call from the bullpen to save the victory and the season for the Pirates.

Gant drove a Belinda delivery to the 330-foot sign in left field, and Bonds caught up with the smash, making the catch. Pendleton trotted home from third, narrowing the Pirate lead to 2–1. Gant had come within a whisker of hitting baseball's most memorable grand slam.

Damon Berryhill walked on a questionable call by Marsh on a 3–1 pitch, and the bases were full again. That and other calls would bring criticism after the contest about the game's second home-plate umpire's shrinking strike zone. The winning run was now halfway home in the person of Bream.

Cox sent pinch hitter Brian Hunter, a long-ball threat, to the plate. The Pirates breathed a bit easier after Hunter popped to Lind for the second out of the inning.

Cox went to the bench again, for the final pinch hitter there. He called for Francisco "Frankie" Paulino Cabrera. The 6'4", 200-pound Dominican bullpen catcher had been called up from the minors on August 31, just in time to be eligible for a roster spot for the NLCS. In his ten at bats at the major league level, he had delivered three hits, including two home runs. Cabrera had failed to produce in his first pinch-hitting effort in game six.

Belinda's first pitch was a slider outside the strike zone. Then, Cabrera watched a high fastball and the count was 2-0. On the third delivery, Cabrera tagged a low liner down the left-field line. It curved foul and went into the seats.

The next pitch produced a dramatic and memorable moment. Francisco drove Belinda's fourth offering over the outstretched arms of shortstop Bell, and it dropped into left field. As the ball rolled toward Bonds, Justice crossed the plate with the tying run.

Bream, slowed by damaged knees, was waived around third base. Bonds fielded the ball and gunned it on a line to catcher Mike LaValliere. He caught the ball inside the third-base line and made a swipe tag, attempting to get the sliding Bream. Bream lunged across the plate — SAFE — and the Braves had won, 3–2.

As reported in the *New York Daily News*: "Cabrera and pitcher Stan Belinda and Bonds and Bream came together in the old ballpark on Capital St. for a finish as luminous as there has ever been at this time of the year."[6]

On Atlanta radio station WGST, announcer Skip Caray was shouting, "Braves win! Braves win! Braves win! Braves win!"[7] Memories of Russ Hodges' famous explosion after Bobby Thomson's home run in 1951 came to mind.

Van Slyke was seen sitting on the outfield grass once again. This time what was happening was all too real. He appeared bewildered as he sat motionless, staring at the ground. A flashback came of Wade Boggs sitting on the dugout bench with tears in his eyes at the conclusion of game six of the 1986 World Series.

**October 15, 1992: Francisco Cabrera's winning hit against the Pirates in game seven of
the National League Championship series (AP/Wide World).**

Two days later, Van Slyke spoke about the moments of his bewilderment:
"What people can't fully understand is that my feelings of sadness that night
were of greater depth than the Braves' feeling of excitement. I felt worse than
they felt good."[8]

Cabrera, who early in his career had been dealt to the Braves by their World
Series opponents — the Blue Jays — as "a player to be named later," celebrated
his unexpected role as the hero. He had imagined that his moment of fame
would have ended with the ceremonial first pitch of game seven, which he had
caught from Rubye Lucas, wife of the late Bill Lucas, a former Brave executive.

Francisco, whose surname is translated "one who tends goats," would see
his name become a household word in the Atlanta area, and it would be linked
forever with "Belinda."

After the game, Belinda stood in the clubhouse, speaking with reporters for 45 minutes. He recounted the details of the event, not hiding from or dodging the inevitable questions.

At spring training the following year, he mentioned some of the repercussions from that one pitch he had delivered at 11:53 P.M. on October 14. Belinda said, "I had a lot of hate mail. But these people were judging my whole career on one pitch. They don't remember the situation I was put in, the debatable calls. There was a whole slew of things that went wrong that inning."[9] He went on to recall the pitch to Cabrera, saying, "I knew he was a fastball hitter but what else was I going to throw? I'm behind in the count. The strike zone was shrinking — rapidly. I had to go with my No. 1 pitch. I tried to put it on the outside of the plate. I've seen the replay enough to know where it was. He sort of reached out and yanked it (into left)."[10]

As the Braves looked ahead to meeting the Blue Jays in Atlanta, the instant hero, who had been besieged for interviews and autographs, knew that he was fated to be back in the bullpen, warming up more pitchers and waiting for another call to grab a bat and go to the on-deck circle.

The Braves were poised for the eighty-ninth Fall Classic. As a city Atlanta stood 0–84 in championship attempts in the major sports. Perhaps 1992 had another miracle waiting for them. Or maybe, it did not.

But forever, the city would have the memory of "One play in a baseball game: a hit, a throw, a play at the plate, a collision of careers and destinies, the most bitter possible loss, the most amazing victory."[11]

1993
World Series
Philadelphia Phillies and Toronto Blue Jays

Fourth Game — October 20 at Philadelphia

Toronto	3	0	4	0	0	2	0	6	0	15 18 0
Philadelphia	4	2	0	1	5	1	1	0	0	14 14 0

Stottlemyre, Leiter[3], Castillo[5], Timlin[8], Ward[8]
Greene, Mason[3], West[6], Andersen[7], M. Williams[8],
               Thigpen[9]

Sixth Game — October 23 at Toronto

Philadelphia	0	0	0	1	0	0	5	0	0	6 7 0
Toronto	3	0	0	1	1	0	0	0	3	8 10 2

Mulholland, Mason[6], West[8], Andersen[8], M. Williams[9]
Stewart, Cox[7] Leiter[7], Ward[9]

When we recall the most outstanding World Series, there are at least three different types of memories. First, there is the collection of outstanding games that hold together as a set of exciting back-and-forth thrillers. Next, there is the individual contest within a series that stands out for some special reason. It may be the delight of the Larsen perfect game or a group of outstanding plays that set a particular contest apart from the rest. Finally, there is the Fall Classic that is remembered solely for the magic moment that comes out of nowhere and is held in memory forever.

The 1993 World Series will long be remembered for reasons of the second and third types. Game four was a zany extravaganza of unexpected happenings. On that night records fell like the rain, which dampened the contest, as run after run crossed the plate into the early hours of the following morning. And there was also the memorable moment in the sixth game when, for the second time in the history of the Fall Classic, a home run served as the exclamation point.

The ninetieth World Series opened in Toronto's SkyDome on Saturday, October 16. The previous season's World Champion Blue Jays were in their home stadium to welcome the Philadelphia Phillies. The Phils had become only the third National League club to go from worst-to-first in a single season. In 1992 Philadelphia had struggled to a 70–92 record, finishing in the basement of the Eastern Division of the Senior Circuit.

Philadelphia reversed its plight, going 97–65 in 1993, outdistancing the Montreal Expos by three games. Their amazing turnaround put them in the National League Championship Series against a dominating Atlanta Braves team that had captured 104 victories in their division.

The Phillies bested the Braves in six games. The NLCS saw the two clubs split the first two contests, which were played in Philadelphia's Veterans Stadium. Atlanta took the third game in Fulton County Stadium to build a 2–1 playoff lead. Philadelphia rebounded, winning three consecutive contests to achieve their 4–2 margin of victory.

By the end of the regular season, Toronto had built a seven-game cushion over the New York Yankees. Their 95–67 mark had sent the Eastern Division champs to meet the Chicago White Sox, who had captured the top spot in the American League West.

The American League Championship Series also lasted six games. Each club won two-game sets. The difference was that the Blue Jays accomplished the feat twice. Toronto captured a pair of games in Chicago's Comiskey Park before returning home to their own ball yard. Chicago evened up the ALCS by taking the next two contests from the Blue Jays. Toronto managed to win the final game of the three-game set in SkyDome and then added another victory back in the Windy City, claiming the American League title, four games to two. In game six Dave Stewart won the fourth playoff clincher of his career. The right-hander had come to Toronto from the Oakland A's in a December 1992 free-agent signing. Overall, "Mr. Playoff" had an 8–0 record in his ALCS games and sported a 2.03 ERA.

Although their roads through the playoffs were similar, the teams that arrived at the gate for the 1993 Fall Classic were vastly different. Toronto, hoping to wear consecutive championship crowns, was chasing an achievement that had not occurred since the New York Yankees accomplished it in 1977 and 1978. The Blue Jays were a team that had been rebuilt since the previous season. Mainstays such as David Cone, Tom Henke, Jimmy Key, and Dave Winfield had departed for other clubs. Twelve new names were on the 1993 World Series roster. "General manager Pat Gillick had carefully assembled a string of the Gary Cooper–meets–John Wayne types like (John) Olerud and Cito Gaston and Joe Carter and Dave Stewart and Paul Molitor and Duane Ward and Roberto Alomar."[1]

The Phillies, on the other hand, were an odd lot. From the clubhouse to the ball field, their act was bizarre. "You see the Phillies and you see a team put together in the dark by a reform school shop class with unauthorized access to the welding tanks. A series of odd lots, irregular cut and off-the-rack mock suede swatches that somehow defy all the laws of fashion, physics and drink in the workplace. General manager Lee Thomas has, well, trolled for and duct-taped together a dinner theatre rendition of 'The Dirty Dozen.'"[2]

The blue-collar Phils stood in sharp contrast to the polished gentlemen from Canada. For the squad from "the City of Brotherly Love," a tattered T-shirt was considered formal attire. "Nails" Dykstra's flair, John Kruk's girth, Mitch "Wild Thing" Williams's relief act, 40-year-old Larry Andersen's humor, and the Darren Daulton–Dave Hollins–Kruk–Williams long, straggly hair-styles created the tone for the strange band of ballplayers who had climbed to the pinnacle of the Senior Circuit. For some, they might have been confused with the champs of the local over-30 softball league. As Williams, who had picked up two wins and two saves in the NLCS, said, "Long hair and fat stomachs don't mean anything. If you have talent, you have a chance to win. If you don't, you won't. We have talent. That is why we are here."[3]

Toronto's potent bats provided security for their pitching staff. The Blue Jays were fearsome at the plate. Olerud (.363), Molitor (.332), and Alomar (.326) had finished 1-2-3 in the American League batting race, the first teammates to do so in a century. Molitor's 111 RBIs were only four better than Olerud's. Carter had led the onslaught, with 33 home runs and 121 RBIs. The bats had stayed hot during the ALCS, with the club pounding the ball at a .301 clip.

Pat Hentgen, in his first full major-league season, had a 19–9 record and a 3.87 ERA. He was the only one of the team's top four starters to finish with an ERA under four. Juan Guzman (14–3), Stewart (12–8), and Todd Stottle-myre (11–12) were the other starters, and Ward headed the bullpen, having collected 45 saves during the regular season.

Philadelphia's offensive stats were not as gaudy. Kevin Stocker and Jim Eisenreich, who each had a limited number of at bats, finished the regular season .324 and .318 respectively. Kruk had hit .316, and Dykstra finished at .305. Dykstra had crossed the plate 143 times, an amazing feat. Daulton, the elder statesman on the Phillies roster, was considered by many to be the heart of the team. The 31-year-old receiver was the only Phil to reach the century mark in RBIs, driving in 105.

The Phillies pitchers had balance in their rotation. Terry Mulholland (12–9) and Danny Jackson (12–11) came at the hitters from the port side, and the Blue Jays appeared to be vulnerable against left-handers. During the regular season they had been 22–25 against them. Tommy Greene (16–4) and Curt Schilling (16–7) were formidable right-handers. And waiting in the wings to bail them out of trouble was the "Wild Thing."

The Philadelphia and Toronto spring training facilities were the closest of all of the major-league camps. A short five-minute drive separated Clearwater and Dunedin, Florida. The teams had met in four "A" games in the spring, and Philadelphia had won them all. That was the number of victories the Phillies had set for their October goal.

The first game of the World Series pitted the Jays' Guzman, who had never lost in postseason play (5–0), against the Phillies' Schilling, who had never won. Schilling had pitched two strong games in the NLCS but wasn't credited with the victories. He did pick up the MVP award for his work in the playoffs, becoming the first pitcher to capture that honor in the LCS without having registered a win or a save.

Guzman was shaky at the start. Although he struck out the side in the visitor's first at bat, he also walked a pair of batters and gave up run-scoring singles to Kruk and Daulton. It took the Blue Jays right-hander 35 pitches to finally retire the side.

Toronto tied the game, 2–2, in the bottom of the second. Devon White's hitting was key to the Blue Jays' offense in game one, and Alomar provided defensive gems in the fifth and sixth innings to prevent rallies by the Phillies. Olerud's solo homer off Schilling in the bottom of the sixth put Toronto ahead to stay, 5–4.

The major damage for Philadelphia took place one inning later. Left-hander David West was called from the bullpen with one out and runners at first and third. He surrendered doubles to White and Alomar, and the score ballooned to 8–4. That outing was an extension of the frustrations West had suffered in his previous World Series appearances. With the Minnesota Twins in 1991, he had faced six batters, walking four and giving up two hits. After his 1993 effort, he was zero-for-eight batters with "infinity" as an ERA.

The Phils added a single run in the top of the ninth on Eisenreich's single, but the contest went to Toronto, 8–5. The Blue Jays were off and running in their quest for their second consecutive championship.

The Phillies rebounded the next day, capturing game two by the score of 6–4. Stewart, the Blue Jays' pitching stalwart in the ALCS, had his worst-ever postseason outing and was bombarded for five runs in the top of the third inning. Eisenreich's three-run homer highlighted the attack. In comparison to his teammates, this Philadelphia outfielder was cut from different cloth. Short-haired and beardless, his experiences provided the basis for a human interest story. Early in his major-league career, Tourette syndrome had forced him out of baseball for five years. Eisenreich had displayed significant offensive talents, but the untreated disease had always won out. Having found an effective drug treatment, he was now experiencing the joys and satisfactions of the game.

Mulholland pitched into the sixth and held a 5–3 lead when he departed. Carter's two-run homer in the fourth was the only big blow against him. Dykstra added to the Phils' margin, slamming a seventh-inning home run.

The center of attention and excitement in the 1993 World Series focused on the Philadelphia bullpen and on Mitch Williams in particular. Would manager Jim Fregosi call on him to save the game for the Phils? And if "Wild Thing" made an appearance, what new and strange thing would happen?

His teammates had lived a season on the brink with Williams. Always an event when he entered the game, Williams did record 43 saves to place near the top of the league in that category. When "Wild Thing" took the mound, Schilling had begun the practice of draping a towel over his head as he sat in the dugout for the performance. He remarked, "I do it for two reasons. To keep my sanity and so I won't throw up on the bench."[4] Eisenreich, the hero of the second game, added, "We're all nervous when Mitch comes in. He puts guys on, but he comes back and gets them. He's not the "Wild Thing" for nothing. We're nervous obviously, but at the same time we're confident because he got the job done."[5]

Williams took his club on its usual roller-coaster ride through the last two innings of the contest. He made his appearance with Molitor, who had doubled, on second base with one out. Molitor stole third and scored on Olerud's sacrifice fly to right field, making the score 6–4. Mitch walked Alomar, who successfully stole second to put himself in scoring position. Out of the corner of his eye, Williams caught Alomar taking off for third. He stepped off of the rubber and threw the ball to Hollins at third base. It was waiting for Alomar when he arrived.

In the bottom of the ninth, "Wild Thing" walked Tony Fernandez on four pitches to lead off the frame. Ed Sprague grounded into a force out on a 3-2 pitch. Pat Borders ended the game by bouncing into a 6-4-3 double play. Williams had his save, and the Phillies had captured game two. Stewart, who had been unbeatable during a string of LCS games, was now 2–4 in his Fall Classic appearances.

The major dilemma facing Toronto manager Gaston for game three was what to do with Molitor, the Blue Jays' designated hitter and the league's runner-up batting champ. When the series moved to Philadelphia's Veterans Stadium, the designated-hitter role did not go with it. Gaston had to devise a lineup that had the pitcher batting in the ninth position.

Molitor, the Jays "DH," had continued his strong hitting, going three-for-seven in the first two games. During his only other World Series appearance, in 1982 with the Milwaukee Brewers, he had hit .355 against St. Louis Cardinal pitching. He had fashioned the Fall Classic's first five-hit game and had added six more singles during the Brewers 4–3 Series loss to the Cards.

Molitor could play left field and replace Rickey Henderson, who had struggled with the bat since coming to Toronto from Oakland on August 28. His .202 average with the Jays was far less impressive than Molitor's. As strong as Molitor's bat was, his arm was another story. Shoulder miseries made any throw a weak and painful one. That was the reason he did not appear to be a candidate for third base, although he had taken some ground balls there during the workout on the off day before the third game.

When the lineup card for game three was posted, Molitor was written in at first base. He had been there 23 times during the 1993 season. But the decision by Gaston meant that Olerud, the American League's leading hitter would be "riding the pines." It was only the third time in World Series history that a batting champ had gone to the bench for a game. (For trivia buffs, Chick Hafey and Willie McGee had also been there.)

Gaston's gamble paid off. Toronto pounded Philadelphia in a 10–3 rout. Following a 72-minute rain delay, Molitor delivered a two-run triple to right center and later scored as the Blue Jays jumped in front, 3–0, in the top of the first inning. He added a home run and a single later in the contest. Alomar contributed four hits, and Henderson, who had been one-for-six in the Series, ignited a pair of three-run outbursts with a single and a double. Jackson, the Phils' starter, was the victim of the early uprising. In the seventh inning, after Philadelphia had scored a run, Molitor started a nifty 3-4-3 double play to bail Toronto out of a bases-loaded jam.

Hentgen, who had been the Jays' "ace away from home," continued his mastery of opponents in ballparks other than SkyDome. He was also the benefactor of the ten-run uprising. During the regular season, he had been 7–6 at home but had rung up a 12–3 record on the road.

Game four was an experience to remember. A prelude of what was to come occurred in the first inning, when each of the starting pitchers walked in the first run. The Phillies had sent Greene to the mound to try to derail the Blue Jays. He had been successful in a similar assignment against the Braves in game six of the NLCS. Greene had been unbeatable at The Vet during the regular season, going 10–0. He had taken a pounding there from Atlanta in the second game of the LCS but had recaptured his winning ways in the series finale.

Greene found the going rough on the rainy night in Philly. He surrendered seven runs in less than three innings. Fortunately for his team, Toronto's starter didn't fare much better. Stottlemyre, who became part of the first father-son team to start World Series games (his father, Mel, had started three games for the New York Yankees in 1968), didn't last long enough to celebrate the occasion. He served up six hits, four consecutive walks, and six runs in two innings.

The Phillies added another tally in the bottom of the fourth and the score was knotted, 7–7. The fun was just beginning. By that time, Dykstra had already walked, hit a two-run homer, and doubled. Fernandez had driven in three Blue Jays with a pair of hits, and Molitor had two RBIs on a bases-loaded walk and a single. The first baseman from game three had moved over to third base — bad arm and all — and Olerud was back in the lineup.

Al Leiter bore the brunt of the next Philadelphia attack. A home run by Daulton and Dykstra's second four-bagger of the game powered the Phils' five-run fifth, making the score 12–7.

In the top of the sixth Toronto moved closer, adding a pair of tallies and closing the gap to 12–9. The big news in the inning was that West finally retired a World Series batter — in fact he retired three. However, before he got Carter to fly out for the historic first, White doubled to left and Alomar singled to center. They both hit first pitches from West. The streak ended at ten straight batters getting on base, and West's Fall Classic ERA dropped from infinity to 54!

Philadelphia added singletons in their next two at bats and carried a 14–9 lead into the top half of the eighth inning. And then more wild things happened.

With one away Carter singled to right off Andersen. Olerud followed with a walk, and Molitor continued his torrid hitting, doubling to left field and driving Carter home. Molitor's hit past Hollins at third was originally ruled an error, but it was changed to a double after the game.

Fregosi dialed the bullpen, and Williams took the mound. Fernandez greeted "Wild Thing" with a single, scoring Olerud. The score was now 14–11. Borders walked. Philadelphia fans were able to breathe again when Williams fanned Sprague, a Blue Jays pinch hitter, for the second out. But relief was brief, as Henderson singled to center, driving home Molitor and Fernandez, making it a one-run contest.

White delivered the killer blow, a triple that dropped beyond Dykstra in center field. The tying and go-ahead runs were on the scoreboard. Mercifully, Alomar grounded out to end the inning.

No more runs scored that night — or morning. Mike Timlin and Ward shut the Phillies down in their final two at bats. Tony Castillo, with 2⅓ innings of middle relief, picked up the victory. Mitch Williams, with ⅔ of an inning of late horror, took the defeat in the 15–14 slugfest, which ended at 12:28 A.M.

Thirteen World Series records were broken or tied in the 4-hours-and-14-minute game, the longest ever in the 532-game history of the Fall Classic. Among them were the marks for the most runs by two teams and the most runs by a losing team.

However, the Phillies had failed to surpass their 1993 regular season late-night heroics. A previous single game had ended at 1:47 A.M., and the curtain had not fallen on a doubleheader with San Diego until 4:40 A.M.

Dykstra's four runs scored tied the record in that category. He had put on an amazing offensive show. His two home runs, a double, and a walk had also produced four RBIs. When he struck out against Ward in the ninth for his only out of the game, he fired his helmet and bat in utter frustration. Later he remarked, "It's the toughest loss I've ever been in. Fourteen runs is usually enough."[6] Although not record-setting but certainly impressive, Fernandez and Milt Thompson each delivered five-RBI games.

Sanity returned to the World Series in the fifth game. Schilling gave his team's battered bullpen a welcomed night off and hurled Philadelphia to a 2–0 victory — the team's first-ever postseason shutout. The right-hander's 148-pitch outing before 62,706 fans in The Vet gave the Phillies another chance. The Blue Jays, who had scored 25 times in the two previous games, failed to cross the plate. Guzman, the Toronto starter, allowed five hits in seven innings of work, surrendering the victor's runs in the opening two frames. The defeat was his first postseason loss after five victories. Toronto's lead was 3–2 as the clubs headed north to SkyDome.

Prior to the sixth game, Ronald Blum of the Associated Press wrote, "In the World Series, Game 7 is the ultimate. But in recent years, Game 6 has been the best. Carlton Fisk, Don Denkinger, Bill Buckner, Kirby Puckett. They all have Game 6s named after them. Their heroics and their failures in those games have defined their careers."[7] With the final swing of the bat of the sixth game of the 1993 Fall Classic, Joe Carter's name was added to the list.

Stewart and Mulholland were the opposing pitchers in what would be the last game. Stewart held the Phils in check through six frames, giving up one run on two hits. Toronto got to Mulholland early, scoring three times in the bottom half of the first. Timely hits by Molitor, Olerud and Alomar were the decisive blows in the inning. The Jays added a single tally in their next at bat, and Molitor homered in the fifth to give Toronto the lead, 5–1.

As the capacity crowd at SkyDome was preparing to celebrate the first World Championship captured on Canadian soil, the Phils jumped ahead in the seventh when five runs crossed the plate. The highlight of the inning was a dramatic three-run blast by Dykstra, which sent Stewart to the showers. Hollins and Pete Incaviglia drove home the other pair of runs.

The Phillies carried a 6–5 lead and their hope for a seventh game into the bottom of the ninth. "Wild Thing" was summoned from the bullpen to protect the narrowest of margins.

Bill Giles, the president of the Phillies had reported that Williams had received at least two death threats since his failure in game four. Policemen had been sent to surround his New Jersey home. The immediate problem facing "Wild Thing," as he strode from the bullpen, was the top of Toronto's menacing order.

Henderson trotted to first base after watching four pitches out of the strike zone. White flied out to left field for the first out. Molitor banged a single, his twelfth hit in 24 at bats, moving Henderson to second.

Carter was the next batter. He had gone zero-for-three, with a sacrifice fly. A television shot of Schilling showed him seated in the Philadelphia dugout with a towel in place over his head and his eyes, painfully awaiting the outcome.

With the count at 2-2, Carter swung at Williams's next pitch, a fastball down and in. History making was in process. Carter drove the ball deep to left. He took three bounding steps up the first base line. Later he would say that he lost the ball in the lights until he was close to the first base bag. Approaching first, he picked it up again, near the end of its 379-foot journey into the Blue Jays bullpen. Carter floated around the bases, making sure to touch them all. The new hero arrived at home plate to the greetings of the

October 23, 1993: Joe Carter delivers the championship to Canada (AP/Wide World).

victorious throng, which had welcomed Henderson and Molitor before him. The final score was Toronto 8–Philadelphia 6.

A dejected "Wild Thing" left the mound and prepared to face his fate as another memorable name in the lore of the Fall Classic.

For the third straight season, the final game of the year had ended dramatically. Two years earlier, Jack Morris had pitched the Minnesota Twins to a 1–0, ten-inning victory over the Atlanta Braves in game seven. In 1992

Atlanta's Otis Nixon had singled home the tying run in the bottom of the ninth inning of the sixth game, sending it into extra innings. After Winfield's two-run double in the top of the eleventh put Toronto back on top, 4–2, the Jays had to shut down the Braves in their at bat after they had scored a run to pull within one. On Saturday October 24, 1993, at 11:39 P.M. in Toronto, Joe Carter began his historic trip around the bases, capping off another magic moment.

Carter had become only the second player to end a World Series with a home run, and he would be linked with Bill Mazeroski forever. Also, following the lead of Francisco Cabrera in the 1992 NLCS, Carter was only the second player in postseason play to make a team that was trailing in a game into the winner and champion on the last pitch of the final contest.

Dykstra, the series hero for the Phillies, said, "I really thought there was going to be a seventh game.... I feel this [another game] was meant to be. It was a weird feeling watching that ball fly out. I can't describe it."[8] He went on to support his teammate, who had suffered his second consecutive heart-breaking defeat: "Yeah, he did make it exciting out there at times. Everybody knows the story in that. He's got a lot of heart. The bottom line is he wants the ball and he does his best out there."[9]

After the game, Williams prepared to answer questions that would come to him in one form or another for the rest of his days. They hadn't eluded Ralph Branca or Ralph Terry. They had become too much for Donnie Moore.

Williams sat at his locker and faced the reporters, fielding their questions bravely and openly. He said: "I didn't do the job in a couple of games in the World Series. It's happened before when I didn't do the job in a couple of games. I have to look at it like maybe we wouldn't have been there if I hadn't done the job I did during the year. Well, we got here and I let us down. I'm not going to sit here and make excuses. I threw the pitch that cost us the World Series. That's tough to deal with, but I'm going to deal with it."[10]

Looking ahead, he added, "I let my team down but I'm not going to go home and commit suicide or hang my head all winter. I've got a job to do. I want to come back next year and do the same thing I did this season."[11]

Williams did return to The Vet the next season, but it was in the uniform of the Houston Astros, to whom he had been traded during the off-season.

The Philadelphia manager was questioned about his choice of Williams instead of Greene, Ben Rivera, or Bobby Thigpen. He was clear about his decision: "'If you could tell me who else I was going to use, I'd be happy,' Fregosi snapped after the game. 'Without Mitch Williams we wouldn't have been here. He saved 43 games during the season. There were no options.'"[12]

At the other end of the continuum created by the magic moment, Carter relished the joy of the event. He had driven that particular pitch by Williams, but he added, "Ninety out of 100 times I hook that ball foul."[13]

When asked about his feelings as he rounded the bases, the celebrating hero said, "They haven't made the word up yet to describe this feeling. You want to see the reaction of the fans, your teammates, but most of all I want to see what my reaction is. As a batter you can't believe it. You want a base hit and you hit a homer to win the sixth game of the World Series."[14]

It would take time for the full impact of the moment to register. Two months later, Carter said: "What I did really has not set in, maybe when I'm 70 or 80 years old and I'm sitting watching a game and it will come on, showing me hitting that home run just like Bobby Thomson did or Mazeroski, maybe it will set in.... I'm not going around gloating that I hit the home run that won the World Series and talking about Mitch. I know very well that I could have made an out, or hit into a double play. Those things happen in baseball."[15]

Many played a part in the memorable and zany fourth game. Carter delivered the blow that created the 1993 magic moment. But when all was said and done, the Series belonged to the 37-year-old designated hitter, first baseman, and third baseman of the World Champion Toronto Blue Jays, Paul Molitor. After 16 years in the major leagues, the first 15 with the Milwaukee Brewers, he had come to Toronto in search of the crown and the ring.

In the 1993 Fall Classic Molitor had done it all and was chosen MVP. He was 12-for-24, including two doubles, two triples, and two home runs. He drove in eight runs and crossed the plate ten times, the winning run of the series being the most important. Molitor had waited a career to claim his crown. The baseball world had waited for its longest period in history to have a repeat champion. Both were realized at the same instant, when Carter created his memorable moment.

1996
World Series

Atlanta Braves and New York Yankees

Fourth Game — October 23 at Atlanta

New York	0	0	0	0	0	3	0	*3*	0	2	8	12	0
Atlanta	0	4	1	0	1	0	0	0	0	0	6	9	2

Rogers, Boehringer[3], Weathers[5], Nelson[6], Rivera[8], Lloyd[9], Wetteland[10]

Neagle, Wade[6], Bielecki[6], Wohlers[8], Avery[10], Clontz[10]

Home runs ruled baseball's 1996 regular season. The 28 major-league clubs combined for a record 4,962 round-trippers. The Baltimore Orioles slammed 257 to break the New York Yankees' single-season mark, which they had set in 1961 when the "M and M Boys" — Roger Maris and Mickey Mantle — totaled 115 between them. Seven Orioles hit more than 20 homers (another all-time record), led by leadoff hitter Brady Anderson's 50 four-baggers. One year earlier, Anderson hit a mere 16 home runs. All told, ten teams topped their franchise's best output for homers in a season, and nine players set single-season records for their clubs.

The two World Series combatants, the Atlanta Braves and the New York Yankees, featured an impressive collection of Cy Young Award winners — past and present. After a season of long-ball, would this group of moundsmen mute the bats and dominate the Series?

The first game was far from a pitchers' duel! Atlanta pounded New York, 12–1, helped along by three round-trippers. However, the pitchers controlled the next two contests, and the home run took a back seat. But in game four a memorable blast by part-timer Jim Leyritz would rescue the Yankees' faltering hopes and set them on the path to a World Championship. Long live the home run!

The Yankees began their march to the title at the franchise's new $20 million training complex in Tampa, Florida, returning to Hillsborough County after 34 springs in Ft. Lauderdale. The centerpiece of the complex was 10,000-seat Legends Field, a ballpark with a decorative frieze on the wall and playing-field dimensions crafted to reflect the legendary "House That Ruth Built" in the Bronx. Twelve air-conditioned luxury suites with a private entrance and elevator access to them represented the modern economic realities of the game.

In addition to the change in scenery, alterations were also made to strengthen the Yankee team for the new campaign. Joe Torre, longtime National League player and manager, was hired as skipper to replace popular Buck Showalter, a move that was roundly criticized by many in the New York media. Torre, holder of the dubious record of having played and managed in the most major league games without ever appearing in a World Series, brought the Senior Circuit's style of play to a team of American Leaguers. His goal was to blend a group of high-priced stars and promising youth into a scrappy, aggressive, base-stealing, run-manufacturing team.

Slugging first baseman Tino Martinez was acquired in a five-player deal with the Seattle Mariners to replace Don Mattingly, who had retired after the 1995 season. Yankee owner George Steinbrenner opened his checkbook and signed him to a five-year, $20.25 million contract.

Four other players were added in the off-season as Steinbrenner spent millions of dollars in his quest for a championship: Tim Raines, a former batting champ, to fill the leadoff spot; Joe Girardi to strengthen the defense behind the plate; Mariano Duncan to back up all around the infield; and Jeff Nelson to bolster the bull pen.

David Cone appeared ready to be the workhorse on the mound. "Hopeful" was the operative word to describe the rest of the staff. Andy Pettitte, the 24-year-old sophomore left-hander, was hoping to continue the progress he had made in his rookie season. Another lefty, Jimmy Key, was coming off rotator cuff surgery in 1995 and was hoping to regain the dominance he had shown during the two seasons before his injury, when he had gone a combined 35–10 for the Yanks. Right-hander Scott Kamieniecki was trying to make it back from elbow surgery. Steinbrenner signed Texas Ranger free agent southpaw Kenny Rogers to a four-year, $20 million contact, and the Yanks owner was hoping that his new pitcher could match his 17–7 record and 3.38 ERA in 1995. Torre also hoped to find an effective setup man to team with John Wetteland, the club's closer.

Hope also focused on a Steinbrenner reclamation project. In October 1995 George signed Dwight Gooden, who had just ended his year of suspension from baseball for a repeat drug offense. Gooden appeared to have his life back in order, but there were lingering questions about what remained of the skills he had displayed as a hard-throwing phenom with the New York Mets a decade earlier.

Through most of the first month of the season, Gooden and Key struggled, and Rogers was in an extended spring training because of an injury. Cone, Pettitte, and strong performances by pitchers out of the bull pen helped the Yankees get off to a fast start. On April 30, the Yanks beat the Orioles in

Baltimore, 13–10, in the longest nine-inning game in major league history. The next night Martinez hit a grand slam in the top of the fifteenth inning to bring the Bronx Bombers an 11–6 victory. Pettitte came out of the bull pen to pick up the win after having been blasted from the hill a day earlier. The Yankees were alone at the top of the American League East for the first time, and they would stay there for the remainder of the season.

But the campaign was not without its hurdles. Early in May the club lost Cone to potentially season-ending surgery after he developed an aneurysm in his right shoulder. Gooden, who on April 27 had been placed on waivers in order to send him back to the minors (he was quickly pulled off the waiver wire when the Orioles put in a claim for him), took up the slack and highlighted his efforts with a no-hitter — a 2–0 gem against the powerful Mariners. The team rode stellar performances by Pettitte and setup, middle-reliever Mariano Rivera to move to ten games above .500 by the first of June. Wetteland was equally as stellar as the closer, setting a major-league mark with saves in 20 consecutive appearances.

Between games of a doubleheader on June 21, Torre received tragic word that older brother, Rocco, had died of a heart attack. Rocco, one of the three Torre boys who had learned to play baseball on the sandlots of Brooklyn, had been watching the Yankees win the first game on TV, and dropped dead shortly after its conclusion. A second adversity beset Torre during his team's march to the World Series. Frank, Joe's other brother, who had played in the majors from 1956 to 1963, spent the summer in a New York hospital awaiting a heart transplant to save his life.

New York held a six-game lead over Baltimore at the All-Star break in mid–July. They extended it to ten lengths shortly thereafter, when two ex–Mets — Gooden and Darryl Strawberry — took center stage during a series with the Orioles.

Strawberry, who had been suspended from baseball for the start of the 1995 season for violating provisions in his drug after-care program, had been signed by the Yankees in June of that year, when he became eligible to play. However, not re-signed by the Yankees for 1996, he hooked on with the St. Paul Saints of the independent Northern League and posted numbers impressive enough to regain Steinbrenner's interest. On July 4, George bought himself a birthday present, inking Darryl to a new contract. After a short stay with Columbus of the Triple-A International League, the 34-year-old Strawberry was recalled by the parent club. He had hit 21 homers in 30 games during his two minor-league stops on his way to the Bronx. Commenting on his display of power, Strawberry said, "Right now it reminds me of earlier in my career.... I'm just doing the things that I have to do as far as a hitter. I have never been on a tear that is so tremendous, so consistent. Hopefully, I can keep it going."[1]

Indeed he did. Back in pinstripes, Darryl's first two hits landed in the outfield seats! On the mound, contributing to this unlikely flashback to the 1986 Mets, Gooden picked up his sixth consecutive victory in the nightcap of a doubleheader sweep of Baltimore.

The final piece of the pennant puzzle fell in place on July 31. Shortly before the midnight trading deadline, the Bronx Bombers sent malcontent Ruben Sierra to the Detroit Tigers in exchange for Cecil Fielder. Fielder, the major leagues' home run and RBI leader in the 1990s, who had hit 26 homers for the Tigers in 1996, powered five more dingers for his new club during the month of August.

Baltimore made a run at the Yankees during the final two weeks of August and in early September, cutting New York's 12-game lead to a slender 2½-game margin. The Yanks rebounded and captured two of the three games played against Baltimore in a critical series in the Bronx and went on to clinch the Eastern Division Championship on September 25. They finished the season 92–70, four lengths in front of the Orioles.

Duncan hit .340 in 109 games to lead the club, and Derek Jeter, who would be named the American League's Rookie of the Year, followed at .314. Wade Boggs, Bernie Williams, and Paul O'Neill all finished above .300. Williams contributed 29 homers and Martinez added 25. Pettitte's 21–8 mark topped the pitchers. Rogers and Key finished with 12 victories apiece, and Gooden added 11. Rivera, who led the staff with a 2.09 ERA and received serious consideration for the Cy Young Award — an honor unheard of for a setup man — limited the first batters he faced to an anemic .089 batting average. Early in the season he put together a string of 15 consecutive hitless innings in relief. When Rivera finished his work, Wetteland put the final touches on the games and collected 43 saves in 47 chances. Rarely, if ever, had a pair of relievers been so largely responsible for a team's success: the Yankees posted an unprecedented 79–1 record in games in which they were ahead after seven innings.

In contrast to the Yankees, the Atlanta Braves made very few changes to their 1995 World Championship roster in preparation for the 1996 season. Five fringe players departed to other clubs and only one veteran — reserve outfielder Jerome Walton — was added.

Some who observed the pitching-rich Braves, who had been in postseason play since 1991 (with the exception of 1994, when the strike stopped the season in August), saw two major opponents for the new campaign: the Florida Marlins and complacency. The Marlins had spent a significant amount of free-agent money to strengthen their ball club. Complacency, however, stood as a more formidable foe.

The Braves' top four hurlers — Steve Avery, Tom Glavine, Greg Maddux, and John Smoltz — had gone to the mound regularly and had provided masterful pitching. They had experienced very few poor starts and fewer missed starts during the Braves' domination of the National League East. Greg McMichael and Mark Wohlers were reliable arms out of the bull pen.

Although the team's major strength was on the mound, the offense also bore the imprint of general manager John Schuerholz's and manager Bobby Cox's building plan. Marquis Grissom, Chipper Jones, Dave Justice, Ryan Klesko, Javier Lopez, and Fred McGriff provided an effective mix of power and speed.

At the beginning of May the Braves were 16–11 and sat 1½ games behind the Montreal Expos. An 18–8 surge during the month vaulted them into first place in the NL East, a position they held the rest the way. After dropping his first decision, Smoltz jumped to the head of the staff, registering 14 consecutive wins.

In mid–July, the Braves turned over Atlanta to the Olympic Summer Games and went on the road for three weeks. During their sojourn, they maintained a comfortable lead over their nearest division rivals.

Two injuries created a slightly different look to the lineup. In May, Justice, the club's right fielder, underwent surgery for a dislocated right shoulder and was lost for the season. Avery suffered a rib cage injury, which hampered the left-hander through most of the campaign, and he finished with a subpar 7–10 record. At the end of August, the Braves obtained another premier lefty, 14-game winner Denny Neagle, from the struggling Pittsburgh Pirates to fill in for the ineffective Avery.

Atlanta's only serious slump occurred in September when they went 12–16, ending an amazing streak of 21 consecutive winning months extending over four seasons.

The Braves finished the regular season at 96–66, eight games in front of the pesky Expos. Chipper Jones hit .309, and Grissom followed at .308. Klesko's 34 home runs and McGriff's 30 led three other players who slammed more than 20. Smoltz finished at 24–8, and Glavine and Maddux added 15 wins apiece. Wohlers registered 39 saves in the closer's role.

Atlanta gained its ticket to the 1996 Fall Classic after a clean sweep of the Los Angeles Dodgers in the Divisional Series.

The National League Championship Series proved to be another matter altogether. After taking game one, Atlanta dropped the next three and were in danger of missing an opportunity to defend their World Championship.

Two of the final three games were Brave blowouts, as both the pitching and hitting excelled. In game four, Atlanta bombed St. Louis, 14–0. They followed with a 3–1 victory, evening the series at three games apiece.

The Braves sent Glavine to the mound in the deciding seventh contest. Tom did it with both his arm and his bat, leading his club back to the Fall Classic. His bases-loaded triple drove in three runs during a six-run, first-inning rally, which propelled the Braves to an NLCS record-setting 15–0 romp.

With their backs to the wall in the final three games, Atlanta outscored St. Louis, 32–1. The club's "big three," Smoltz, Maddux, and Glavine, were primed for the season's most important set of games.

The Yankees, meanwhile, met the Rangers in the American League Divisional Series. Texas won the first encounter, but New York captured the final three games, coming from behind in each of them. The relief corps was dominant as the Yanks became the first team to win a postseason series without getting a victory from a starting pitcher.

The "lone star" for Texas was Juan Gonzalez, who, during the four-game series, slugged five home runs, tying a postseason series mark held jointly by Reggie Jackson and Ken Griffey, Jr.

New York and Baltimore faced each other in the American League Championship Series. Some New Yorkers came to the stadium to give a "Bronx cheer" to the Orioles' bad boy, Roberto Alomar, who, late in the regular season, had spit in the face of umpire John Hirschbeck. Baseball fans were angry about Alomar's childish act as well as American League president Gene Budig's decision to postpone Roberto's five-game suspension until the start of the 1997 season.

The Orioles took an early lead in game one on home runs by Anderson and Raphael Palmeiro. However, with one out in the bottom of the eighth inning and with the Yankees trailing, 4–3, Jeter hit a long fly ball towards Yankee Stadium's right-field wall. It was destined to either bounce off the top of the wall or land in Oriole right fielder Tony Tarasco's glove. Neither happened as Jeffrey Maier, a 12-year-old fan from New Jersey, reached over the wall with his glove, just to the right of the "Nobody beats the WIZ" sign, and brought the ball into the stands. He committed a series of errors on the play. He bobbled the ball and allowed it to fall into the hands of a fan from Connecticut behind him. He also committed a major miscue by interfering with a ball that was still in the field of play.

Right-field umpire Richie Garcia, however, didn't see the second error and ruled Jeter's hit a game-tying home run. He believed (wrongly, as the replays would show) that the ball was in the stands before Maier got his black glove on it. Tarasco, who saw the play "up close and personal," argued vehemently as did other Orioles.

After the game Garcia admitted that Maier had interfered on the play, and he should have put Jeter on second base but not call him out. The umpire was applying Rule 3.19 which states that the batter is to be called out only if the interference "clearly prevents a fielder from catching a flyball."[2] After reviewing the tape, Garcia did not believe that was the case.

Had Jeter been returned to second base, the result might have been the same because Raines followed with a single to right field, which would have probably scored Derek. But "probably" didn't satisfy the Orioles.

The two teams battled into the bottom of the eleventh inning, and Williams brought the Yanks victory with a "no-question-about-it" home run.

Following the game, Baltimore lodged an official protest of Jeter's home run, although an umpire's judgment call cannot form the basis for such a protest. The decision on the Orioles' action did not change the game's outcome.

The part Maier played in the Yankees' opening-game victory set off a variety of reactions. The next day's newspaper headline, "A 12-Year-Old Legend Is Born in Right Field,"[3] heralded the youngster as if he were a new member of the Yankee pantheon. In the minds of some, he joined Ruth, Gehrig, DiMaggio, and, most recently, Mantle, whose monument had been unveiled on August 25 in Monument Park just beyond the left-center-field wall. The article under the headline commented, "New York now has another epic to go along with Don Larsen's perfect game for the Yankees in 1956 or the night Mookie Wilson's grounder slithered through Bill Buckner's legs in 1986."[4]

Maier appeared on ABC-TV's "Good Morning America" the following day, after having been "secured" in a Manhattan hotel for the night. However, he turned down an invitation from David Letterman to be on his show.

As a reward for his "hometown heroics," Jeffrey was seated in a box along the first baseline for the second game. The boy-hero was adorned in a Yankee cap, which had not been part of his "uniform" the day before.

Not all of the reports about the Maier-miracle were positive. Some noted that the 12-year-old was a truant from school who was at an afternoon ball game. He had also, after all, committed an act punishable by expulsion from the ballpark — as every fan, young and old — is reminded at every major-league game in every major-league park.

Some went further and saw the event which had begun with a boy, a glove, and a ball as a home run with a moral twinge. Burt Solomon, writing in the *New York Times,* editorialized:

> It wasn't that the boy crossed the line. It was that adults all over New York hailed him as a hero when he should have been scolded and tossed from the ball park. The TV talk shows fought over him. ABC's "Good Morning America" put him up in a suite at the Plaza Hotel. Mayor Rudolph W. Giuliani and Gov. George E. Pataki defended him. Sen. Alfonse D'Amato called his interference "almost a miracle."
> This is what is wrong with Yankees fans — and with more and more fans everywhere. Winning is everything and knowing right from wrong ... well, that's no big deal.[5]

Legitimate home runs marked the rest of the ALCS. Fifteen more were hit in the next four games to set a League Championship Series record of 19. The Orioles won the second game to bring them even, 1–1, but the Bronx Bombers took the next three to capture the American League crown. Strawberry had a power-series with a 1.167 slugging percentage — a record for a five-game ALCS.

New York joined Atlanta in the Fall Classic, scheduled to begin on October 19 in Yankee Stadium. The Yanks were in the World Series for the first time since 1981 and sought their first championship since 1978 — a mighty drought for the Bronx Bombers' legendary franchise. Torre was eager for his first World Series appearance, after having played and managed in 4,272 major-league regular-season games and having spent 31 idle Octobers.

The pitchers were ready to go to battle with the sluggers who had enjoyed "Homer Summer." They did not represent the dilution of pitching talent that had been brought about through expansion and that was part of the rationale offered to explain the 1996 power surge. The Braves had Maddux, who had four "Cys" on his mantle, and Glavine, a Cy Young winner in 1991. Smoltz appeared to have a lock on the 1996 award. In the bull pen, Mark Wohlers had been overpowering in the closer role.

The Yankees countered with Cone, who had beaten the odds and made it back from arm surgery in time for the September stretch drive. On September 2, he accentuated his return with a no-hitter through seven innings against the Oakland A's. He was removed before the eighth, having reached the designated pitch count for his first outing. Cone had won the Cy Young Award in 1994 while he was with the Kansas City Royals. Pettitte, coming off his outstanding season, would be edged out by the Toronto Blue Jays' Pat Hentgen for the American League's award in 1996. The Yankees also had a pair of devastating relievers to throw at the Braves. Unfortunately, Gooden would not go to the hill; he had been removed from the roster for the ALCS and the World Series because of an inflammation in his rotator cuff.

After a rain-out of the scheduled opener, the clubs met the following day. Only one of the pitching staffs did its job. The Yankees got to Smoltz in the bottom of the fifth inning for their only run. Jeter drew a two-out walk and scored on Boggs's double. The Braves scored 12 times.

Andruw Jones, who had started the season at Class A and had then moved through AA and AAA before arriving in Atlanta in mid–August, was in left field for defensive purposes. Klesko, whose position Jones had taken, was in the lineup as the designated hitter, a benefit of playing in an American League park. Jones belted a two-run homer in the top of the second inning. The blast broke Mantle's record for the youngest player to hit a World Series home run — and the 19-year-old Brave did it on Mickey's birthday.

Andruw followed with a three-run blast the next inning to match Oakland's Gene Tenace's accomplishment of hitting home runs in their first two Fall Classic at bats. McGriff made the score 9–0 in the fifth with a drive off the right-field foul pole. Pettitte was the victim of the early Brave uprising, surrendering seven runs in just 2⅓ innings of work. Atlanta's 12–1 thumping represented the Yankees' worst World Series loss ever.

The following day Maddux bested Key, shutting out the Bronx Bombers, 4–0. It was a typical Maddux outing as he threw 82 pitches in eight innings, 62 of which were strikes. Wohlers preserved the win, striking out three Yankee hitters in the ninth.

Having dropped the first two games and having been outscored, 16–1, the Yanks headed to the home of the Tomahawk Chop.

In game three, Cone was the Yankee stopper. He took the team into the late innings with a 5–1 lead, and then turned the game over to Rivera and Wetteland. The Braves scored once off Rivera, but the Yanks registered a 5–2 win. The Bronx Bombers manufactured their first run off Glavine in the top of the first frame. Raines walked, was sacrificed to second base by Jeter, and scored on a single by Williams. Three innings later, the Yankees went ahead, 2–0, on an error, a walk, a base-advancing fly out, and Strawberry's single. Torre's "National League Yankees" were back in it.

Atlanta took a 2–1 series lead into the fourth game. On October 23, Atlanta–Fulton County Stadium became the site of yet another of the National Pastime's memorable postseason moments.

Rogers had a horrendous outing and was relieved by Brian Boehringer in the third inning with no outs and runners at the corners. Rogers was charged with Atlanta's first five runs. The Braves added a singleton in the fifth to take a 6–0 lead. New York bounced back with three tallies in the top of the sixth before a batter was retired, but reliever Mike Bielecki registered three consecutive strikeouts to silence the Bronx Bombers.

Without a rally, the Yankees faced a 3–1 series deficit and the prospect of facing Smoltz in the fifth and, possibly, final game. With Atlanta ahead, 6–3, in the top of the eighth, the stage was set for "the moment."

Charlie Hayes led off the inning with a dribbler down the third-base line that refused to roll foul. Strawberry followed with an opposite-field single to left, sending Hayes to second. Duncan hit a "tailor-made" double-play ball, but slick-fielding shortstop Raphael Belliard bobbled it and was only able to retire one runner.

Up to the plate stepped Leyritz to face Wohlers and his menacing 100-mph fastball.

The Yankees' backup catcher had appeared in 88 games during the regular season, hitting .264, with seven home runs, in 265 at bats. In his 72 starts, he was behind the plate in 50 games, at third base 10 times, was the designated hitter in 10 games and started in left field twice. He had become "Pettitte's catcher" and was in the lineup for most of the games when the ace left-hander took the mound.

Throughout the season, Leyritz had played "second fiddle" to Girardi. It was the same on this memorable evening in Atlanta. Torre pinch-hit O'Neill for Girardi during the sixth-inning rally, and Leyritz went behind the plate in the bottom of the inning.

Leigh Montville in *Sports Illustrated* described Jim's plight: "Leyritz was caught in a role he could not shake, forever Kramer to someone else's Seinfeld. He was always seen as this squat guy with the Popeye forearms, an undrafted kid out of Anderson Township, Ohio, and the University of Kentucky who could catch a little, play a little at first base, maybe even third or the outfield if necessary, nice to have around, but certainly no marquee player."[6]

Cox, realizing the importance of the win and wanting to nail it down, brought in Wohlers, his closer, to start the eighth rather than save him for his normal one-inning stint. Wohler's first four pitches to Leyritz were fastballs. After fouling off two of the right-hander's heaters and watching two others zoom out of the strike zone, Leyritz was geared for another fastball. Wohlers changed the pattern and tried a slider — a high, hanging slider. Montville recounted the batter's reaction: "Leyritz remembers starting to swing for the fastball that didn't come and watching this slider that didn't slide moving into the picture. His bat was already there and made contact, and the ball headed for the left field wall at Atlanta–Fulton County Stadium. 'I didn't style or anything at the plate because I didn't know if it was going to go out of the park.... But I also didn't run hard to first because I knew the ball was going to be either over the fence or caught. I just watched to see what would happen.'"[7]

The blast eluded the leaping Andruw Jones's outstretched glove and bounced off the top of the wall for a home run. Three Yankees crossed the plate, quickly tying the game, 6–6, and stunning the crowd of 51,881— most of them tomahawk-chopping Brave fans.

Unlike the memorable home runs of Mazeroski, Fisk, and Carter, which had delivered victory to their clubs, Leyritz's rescued his team from impending defeat.

The Braves threatened to take the lead in the bottom of the eighth, but Rivera held them scoreless. The Yanks then loaded the bases with two out in their at bat, but Wohlers pitched out of the jam. Lefty Graeme Lloyd replaced Rivera in the bottom of the ninth with Braves at first and second with one out, and he got McGriff to ground into a double play, sending the game into extra innings.

Avery, who had lost his place in Atlanta's starting rotation, relieved Wohlers and retired the first two Yankees to face him. He walked Raines on four pitches and Jeter singled Raines to second. Cox decided to walk Williams intentionally with Andy Fox in the on-deck circle. It was a risky move that not only loaded the bases but advanced Raines to third. Torre called Fox back to the bench and sent Boggs to the plate. In the lefty versus lefty matchup, Avery went ahead in the count, 1–2. Boggs watched the next three pitches miss the strike zone. As he trotted to first base, Raines was scoring from third. The Yankees were on top, 7–6.

Cox's next move was to make a double-switch — a National League specialty — bringing right-hander Brad Clontz in to pitch and sending Klesko to first base. Hayes smashed a liner at Klesko, which the new first sacker booted for an error, allowing Jeter to score the Yanks' final run. Lloyd and Wetteland shut down the Braves, but not before Jermaine Dye and Terry Pendleton hit shots to the warning track for the final two outs.

With the dramatic 8–6 extra-inning win, New York had evened the series, 2–2, in the longest game in Fall Classic history — four hours and 17 minutes.

After the game, Wohlers, whose name would be linked forever to a player and a monumental home run — like other pitchers before him — spoke about the non-sliding slider. "I tried to throw him a slider and left it up…. He got good wood on it," Wohlers recalled. "I didn't think it was gone, but obviously it was. It didn't sound like a normal home run sound."[8]

Steinbrenner talked about what had transpired with words that were reminiscent of descriptions offered about other games in other places that live in the memories of so many. The Boss said, "This was a great game…. This was great for baseball. If you wanted to go to bed, you couldn't. You had to stay up late to watch. If you were in New York, you stayed up. In the bars and everywhere. I bet they're still going crazy. Man, I'd like to see that."[9]

Pettitte took the mound for the fifth game, and Leyritz was behind the plate. Andy was hoping to atone for the stunning defeat he had suffered in game one. The Yankees were hoping to add one more victory to their perfect 7–0 mark for wins on the road in 1996 postseason play.

The American League's top winner hooked up with Smoltz, the National League's best. New York scored their only run in the top of the fourth inning when Fielder doubled to drive in Hayes. With two outs in the bottom of the ninth and with Braves on first and third, O'Neill, who was hobbled by a painful hamstring injury, made a remarkable running, over-the-shoulder catch of a drive by Atlanta pinch hitter and former-Yankee Luis Polonia to end the game. Pettitte allowed only five hits in 8⅓ innings and, with Wetteland's help, the Yankees held on to win, 1–0.

The teams traveled to New York to await game six. On October 25, an off day, Torre celebrated again. His brother Frank received a new heart. For months, Frank had been hospitalized, too weak to go home, and desperately in need of a transplant to save his life. From his hospital room he had watched his brother guide the Yankees to a pennant and then towards a Fall Classic Championship and a ring. Frank had gotten his World Series ring in 1957 as a member of the Milwaukee Braves, who had defeated the Yankees. He was pulling for his brother to get his.

Frank's attachment to the 1996 Yanks had kept him going during the long and difficult summer. Occasionally he suggested strategy to his younger brother. "'Frank loves managing,' Joe said. 'He gets on me, telling me I've got to do something about this guy or that guy. When the race got close, he told me I had to forget about hurting a guy's feelings if I have to bench him. It's given him something to think about instead of just sitting there waiting for a heart.'"[10]

Frank had given Joe something to think about besides baseball. Often his brother's plight took away some of the seeming importance of a game of ball.

Joe visited Frank in the hospital after the surgery and wanted to present him with a special memento— the ball from the final out of game three, Joe's first World Series victory. Unfortunately, Joe had to leave the unsterilized trophy outside his brother's room.

The following evening, October 26, the Yankees won their twenty-third and long-awaited World Championship, beating the Braves, 3–2. The stars were out that night as Matthew Broderick, Billy Crystal, Matt Dillon, Mel Gibson, Spike Lee, Eddie Murphy, Julia Roberts, Susan Sarandon, and other notables from show business were in the crowd of over 56,000 at the Stadium. Vice–presidential candidate Jack Kemp, New York governor George Pataki, New Jersey governor Christine Whitman, and New York City mayor Rudy Giuliani represented the political establishment.

Key outdueled Maddux, and, as he had done all season, Wetteland put the icing on the Yankees' championship cake. With two out, the tying run at second base and the go-ahead run at first in the top of the ninth, Wetteland got Mark Lemke to hit a towering foul pop fly near the third-base dugout. The ball just eluded Hayes's outstretched glove. Torre heard Don Zimmer, whom Joe had urged out of retirement that season to serve as his bench coach, say, "Don't worry about it…. This is the one for Frank. This is the last pitch."[11] Wetteland delivered again and Lemke lifted another foul ball in the same direction. This time, Hayes hauled it in. The Yank's closer recorded his fourth save — a Fall Classic record.

Joe had his ring, and Frank, with his new heart, appeared to be on the way to recovery. Baseball had another memorable moment to savor — a game four, game-tying, three-run homer off the bat of Jim Leyritz that was to power the Yankees' dramatic turnaround.

During the roaring on-the-field-celebration, Boggs climbed on a horse, and he and the mounted policeman took a joyous gallop around Yankee Stadium. Wade, too, had his first ring. One might have recalled the same Boggs sitting alone in a dugout with tears streaming down his face after a previous World Series Championship had slipped from his grasp. That was a decade earlier — on October 27, 1986, in Shea Stadium, Flushing, New York.

Notes

Introduction

1. Russ Hodges and Al Hirshberg, *My Giants* (Garden City, N.Y.: Doubleday, 1963), 113.
2. George Will, "A Mosaic of Memories," *Major League Baseball Official World Series Program*, 1988: 13.
3. *The Sporting News*, 25 Oct. 1980, 25.
4. *USA Today*, 14 Oct. 1988, 2A.
5. W. R. Kinsella, *Shoeless Joe* (New York: Ballantine Books, 1982), 212.
6. David Halberstam, "Why Men Love Baseball," *Parade Magazine*, 14 May 1988, 16.
7. John Updike, *Forever Baseball*, PBS Television Production, Drasnin Production, for the American Experience, 1989.
8. Updike.
9. Thomas Boswell, *How Life Imitates the World Series* (Garden City, N.Y.: Doubleday, 1982), 238.

1940 World Series

1. "Seesaw Series Gives Fans a Fight to the Finish Between Reds' Pitching Stars and Tigers' Power," *New York Times*, 14 Oct. 1940, 56.
2. John Drebinger, "National Winners, Who Spread-Eagled Field, Enter Classic with Assurance — Tigers Upset American Loop's Pattern," *New York Times*, 30 Sept. 1940, 21.
3. James P. Dawson, "Rowe and Walters Are Today's Pitching Choices," *New York Times*, 3 Oct. 1940, 34.
4. John Gardner, "The One and Only Bobo," in Charles Einstein, ed., *The Second Fireside Book of Baseball* (New York: Simon and Schuster, 1958), 226.
5. "Mighty Master of Three-Hit Shutout Sobs Out Grief in Tiger Clubhouse," *Boston Daily Globe*, 7 Oct. 1940, 6.
6. Hy Hurwitz, "Newsom on Detroit Mound by Request, Baker Reveals," *Boston Evening Globe*, 8 Oct. 1940, 21.
7. Hurwitz, "Newsome," 21.
8. John Kieran, "Red Is the Winning Color," *New York Times*, 9 Oct. 1940, 34.
9. H. G. Salsinger, "'Home!' Is Shriek Bartell Fails to Hear," *Detroit News*, 9 Oct. 1940, 21.
10. Dick Bartell with Norman L. Macht, *Rowdy Richard* (Berkeley, Calif.: North Atlantic Books, 1987), 303–4.
11. Bartell with Macht, 303.
12. Grantland Rice, "Derringer Stops Tigers 2–1, and Reds Win the World Championship," *Boston Daily Globe*, 9 Oct. 1940, 20.
13. Gerry Moore, "Bartell, Back to Plate, Holds Ball as Reds Tie Score, Then Go on to Win," *Boston Daily Globe*, 9 Oct. 1940, 20.

14. Hy Hurwitz, "Reds Beat Tigers, 2–1, in Decisive Game of Series," *Boston Evening Globe*, 8 Oct. 1940, 21.

15. Eddie Joost, letter, 1996.

16. Eddie Joost, letter, 1988.

17. Charles Gehringer, letter, 1988.

18. Bartell with Macht, 304.

19. Dick Bartell, letter, 1990.

20. Bartell with Macht, 305.

1941 World Series

1. John Kieran, "Coming Up to the Plate," *New York Times*, 1 Oct. 1941, 27.

2. "Yanks Stay Ahead after the Second," *New York Times*, 2 Oct. 1941, 32.

3. John Devaney and Burt Goldblatt with Barbara Devaney, *The World Series* (Chicago: Rand McNally, 1981), 173.

4. Gerry Moore, "Owen Weeps at Fatal Muff," *Boston Daily Globe*, 6 Oct. 1941, 1.

5. Moore, 1.

6. "'Owen, Ya Bum,' Chorus in Flatbush After Fatal Ninth," *Boston Daily Globe*, 6 Oct. 1941, 8.

7. Sid Feder, "'It Shoulda Happened to Hitler,' Sobs Tear-Faced Kid, Leaving Game," *Boston Daily Globe*, 6 Oct. 1941, 8.

8. John Lardner, "Mickey Owen's Classic Muff Makes History," *Boston Daily Globe*, 6 Oct. 1941, 9.

9. John Drebinger, "Yanks Win Series as Bonham Beats Dodgers, 3–1," *New York Times*, 7 Oct. 1941, 1.

10. Donald Honig, *The World Series* (New York: Crown, 1986), 112.

11. Roscoe McGowen, "Dodgers Stress Luck of Rivals," *New York Times*, 6 Oct. 1941, 21.

12. Dave Anderson, Owen, Henrich Say Casey Threw a Curve," *New York Times*, 12 June 1988, sec. 8, 3.

13. Mickey Owen, letter, 1990.

14. Robert Obojski, "Tommy Henrich," *Sports Collectors Digest*, 10 March 1989, 172.

15. Anderson, sec. 8, 3.

16. Leo Durocher with Ed Linn, *Nice Guys Finish Last* (New York: Simon and Schuster, 1975), 129.

17. Owen, letter.

18. Owen, letter.

19. Owen, letter.

1946 World Series

1. "Old-Timers Classic Provides Memories," *Springfield* (MA) *Union-News*, 28 June 1988, C4.

2. John Drebinger, "Cards Take Series as Brecheen Beats Red Sox for 3d Time, 4–3," *New York Times*, 16 Oct. 1946, 1.

3. Donald Honig, *The World Series* (New York: Crown, 1986), 114.

4. Ted Williams with John Underwood, *My Turn at Bat: The Story of My Life* (New York: Simon and Schuster, 1969), 127.

5. "What Williams Did," *Boston Evening Globe*, 7–16 Oct. 1946.

6. Williams with Underwood, 126.

7. Whiteney Martin, "Slaughter Run Like Paul Revere's Ride," *Boston Daily Globe*, 16 Oct. 1946, 19.

8. Harold Kaese, "Why Did Sox Lose? Series Inexperience, Soft Pennant Race and Williams Slump," *Boston Daily Globe*, 16 Oct. 1946, 20.

9. Johnny Pesky, letter, 1988.

10. Johnny Pesky, letter, 1996.

11. Dominic DiMaggio, phone conversation, 18 July 1988.

12. Williams with Underwood, 128.

13. Dave Ferriss, letter, November 1990.

14. Bobby Doerr, letter, November 1990.

15. John B. Holway, *USA Today Baseball Weekly*, 20 Dec. 1991–2 Jan. 1992, 23.

16. Holway, 23.

17. John Devaney and Burt Goldblatt with Barbara Devaney, *The World Series* (Chicago: Rand McNally, 1981), 195.

18. Devaney and Goldblatt, 195.

19. Drebinger, 37.

1947 World Series

1. RCA Victor advertisement, *New York Times*, 29 Sept. 1947, 15.

2. Arthur Daley, "Opening Day at the Stadium," *New York Times*, 1 Oct. 1947, 38.

3. Clyde Sukeforth, letter, 1996.

4. Arthur Daley, "Yankee Doodle Dandy," *New York Times*, 2 Oct. 1947, 34.

5. Arthur Daley, "Change of Scenery," *New York Times*, 3 Oct. 1947, 33.

6. Bobby Brown, letter, 1995.

7. Curt Smith, *Voices of the Game* (South Bend, Ind.: Diamond Communications, 1987), 109.

8. Smith, 109.

9. Harold Kaese, "'Hit' Order Surprises Cookie," *Boston Daily Globe*, 4 Oct. 1947, 1.

10. Kaese, 1.

11. Peter Golenbock, *Bums* (New York: G. P. Putnam's Sons, 1984), 175.

12. Donald Honig, *The World Series* (New York: Crown, 1986), 115.

13. Arthur Daley, "It Happened in Brooklyn," *New York Times*, 4 Oct. 1947, 12.

14. Dick Young, "1947: Brooklyn Dodgers 3, New York Yankees 2," in Charles Einstein, ed., *The Baseball Reader* (New York: Lippincott & Crowell, 1980), 357.

15. Albert B. Chandler, letter, 1989.

16. Bobby Brown, letter, 1989.

17. Louis Effrat, "Stunning Climax Sets Off Bedlam as Elated Brooklyn Fans Go Wild," *New York Times*, 4 Oct. 1947, 12.

18. John Drebinger, "Dodgers Set Back Yankees by 8–6 for 3–3 Series Tie," *New York Times*, 6 Oct. 1947, 28.

19. Phil Rizzuto, letter, 1988.

20. "Nothing Like It," *Time*, 13 Oct. 1947, 75.

21. "Heartthrob Series: The Yanks Take It, 4–3," *Newsweek*, 13 Oct. 1947, 76.

1948 World Series

1. "Dom DiMaggio's Circuit Smash in Eighth Inning Beats Indians for Red Sox," *New York Times*, 14 Sept. 1947, sec. 5, 2.

2. "Veeck Sure of Boudreau," *New York Times*, 17 Sept. 1947, 32.

3. Bill Veeck with Ed Linn, *Veeck — As in Wreck* (New York: G. P. Putnam's Sons, 1962), 97.

4. "Boudreau on Block! Veeck Dickering with St. Louis," *Boston Daily Globe*, 4 Oct. 1947, 4.

5. Veeck with Linn, 153.

6. Veeck with Linn, 154, 155.

7. Veeck with Linn, 156.

8. John Drebinger, "Indians Win American League Flag, Beating Red Sox in Play-Off, 8–3," *New York Times*, 5 Oct. 1948, 32.

9. Tommy Holmes, letter, 1988.

10. Clif Keane, "Boudreau Disputes Decision," *Boston Daily Globe*, 7 Oct. 1948, 1.

11. "Ump Said 'Safe'; Camera Says 'Out,'" *Cleveland News*, 7 Oct. 1948, 1.

12. Lucien Thayer, "Do Pictures Prove Masi Was Out?" *Boston Evening Globe*, 7 Oct. 1948, 25.

13. "Photo of Pick-Off Play Is Revealing," *Cleveland Plain Dealer*, 7 Oct. 1948, 22.

14. Herman Goldstein, "'Haunted,' Feller Says, By 'Base on Balls,'" *Cleveland News*, 7 Oct. 1948, 1.

15. John Devaney and Burt Goldblatt with Barbara Devaney, *The World Series* (Chicago: Rand McNally, 1981), 205.

16. Mel Harder, letter, 1988.

17. Sibby Sisti, letter, 1989.

18. Earl Torgeson, letter, 1989.

19. Ed McAuley, "Boudreau Not Disturbed by Second Guessers," *Cleveland News*, 7 Oct. 1948, 24.

20. "Braves Fans Sing Sain, Spahn, Rain," *Cleveland Plain Dealer*, 7 Oct. 1948, 1.

21. Arthur Daley, "With a Dash of Lemon," *New York Times*, 8 Oct. 1948, 34.

22. "Pitching Pays," *Time*, 18 Oct. 1948, 81.

23. "Pitching Pays," 81.

24. Arthur Daley, "Champions at Long Last," *New York Times*, 12 Oct. 1948, 35.

1951 National League Playoff

1. Monte Irvin, letter, 1989.

2. Wes Westrum, letter, 1989.

3. Larry Jansen, letter, 1989.

4. Russ Hodges and Al Hirshberg, *My Giants* (Garden City, N.Y.: Doubleday, 1963), 110.

5. "Wishful Thinking," *Boston Daily Globe*, 4 Oct. 1951, 16.

6. Whitey Lockman, letter, 1989.

7. Carl Erskine, letter, 1989.

8. Carl Erskine, letter, 1996.

9. Hodges and Hirshberg, 113.

10. Hodges and Hirshberg, 113, 114.

11. Erskine, letter, 1996.

12. Hy Hurwitz, "Thomson's Homer Climaxes Giants' Saga," *Boston Daily Globe*, 4 Oct. 1951, 1.

13. Bobby Thomson, as told to the United Press, "Rode 'on a Cloud' on Tour of Bases," *New York Times*, 4 Oct. 1951, 42.

14. Bobby Thomson, letter, 1988.

15. Lawrence Ritter and Donald Honig, *The Image of Their Greatness* (New York: Crown, 1979), 248.

16. Donald Honig, *The October Heroes* (New York: Simon and Schuster, 1979), 69.

17. John Griffin, "Like World's End for Branca," *Boston Daily Globe*, 4 Oct. 1951, 18.

18. "Baseball's 'Haunted' List Lengthy," *Springfield* (MA) *Sunday Republican*, 23 July 1989, sec. C, 16.

19. Dave Anderson, "Sports of the Times," *New York Times*, 6 June 1991, sec. B, 13.

20. Honig, 80, 81.

21. Honig, 81.

1954 World Series

1. John Drebinger, "Giants Boast a Tighter Defense, but Indians Hold Pitching Edge," *New York Times*, 27 Sept. 1954, 25.
2. Drebinger, "Giants Boast," 25.
3. John Drebinger, "Giants Have an Edge over Tribe with Their Diversified Attack," *New York Times*, 28 Sept. 1954, 35.
4. Drebinger, "Giants Have an Edge," 35.
5. Drebinger, "Giants Have an Edge," 35.
6. Don Liddle, letter, 1988.
7. Liddle, letter, 1988.
8. Arnold Hano, "A Day in the Bleachers," in Charles Einstein, ed., *Fireside Book of Baseball* (New York: Simon and Schuster, 1956), 166, 167.
9. Don Liddle, letter, 1995.
10. Davey Williams, letter, 1989.
11. "Never Hit Ball Harder, Wertz Says of Longest Series 'Out,'" *Cleveland Plain Dealer*, 30 Sept. 1954, 25.
12. Geoffrey Fisher, "Allee Samee, Dusty Stays on Bench," *Cleveland News*, 30 Sept. 1954, 21.
13. "Eclipse Gionfriddo," *Cleveland Plain Dealer*, 30 Sept. 1954, 23.
14. Harold Kaese, "'Fenway Park Has Nothing on This Place'—Lemon," *Boston Daily Globe*, 30 Sept. 1954, 30.
15. "Reminder of Gionfriddo," *New York Times*, 30 Sept. 1954, 40.
16. Dave Philley, letter, 1989.
17. Wally Westlake, letter, 1990.
18. Arthur Daley, "The Magic Number Is One," *New York Times*, 2 Oct. 1954, 11.
19. Donald Honig, *The October Heroes* (New York: Simon and Schuster, 1979), 78.
20. Arthur Daley, "It's Not Done with Mirrors," *New York Times*, 1 Oct. 1954, 29.
21. Jim (Dusty) Rhodes, "High Curve Pitch Struck by Rhodes," *New York Times*, 30 Sept. 1954, 40.
22. "Toast of the Town," *Newsweek*, 11 Oct. 1954, 96.
23. Fisher, 21.
24. Gordon Cobbledick, "Amazing Mays Is Giants' No. 1 Hero," *Cleveland Plain Dealer*, 30 Sept. 1954, 23.
25. Bert Randolph Sugar, *Baseball's 50 Greatest Games* (New York: Exeter Books, 1986), 103.
26. Louis Effrat, "Lopez Lauds 'Hot' Giants Who Did Everything Right Against 'Cold' Indians," *New York Times*, 3 Oct. 1954, sec. 5, 2.
27. Wally Westlake, letter, 1989.
28. Al Rosen, letter, 1989.

1955 World Series

1. Roscoe McGowen, "Dodgers Have a Confident Look and Alston a Confident Feeling," *New York Times*, 28 Sept. 1955, 41.
2. Arthur Daley, "Series Speculations," *New York Times*, 27 Sept. 1955, 46.
3. Arthur Daley, "A Day of Decision," *New York Times*, 28 Sept. 1955, 45.
4. Bert Randolph Sugar, *Baseball's 50 Greatest Games* (New York: Exeter Books, 1986), 88.
5. Sugar, 89.
6. Arthur Daley, "Flatbush Fantasy," *New York Times*, 6 Oct. 1955, 35.
7. "'Just Developed,' Says Reese of Key Double Play," *Boston Daily Globe*, 5 Oct. 1955, 22.

8. Gil McDougald, letter, 1989.

9. Peter Golenbock, *Bums* (New York: G. P. Putnam's Sons, 1984), 396.

10. John Lardner, "El Catch," *Newsweek*, 17 Oct. 1955, 105.

11. Arthur Daley, "At Long Last," *New York Times*, 5 Oct. 1955, 43.

12. Johnny Podres, letter, 1989.

13. "Joy in Brooklyn," *Time*, 17 Oct. 1955, 65.

1956 World Series

1. Arthur Daley, "A Matter of Resiliency," *New York Times*, 2 Oct. 1956, 41.

2. The author played against Podres twice in 1956, as a member of the University of Delaware baseball team.

3. "Antique Series," *Time*, 15 Oct. 1956, 69.

4. "Perfectionist of Sorts," *New York Times*, 9 Oct. 1956, 38.

5. "Perfectionist of Sorts," 38.

6. Arthur Daley, "Day of Decision," *New York Times*, 28 Sept. 1955, 45.

7. Louis Effrat, "Larsen Says His No Wind-Up Delivery Aided Control and Kept Batters Tense," *New York Times*, 9 Oct. 1956, 38.

8. John Devaney and Burt Goldblatt with Barbara Devaney, *The World Series* (Chicago: Rand McNally, 1981), 237.

9. "1956: New York Yankees 2, Brooklyn Dodgers 0," in Charles Einstein, ed., *The Fireside Book of Baseball* (New York: Simon and Schuster, 1956), 346B.

10. Shirley Povich, "1956, New York Yankees 2, Brooklyn Dodgers 0," in Charles Einstein, ed., *The Second Fireside Book of Baseball* (New York: Simon and Schuster, 1958), 284.

11. Povich, 284.

12. Hy Hurwitz, "Ump Weeps," *Boston Daily Globe*, 9 Oct. 1956, 20.

13. Gil McDougald, letter, 1989.

14. Arthur Daley, "As One More Spectacular Baseball Drama Unfolded," *New York Times*, 10 Oct. 1956, 51.

15. "Perfectionist of Sorts," 38.

1960 World Series

1. "Quotable Berra," *New York Times*, 22 Sept. 1984, 14.

2. John Drebinger, "Series Batting: Yanks Imposing," *New York Times*, 4 Oct. 1960, 54.

3. Arthur Daley, "With Undue Emphasis," *New York Times*, 13 Oct. 1960, 45.

4. "Baseball in Shoe Is Turley Tip-Off," *New York Times*, 14 Oct. 1960, 37.

5. Vernon Law, letter, 1989.

6. Law, letter.

7. Bobby Shantz, letter, 1989.

8. Arthur Daley, "Destiny's Darlings," *New York Times*, 14 Oct. 1960, 36.

9. Bob Friend, letter, 1989.

10. "Champions of the World," *Newsweek*, 24 Oct. 1960, 80.

11. John Devaney and Burt Goldblatt with Barbara Devaney, *The World Series* (Chicago: Rand McNally, 1981), 253.

12. "Look What I Got, Kids," *New York Times*, 14 Oct. 1960, 37.

13. Thomas Lavin, "Harvey Haddix: An Unsung Hero of the 1960 World Series," *Baseball Digest*, Oct. 1985, 28.

14. Harvey Haddix, letter, 1989.

15. Bill Virdon, letter, 1988.

16. Mickey Vernon, letter, 1988.

17. "Supreme Court Throws Out Ditmar's Bid to Revive Suit," *Springfield* (MA) *Union-News*, 12 Oct. 1988, 43.
18. "Supreme Court Throws Out," 43.

1962 World Series

1. Art Rosenbaum and Bob Stevens, *The Giants of San Francisco* (New York: Coward-McCann, 1963), 182.
2. Arthur Daley, "Gold at the Golden Gate," *New York Times*, 12 Oct. 1962, 36.
3. Rosenbaum and Stevens, 191.
4. Tony Kubek, letter, 1989.
5. Roger Birtwell, "Whew ... and Still Champions," *Boston Globe*, 17 Oct. 1962, 24.
6. John Drebinger, "Yanks Beat Giants, 1–0; Win World Series," *New York Times*, 17 Oct. 1962, 42.
7. Rosenbaum and Stevens, 192.
8. John Devaney and Burt Goldblatt with Barbara Devaney, *The World Series* (Chicago: Rand McNally, 1981), 263.
9. TV *Game of the Week* (NBC) from Yankee Stadium (Old-Timers Day), 16 July 1988.
10. Bill Madden, *Sporting News*, 18 Oct. 1982, 13.
11. Rosenbaum and Stevens, 189.
12. "Philosophical Pitcher — Ralph Willard Terry," *New York Times*, 17 Oct. 1962, 42.
13. Arthur Daley, "No Game Today," *New York Times*, 18 Oct. 1962, 50.
14. "Baseball's 'Haunted' List Lengthy," *Springfield* (MA) *Sunday Republican*, 23 July 1989, sec. C, 16.
15. Rosenbaum and Stevens, 192, 193.

1969 World Series

1. Arthur Daley, "Triumph for Justice," *New York Times*, 10 Oct. 1969, 59.
2. Joseph Durso, *Casey* (Englewood Cliffs, N.J.: Prentice-Hall, 1967), 161.
3. Durso, *Casey*, 163.
4. Durso, *Casey*, 165.
5. Daley, "Triumph," 59.
6. Arthur Daley, "The Bubble Bursts," *New York Times*, 12 Oct. 1969, sec. 5, 2.
7. Arthur Daley, "Quality of Being Amazing," *New York Times*, 15 Oct. 1969, 51.
8. Harold Kaese, "Agee's Two Circus Catches Spark Mets, 5–0," *Boston Globe*, 15 Oct. 1969, 1.
9. Leonard Koppett, "Agee Says Second Catch Was Easier Because It Was 'on My Glove Side,'" *New York Times*, 15 Oct. 1969, 50.
10. Koppett, 50.
11. Koppett, 50.
12. Clif Keane, "Mets Take 3–0 Lead on Orioles' Mistake," *Boston Globe*, 16 Oct. 1969, 64.
13. Joseph Durso, "Mets Triumph, 2–1, on Error in 10th; Lead Series by 3–1," *New York Times*, 16 Oct. 1969, 58.
14. Ron Swoboda, letter, 1989.
15. William Leggett, "Never Pumpkins Again," *Sports Illustrated*, 27 Oct. 1969, 14, 15.
16. Arthur Daley, "Defying Belief," *New York Times*, 17 Oct. 1969, 59.

1970 World Series

1. Arthur Daley, "Birds on the Wing," *New York Times*, 11 Oct. 1970, sec. 5, 2.
2. William Leggett, "Flying Start for the Big Bad Birds," *Sports Illustrated*, 19 Oct. 1970, 16.
3. Daley, sec. 5, 2.
4. Robert Lipsyte, "The Same Old Reds," *New York Times*, 12 Oct. 1970, 50.
5. Leonard Koppett, "Red Pilot's Lament: Oh, That Brooks Robinson," *New York Times*, 12 Oct. 1970, 51.
6. Koppett, 51.
7. Brooks Robinson, letter, 1988.
8. "Bench Refuses to Put on Film His Expressions About Orioles," *New York Times*, 14 Oct. 1970, 57.
9. "Bench Refuses," 57.
10. "Hero of 3 Games Praises His Club," *New York Times*, 14 Oct. 1970, 56.
11. John Devaney and Burt Goldblatt with Barbara Devaney, *The World Series* (Chicago: Rand McNally, 1981), 307.
12. Brooks Robinson, inscription in a book, Nov. 1989.
13. Robert Lipsyte, "After the Series," *New York Times*, 17 Oct. 1970, 34.
14. William Leggett, "That Black and Orange Magic," *Sports Illustrated*, 26 Oct. 1970, 27.

1972 World Series

1. Roger Angell, *Five Seasons* (New York: Simon and Schuster, 1977), 60.
2. Angell, 53, 54.
3. Arthur Daley, "Long and Short of It," *New York Times*, 17 Oct. 1972, 49.
4. John Devaney and Burt Goldblatt with Barbara Devaney, *The World Series* (Chicago: Rand McNally, 1981), 321.
5. Ron Fimrite, "A Big Beginning for the Little League," *Sports Illustrated*, 23 Oct. 1972, 26.
6. Fimrite, 26.
7. Fimrite, 26.
8. Murray Chass, "3 Runs, 13 Hits, 2 Losses and 25 Red Faces," *New York Times*, 16 Oct. 1972, 50.
9. Arthur Daley, "Rudi Snares a Ranking with Gionfriddo, Mays," *New York Times*, 16 Oct. 1972, 49.
10. Daley, "Rudi Snares," 49.
11. Daley, "Rudi Snares," 49, 51.
12. Daley, "Long and Short," 49.
13. Leonard Koppett, "Trick Play Produces Conflicting Statements," *New York Times*, 19 Oct. 1972, 62.
14. Devaney and Goldblatt with Devaney, 321.

1975 World Series

1. Roger Angell, *Five Seasons* (New York: Simon and Schuster, 1977), 295.
2. Clif Keane, "Fisk: It Was Like Smashing into a Linebacker," *Boston Globe*, 15 Oct. 1975, 56.
3. Murray Chass, "Infuriated Losers Blame the Umpire," *New York Times*, 15 Oct. 1975, 30.
4. John Devaney and Burt Goldblatt with Barbara Devaney, *The World Series* (Chicago: Rand McNally, 1981), 361.

5. Chass, 30.

6. Chass, 27.

7. Ron Fimrite, "Stormy Days for Series," *Sports Illustrated*, 27 Oct. 1975, 22.

8. Ray Fitzgerald, "After Tumult, the Shouting," *Boston Globe*, 15 Oct. 1975, 51.

9. Elena Oliver, "Ump Barnett Makes Good Call on Veterans in Northampton," *Springfield* (MA) *Union-News*, 5 Nov. 1991, 32.

10. Ron Fimrite, "Everything Came Up Reds," *Sports Illustrated*, 3 Nov. 1975, 26.

11. Bert Randolph Sugar, *Baseball's 50 Greatest Games* (New York: Exeter Books, 1986), 30.

12. Bob Ryan, "Back in His Chosen Field," *Boston Globe*, 27 Sept. 1989, 49.

13. Dwight Evans, as told to George Vass, "The Game I'll Never Forget," *Baseball Digest*, June 1988, 45.

14. Dennis Tuttle, "75 Is Still Alive," *USA Today Baseball Weekly*, 4–10 Oct. 1995, 25.

15. *Heroes and Heartaches*, Phoenix Communications Group, 1987, videotape.

16. Roger Angell, "Celebration," *The New Yorker*, 22 Aug. 1988, 54.

17. Don Conkey, "A Rosy Weekend for A's, Red Sox at the Fenway Museum," *Springfield* (MA) *Union-News*, 22 Aug. 1988, 29.

18. Ray Fitzgerald, "The Best Game Ever!" *Boston Globe*, 22 Oct. 1975, 21.

19. Red Smith, "So You Thought It Would Never End," *New York Times*, 24 Oct. 1975, 45.

1977 World Series

1. "Jackson: I'm Treated Like Dirt," *New York Times*, 19 June 1977, sec. 5, 4.

2. "Jackson: I'm Treated," sec. 5, 4.

3. Murray Chass, "Yankees' Center of Controversy and Adulation," *New York Times*, 20 Oct. 1977, sec. B, 21.

4. Reggie Jackson with Mike Lupica, *Reggie: The Autobiography* (New York: Villard Books, 1984), 203.

5. Ron Fimrite, "The Good Guys Against the Bad Guys," *Sports Illustrated*, 24 Oct. 1977, 21.

6. Fimrite, 22.

7. "Martin and Jackson: All's Well That Ends Well," *New York Times*, 16 Oct. 1977, sec. 5, 4.

8. Jackson with Lupica, 209.

9. John Devaney and Burt Goldblatt with Barbara Devaney, *The World Series* (Chicago: Rand McNally, 1981), 377.

10. Jackson with Lupica, 211.

11. Red Smith, "The Moving Finger Writes, Etc.," *New York Times*, 19 Oct. 1977, sec. B, 5.

12. Dave Anderson, "Losers Awed by Jackson; The 'Greatest' in a Series," *New York Times*, 19 Oct. 1977, sec. B, 6.

13. Steve Yeager, as told to George Vass, "The Game I'll Never Forget," *Baseball Digest*, May 1986, 78.

14. Bert Randolph Sugar, *Baseball's 50 Greatest Games* (New York: Exeter Books, 1986), 160.

15. Thomas Boswell, *How Life Imitates the World Series* (Garden City, N.Y.: Doubleday, 1982), 259.

16. Ron Fimrite, "Reg-gie! Reg-gie!! Reg-gie!!!" *Sports Illustrated*, 31 Oct. 1977, 35.

1978 American League Eastern Division Playoff

1. Murray Chass, "Hunter Knocked Out; Yanks Lose 5–1 Lead," *New York Times*, 18 July 1978, B, 13.
2. Bert Randolph Sugar, *Baseball's 50 Greatest Games* (New York: Exeter Books, 1986), 109.
3. Murray Chass, "Martin Raps Steinbrenner, Jackson and Jeopardizes Job," *New York Times*, 24 July 1978, C, 1.
4. Moss Klein, "Miracle Finish in '78 Still Vivid for Yankee Fans," *Baseball Digest*, Aug. 1988, 79.
5. Klein, 80.
6. Peter Gammons, "There's Life After Death," *Sports Illustrated*, 9 Oct. 1978, 33.
7. Bill Lee with Dick Lally, *The Wrong Stuff* (New York: Penguin Books, 1984), 186.
8. Gammons, 33.
9. Gammons, 35.
10. *Heroes and Heartaches*, Phoenix Communications Group, 1987, videotape.
11. *Heroes and Heartaches*.
12. Leigh Montville, "So What? We're Used to Waiting," *Boston Evening Globe*, 3 Oct. 1978, 29.
13. *Heroes and Heartaches*.
14. *New York Times News Service and Associated Press*, 3 Oct. 1978, 65, supplementary material.
15. Larry Whiteside, "For Mike Torrez, Second Guessing," *Boston Globe*, 3 Oct. 1978, 36.
16. Leigh Montville, "Should Burleson Have Gone to 3d?" *Boston Globe*, 3 Oct. 1978, 36.
17. Ray Fitzgerald, "A Run for the Money," *Boston Globe*, 3 Oct. 1978, 1.
18. Ernie Roberts, "Destiny 5, Red Sox 4," *Boston Evening Globe*, 3 Oct. 1978, 32.

1984 National League Championship Series

1. Roger Angell, *Season Ticket* (Boston: Houghton Mifflin, 1988), 136.
2. Angell, 139.
3. Joseph Durso, "Tigers, in 11, and Cubs Take 2–0 Playoff Leads," *New York Times*, 4 Oct. 1984, B, 23.
4. Fred Mitchell, "Paradise Lost," *Chicago Tribune*, 8 Oct. 1984, sec. 4, 1.
5. Mitchell, sec. 4, 1.
6. Mitchell, sec. 4, 1.
7. Jerome Holtzman, "Durham's Mistake Wasn't Only Cubs' Shortcoming," *Chicago Tribune*, 8 Oct. 1984, sec. 4, 4.
8. Bernie Lincicome, "The Fold of '84 Came in a Hurry," *Chicago Tribune*, 8 Oct. 1984, sec. 4, 2.
9. Holtzman, sec. 4, 4.
10. Steve Goodman, "A Dying Cub Fan's Last Request" (Red Pajama Records, 1981 on Rhino Records, Santa Monica, CA).

1986 American League Championship Series

1. Michael Martinez, "Pitching Staff with Depth Challenges Heavy Hitters," *New York Times*, 7 Oct. 1986, sec. D, 29.
2. Peter Gammons, "Bosox vs. Angels: A Pair of Heart Stoppers," *Sports Illustrated*, 20 Oct. 1986, 23.

3. "DeCinces' Little Hit Creates Big Dispute," *New York Times*, 11 Oct. 1986, 17.

4. "DeCinces' Little Hit," 17.

5. Gammons, 23.

6. Gammons, 24.

7. Dave Henderson, as told to George Vass, "The Game I'll Never Forget," *Baseball Digest*, July 1988, 40.

8. ABC Game of the Week, 13 July 1989.

9. Gene Wojciechowski, "Henderson," *Los Angeles Times*, 13 Oct. 1986, 13.

10. Michael Martinez, "A Wild Victory for Boston," *New York Times*, 13 Oct. 1986, sec. C, 6.

11. Gammons, 25.

12. Michael Martinez, "Mauch Can't Hide Anguish of Defeat," *New York Times*, 16 Oct. 1986, sec. D, 29.

13. "Baseball's 'Haunted' List Lengthy," *Springfield* (MA) *Sunday Republican*, 23 July 1989, sec. C, 16.

1986 World Series

1. Roger Angell, *Season Ticket* (Boston: Houghton Mifflin, 1988), 336.

2. Ira Berkow, "Red Sox's Buckner Plays With Pain and Enthusiasm," *New York Times*, 20 Oct. 1986, sec. C, 3.

3. Mookie Wilson, as told to George Vass, "The Game I'll Never Forget," *Baseball Digest*, January 1990, 64.

4. Malcolm Moran, "Even Mets Are Amazed," *New York Times*, 26 Oct. 1986, sec. 5, 1.

5. Michael Martinez, "Red Sox Hoping Past Isn't Prologue," *New York Times*, 27 Oct. 1986, sec. C, 3.

6. Rich Marazzi, "Proceeds from 'Mookie Ball' Sale Go to Charity," *Sports Collectors Digest*, 4 Sept. 1992, 134.

7. *Heroes and Heartaches*, Phoenix Communications Group, 1987, videotape.

8. Gerry Finn, "A's Coach Vividly Recalls What Might Have Been," *Springfield* (MA) *Union-News*, 5 Oct. 1988, 41.

9. Michael Martinez, "Red Sox Lose Grip on Vision," *New York Times*, 26 Oct. 1986, sec. 5, 6.

10. Murray Chass, "Rewound Mets Back in the Chase," *New York Times*, 26 Oct. 1986, sec. 5, 1.

11. Peter Alfano, "McNamara Joy Slips into Cruelest Defeat," *New York Times*, 26 Oct. 1986, sec. 5, 3.

12. Larry Whiteside, "Boyd Out; Hurst Gets Call," *Boston Globe*, 27 Oct. 1986, 59.

13. Lou Gorman, letter, 1996.

14. George Vecsey, "Red Sox: 68 Years and Counting," *New York Times*, 26 Oct. 1986, sec. 5, 3.

15. Leigh Montville, "They Were Just One Pitch Away," *Boston Sunday Globe*, 26 Oct. 1986, 1.

16. Dave Anderson, "Not Since Thomson Homer," *New York Times*, 26 Oct. 1986, sec. 5, 1.

17. Angell, 344.

18. Ron Fimrite, "Good to the Very Last Out," *Sports Illustrated*, 3 Nov. 1986, 16.

19. "Baseball's 'Haunted' List Lengthy," *Springfield* (MA) *Sunday Republican*, 23 July 1989, sec. C, 16.

20. Angell, 310.

1988 World Series

1. Bernard Malamud, *The Natural* (New York: Farrar, Straus and Giroux, 1952), 138.
2. Hal Bodley, "Canseco Answers Hecklers," *USA Today*, 6 Oct. 1988, sec. C, 4.
3. Bodley, sec. C, 4.
4. Ron Borges, "Gibson Effect," *Boston Globe*, 14 Oct. 1988, 90.
5. Peter Gammons, "A Big Blast in L.A." *Sports Illustrated*, 24 Oct. 1988, 36, 37.
6. Gammons, 45.
7. Gammons, 45.
8. Joey Johnston, "15 Most Dramatic Home Runs in Big League History," *Baseball Digest*, Nov. 1989, 27.
9. Sam McManus, "Gibson's Shot in the Dark Stuns A's," *Los Angeles Times*, 16 Oct. 1988, sec. 3, 1.
10. CBS Radio account, 15 Oct. 1988.
11. Gammons, 37.
12. "World Series Notebook: Surgery for Tutor?" *Boston Globe*, 21 Oct. 1988, 85.
13. Joan Ryan, "Nobodies Did the Job for L.A.," *San Francisco Examiner*, 21 Oct. 1988, sec. D, 5.
14. Dave Anderson, "Rock Concert of Sluggers," *New York Times*, 17 Oct. 1988, sec. C, 5.
15. Dave Anderson, "The World Series That Still Haunts Oakland," *New York Times*, 12 Mar. 1989, sec. 8, 7.

1989 World Series

1. Hal Bodley, "Series: 'Modest Little Sports Event,'" *USA Today*, 19 Oct. 1989, sec. C, 3.
2. Bodley, sec. C, 3.
3. Mike Littwin, "End Series Now and Call It a Season," *Baltimore Sun*, 20 Oct. 1989, sec. C, 1.

1991 World Series

1. Steve Fainaru, "Native Americans Stage Rally Against Braves' Actions," *Boston Sunday Globe*, 20 Oct. 1991, 56.
2. Fainaru, 56.
3. Michael Madden, "For Atlanta Fans, the Beat Goes On," *Boston Globe*, 14 Oct. 1991, 51.
4. "Lonnie Smith Speaks Out: 'OK, so I Blew Series, OK?'," *Springfield* (MA) *Union-News*, 30 Oct. 1991, 31.
5. Mel Antonen, "Knoblauch Contributed More Than Game 7 Decoy at Second," *USA Today*, 6 Nov. 1991.
6. Jack Curry, "Pendleton Unable to Shake Dome Hex," *New York Times*, 28 Oct. 1991, C4.
7. "Series Provides Lasting Images," *Springfield* (MA) *Union-News*, 29 Oct. 1991, 31.
8. Steve Rushin, "A Series to Savor," *Sports Illustrated*, 4 Nov. 1991, 27.
9. Mike Barnicle, "The Game to Remember," *Boston Globe*, 30 Oct. 1991.

1992 National League Championship Series

1. Tim Kurkjian, "The Cruelist Game," *Sports Illustrated*, 26 Oct. 1992, 23.

2. *New York Times*, 7 Oct. 1992, sec. B, 9.

3. Steve Rushin, "Racing for Home," *Sports Illustrated*, 19 Oct. 1992, 16.

4. Rushin, 17.

5. Bruce Newman, ed., "Deion's Big Splash," *Sports Illustrated*, 26 Oct. 1992, 13.

6. Mike Lupica, "A Play at Plate & Game Again Is Safe at Home," *New York Daily News*, 16 Oct. 1992, 78.

7. Steve Rushin, "Unbelievable," *Sports Illustrated*, 26 Oct. 1992, 20.

8. Kurkjian, 21.

9. "Belinda Talks about 'the Pitch,'" *Springfield* (MA) *Union-News*, 24 Feb. 1993, 35.

10. "Belinda Talks," 35.

11. Lupica, 78.

1993 World Series

1. Ray Ratto, "Series Offers a Diverse Choice," *Springfield* (MA) *Union-News*, 15 Oct. 1993, 44.

2. Ratto, 44.

3. "Looks Can't Kill Phillies' Abilities," *Boston Globe*, 16 Oct. 1993, 71.

4. Steve Rushin, "Slam-Bang Series," *Sports Illustrated*, 25 Oct. 1993, 25.

5. Murray Chass, "Phils Get the Big Hit, Then the Big Outs and the Series Is Tied," *New York Times*, 18 Oct. 1993, sec. C, 1.

6. Nick Cafardo, "Heroic Dykstra's Torment Was No Laughing Matter," *Boston Globe*, 22 Oct. 1993, 80.

7. Ronald Blum, "No Shortage of Drama in Game 6," *Springfield* (MA) *Sunday Republican*, 24 Oct. 1993, sec. D, 1.

8. Ralph Bernstein, "Phils' Surprising Year Has a Shocking Finish," *Springfield* (MA) *Union-News*, 25 Oct. 1993, 29.

9. Jennifer Frey, "'Wild Thing' One Time Too Often," *New York Times*, 24 Oct. 1993, sec. 8, 6.

10. Hal Bodley, "Williams Adds Name to Infamous List," *USA Today*, 25 Oct. 1993, sec. C, 7.

11. Rob Rains, "Dealing with the Failure," *USA Today Baseball Weekly*, 27 Oct.–2 Nov. 1993, 20.

12. Bodley, sec. C, 7.

13. Paul White, "Joe Carter, of Course," *USA Today Baseball Weekly*, 27 Oct.–2 Nov. 1993, 20.

14. "Series Hero Can't Find the Words," *USA Today Baseball Weekly*, 27 Oct.–2 Nov. 1993, 27

15. Evan Weiner, "Series Hero Carter Downplays Big Home Run," *Sport Collectors Digest*, 11 Feb. 1994, 90.

1996 World Series

1. Claire Smith, "Baseball; At Age 34, Darryl Strawberry Grows Up," *New York Times*, 7 July 1996, sec. 8, 1.

2. *Official Baseball Rules* (St. Louis, MO.: Sporting News Publishing Company).

3. George Vecsey, "A 12-Year-Old Legend Is Born in Right Field," *New York Times*, 10 Oct. 1996, sec. B, 17.

4. Vecsey, sec. B, 17.

5. Burt Solomon, "Winning Ugly," *New York Times*, 12 Oct. 1996, sec. 1, 23.

6. Leigh Montville, "Stepping to the Fore," *Sports Illustrated*, 5 May 1997, 40.

7. Montville, 39.

8. George Willis, "World Series '96; On This Night, Wohlers Can't Save Braves," *New York Times*, 24 Oct. 1996, sec. B, 16.

9. Jack Curry, "World Series '96; Steinbrenner Cracks a Smile," *New York Times*, 24 Oct. 1996, sec. B, 15.

10. Dave Anderson, "Sports of the Times; The Torre Brothers Wait for a New Heart," *New York Times*, 22 Sept. 1996, sec. 8, 15.

11. Dave Anderson, "Sports of the Times; Joe and Frank Torre's Dreamland," *New York Times*, 27 Oct. 1996, sec. 8, 3.

Index

*Numbers in **boldface** refer to pages with photographs.*